A School Counselor's Guide to Small Groups

A School Counselor's Guide to Small Groups

COORDINATION, LEADERSHIP, AND ASSESSMENT

SECOND EDITION

Sarah I. Springer, Lauren J. Moss,
and Christine J. Schimmel, Editors

cognella

SAN DIEGO

Bassim Hamadeh, CEO and Publisher
Amy Smith, Senior Project Editor
Abbey Hastings, Production Editor
Jess Estrella, Senior Graphic Designer
Kim Scott/Bumpy Design, Interior Designer
Natalie Piccotti, Director of Marketing
Kassie Graves, Senior Vice President of Editorial
Jamie Giganti, Director of Academic Publishing

Cover image copyright © 2020 iStockphoto LP/Julia Garan.

Printed in the United States of America.

3970 Sorrento Valley Blvd., Ste. 500, San Diego, CA 9212

I dedicate this second edition to the fierce school counselors working tirelessly in the trenches (especially during the COVID-19 pandemic) and continuing to make a difference in the lives of children and adolescents each day. This text is also a tribute to the wonderful school counselor educators who prepare our future practitioners to facilitate group work across K–12 settings. I'm grateful that my daughter will have more resources and support in the schools because of you!

—*Sarah*

This work is dedicated to my daughter, Ava. May the time I spent on this book be an investment in forging a world that is greater for you tomorrow than it is today. I pray this resource is utilized by ambitious school counselors who work every day to nurture kind and insightful students. Also, special thanks to the mentors and supervisors like my beloved friend and former co-counselor, Dr. Christy Land, who inspire the next generation of school counselors to "trust the process"—your impact is truly infinite!

—*Lauren*

This work is dedicated to all the wonderful pre-service school counselors with whom I have been given the privilege of working. I remember when we first began reading the first edition of this text in my group counseling class; your reports of the impact and power this text had on your development as group leaders increased my passion for the content. Imagine how thrilled I was to be asked to join Sarah and Lauren on the second edition! Thank you, Dr. Springer and Dr. Moss, for your tireless work on this book and for allowing me to join the team!

—*Chris*

Brief Contents

Detailed Contents

Preface

Small-group responsive services are an essential component of a comprehensive school counseling program. With the student-to-counselor ratio often well above recommended best practice, group interventions offer vital opportunities for school counselors to effectively meet diverse student needs. Although the benefits of group counseling with children and adolescents are well documented, scholars suggest that inadequate group leader training may result in counselors' hesitancy to lead groups in their schools. A lack of confidence around group leadership may further contribute to an underutilization of group work in school counseling practice. This text was thereby created with these needs in mind as a tool for currently practicing school counselors, school counseling supervisors, school counselor educators, and counselors-in-training to fill gaps associated with their hesitance with respect to group work implementation.

The structure of this book includes two large sections. The first section is composed of 10 mini chapters (including the introduction) designed to help readers consider how to utilize their group leadership skills to support group implementation. This includes how they might use these facilitation skills to effectively lead student and adult groups in the school (RTI/MTSS/504) as well as provide supervision and consultation.

The second section of the text includes more than 50 small-group session plans divided into four categories: Anxiety, Social Skills, Decision-Making, and Grief. These topics were inspired by practitioners around the country who identified these areas based on the needs of their respective schools. The plans themselves include recommended grade level (elementary or middle/high school), stage (orientation, working, closing), American School Counselor Association (ASCA) Mindsets and Behaviors, and learning objectives.

New to This Edition

First and foremost, we welcome new editor Dr. Christine Schimmel, a well-respected school counselor educator and group counseling scholar, to this second edition. Dr. Schimmel, along with her colleague Dr. Jacobs, are well published in the group counseling literature and are perhaps most well known for their text *Group Counseling: Strategies and Skills*, currently in its eighth edition. Since publication of the first edition of *A School Counselor's Guide to Small Groups: Coordination, Leadership, and Assessment*, Dr. Schimmel has eagerly coupled these two texts into her courses to provide rich curricular resources for her preservice school counseling students. We are excited to include Dr. Schimmel's expertise in this newest edition!

Overall, the second edition of this text provides a more concentrated focus on preservice school counselors. Specifically, a new chapter, "Structured Feedback to Enhance Preservice School Counselors' Group Leader Skills," written by Dr. Jonathan Ohrt and colleagues, offers a model for counselor educators and supervisors to assess the development of group leader skills. Additionally, revised existing chapters reflect the fourth edition of the ASCA National Model, updated learning objectives and references, and most notably, sidebar extension activities designed for counselor educators and supervisors to use for reflective practice. These include case studies, supervision questions, advice from the author, and additional resources.

Unique to this edition are two new additional chapters, "Essential Skills for Leading Small Groups in Schools," authored by Dr. Ed Jacobs and school counseling practitioner Wilson Harvey, and "Creative Strategies (Improvisation and Gaming) With School Counseling Small Groups," authored by West Virginia School Counselor Association president (2020) Matthew Tolliver and school counselor colleague Carla Smith. Additionally, Dr. Clare Merlin-Knoblich provides a new perspective specific to "The Importance of Stakeholder Collaboration."

Finally, while group session plans remain similar to the first edition, the introductions for each section (Anxiety, Decision-Making, Grief, and Social Skills) now extend the discussion to include how preservice and practicing school counselors can consider collecting and using data (Participation, Mindsets and Behaviors, and Outcome) from these sessions to enhance and advocate for their school counseling programs.

Acknowledgments

We would like to acknowledge the significant contributions of several individuals who helped to make this text possible. First, thank you to Ms. Ashley Pugliese Bleakley and Mr. Nadar Manavizadeh, who served as student editors of the first edition of this book. When most students in their positions were working to finish papers and internship hours, Ashley and Nadar were exceeding expectations as graduate students while also contributing countless hours to support this work. Their efforts were fundamental in creating this book! Similarly, through her graduate assistantship, Ms. Shelby Tortorello added immeasurable value to the second edition of this text. We are eternally grateful for the energy Ashley, Nadar, and Shelby gave to this work!

Introduction: Group Leadership Considerations for Effective Facilitation in Schools

Sam Steen, PhD
George Mason University

Jennifer Melfie
George Mason University

Annie Carro
George Mason University

with contributions by **Lan Zhu**
and **Elyana Genovese**

LEARNING OBJECTIVES

1. Identify the benefits of group counseling interventions in a school setting.
2. Distinguish between the different types of school counselor-led group formats.
3. Recognize the challenges associated with group leadership in schools and acknowledge related best practices and effective group leader attributes.

CONSIDER THIS SCENARIO

Erika is an elementary school counselor, hoping to run a small group for anxiety in a virtual setting. She suggests this to her school's administration but is told that it is not possible due to scheduling concerns including competing with other core subjects, specials, and important school mandates. The school administration is also concerned about limits to confidentiality due to the inability to keep the students' group sessions private. The school counselor knows that this group would be beneficial to her students who are struggling with coping strategies during this difficult pandemic season but is unsure how to handle the concerns raised by the administration.

CONSIDER THESE QUESTIONS FOR DISCUSSION

- How might you address the confidentiality concerns the principal presented?
- What are some ways in which you could gain buy-in from other stakeholders to help advocate for groups like this?
- If the group is not permitted to be run, what are some alternatives that the school counselor could implement?

Introduction

Group counseling is a necessary and useful intervention for helping numerous students in our nation's public schools. The American School Counselor Association (ASCA) states that "group counseling is a vital part of an effective comprehensive school counseling program supported by school administration and school districts" (American School Counselor Association, 2020, p. 30). Most scholars and practitioners would agree that schools are an obvious place for gaining access to children and adolescents. In fact, it has been documented repeatedly that cognitive, behavioral, and mental health concerns are oftentimes first identified by school personnel (Gueldner et al., 2020; Miller et al., 2015). Therefore, with many students in desperate need of services and effective group counseling potentially offering more benefits than any other single-focused intervention, group work should continue to develop its scope of research and practical application in school settings.

A School Counselor's Guide to Small Groups

In light of the many challenges facing youngsters, effective group counseling interventions provide an avenue through which children and adolescents learn from each other and benefit from peer accountability (McGuire et al., 2015). This is particularly meaningful, as peer interactions are instrumental in helping students develop skills during one of the most difficult and transformative times of their lives. Specifically, group counseling in school settings affords opportunities to bring students together and to help them benefit from the wide range of therapeutic factors that often emerge during this process. Some of these factors include universality (e.g., everyone experiencing similar feelings), interpersonal learning (e.g., positive and negative interactions between each other), instillation of hope (e.g., gaining a sense of positive expectations), catharsis (e.g., release of pent-up emotions), and cohesion or acceptance (e.g., togetherness); each of these is supported in group research with children and adolescents (Erford, 2016). These benefits are often present across many different types of small groups.

Student-Focused Groups

Many types of groups exist in the school setting. These groups are usually described according to the purpose and format associated with each of them. The following summary offers a description of different types of school counselor-led group formats and a brief definition of each.

Classroom Guidance

School counselors use large-group classroom guidance with an entire classroom/grade level to deliver materials related to social/emotional, academic, or career topics. This format affords the counselor an opportunity to deliver information to a large number of students while providing time for self-reflection and critical thinking. In a classroom setting, the group leader needs to be familiar with classroom management skills, as well as the general needs of as many as 20 to 150 students, depending on the role played by the school counselor (e.g., classroom guidance unit, student assembly, college career fair presentation). One of the benefits of this large group intervention is that it offers opportunities for school counselors to collect data (observational, quantitative, and qualitative) to plan future small-group interventions.

While the focus of this text is on small-group counseling, Chapter 3 offers specific data collection strategies that can be used to understand the efficacy of both large and small group counseling interventions in the school setting.

Psychoeducation and Counseling Small Groups

The most common type of group intervention used by school counselors occurs in a small-group setting (Ohrt et al., 2014). In these cases, the school counselor leads or co-leads a psychoeducation or counseling group, typically consisting of three to nine students, to address social/emotional, academic, and/or career-related concerns. In this context, the group leader works with students both individually within the group and collectively as a whole. Students can be encouraged to set individual goals and/or group goals. Small groups are sometimes easier to manage; however, conversations that may emerge during the group process can have serious implications due to the nature of self-disclosures. In some cases, students feel very comfortable sharing what is going on in their worlds. In other instances, the group leader's processing skills help to uncover student issues. In either situation, the school counselor needs to be aware of students' presenting issues and remain prepared to either help them develop strategies to overcome their impasses or provide referrals for more appropriate resources.

Adult-Focused Groups

School counselor group facilitation is not limited to group leadership with students. School counselors demonstrate their group leadership skills working with (and often leading) school personnel-focused and parent-focused groups on behalf of the students in their schools. In these cases, school counselors use their training around group facilitation to ensure that all voices are valued and central to meeting the identified goals. The following briefly discusses how adult-focused groups are often impacted by the effectiveness of the school counselor's group leadership skills.

Parent-Teacher Conferences

School counselors are often called upon to help facilitate dialogue or disseminate information and resources during parent-teacher conferences. The role that a school counselor plays during this group or meeting depends on district expectations. Generally speaking, the school counselor may be responsible for interfacing with parents and family members of students experiencing academic or social/emotional issues in order to help facilitate any post-meeting follow-up. The school counselor's leadership role in this case may involve bridging the perspectives of parents, teachers, and the student in order to support academic, career, and social/emotional progress. The school counselor also has the opportunity to shed light on systemic issues present in the school and/or community, as well as typical developmental stages that could be playing a role in the student's current level of functioning. Rapport and trust building between each of these stakeholders are valuable necessities.

Stakeholder collaboration is discussed further in Chapter 5.

Consultation Groups

School counselors in secondary school settings are often grouped as part of a larger team of school counselors. While this may also occur in elementary settings, these schools are usually smaller in size and are less likely to have more than one full-time school counselor per building. As such, elementary school counselors from many schools in the same district, other districts in the surrounding communities, or in combination with other health professionals in complementary disciplines (e.g., school psychologists, school social workers, student assistance counselors, school-based mental health counselors) may meet semi-regularly in a similar consultative group format.

The small groups described above are often considered task groups formed with the intention of meeting defined goals and objectives specific to the school, district, or larger community. In many of these cases, school counselors serve in a leadership capacity (e.g., department chair, lead counselor, committee chair) and are charged with the task of using their leadership skills to effectively organize the agenda while dually managing group dynamics. For example, the school counselor may be responsible for scheduling meetings, taking meeting notes or minutes, and fostering an environment conducive to individuals using their unique skills to accomplish a particular project or task. In these cases, the school counselor's leadership skills need to include the processing of information and statements related to the observations noted during these meetings. This process requires paying attention to group stages and member roles, which may be influenced by current and prior mentoring, consultative, or evaluative relationships occurring between group members in other capacities. A nuanced set of group leadership skills is necessary in order to manage the potential power differentials inherent within these relationships.

More discussion specific to supervision and peer consultation groups appears in Chapters 9 and 10.

Tiered Support and Progress Monitoring Groups

In some cases, the school counselor is charged with coordinating or chairing many or all of the building-based progress monitoring teams (e.g., Multitiered Systems of Support [MTSS]; Response to Intervention [RTI]; Section 504; Individualized Education Plan [IEP]). One of the major roles of the school counselor in these meetings includes ensuring that all stakeholders involved with the child's success are on board with an appropriate game plan for the student. This includes helping stakeholders understand assessment results (where appropriate), reviewing interventions and associated data, and recommending different or more intense support when necessary. The role a school counselor plays in these processes is critical, whether they are steering the work or simply using their expertise as a member of the team. In these positions, it is necessary for school counselors to be organized and timely, able to use their leadership skills to help define and potentially facilitate challenges associated with member roles and boundaries, able to mitigate any caregiver or teacher anxiety associated with the process, and willing to process observations to ensure that the parents' and children's voices are playing a major role in the decisions made about the students.

More discussion around the role of the school counselor in supporting MTSS teams is shared in Chapter 4.

Group Leader Challenges in Schools

Logistics

Leading any of the aforementioned group types can be challenging in all settings. However, facilitating small-group counseling interventions with children and adolescents in a school setting comes with a particularly complex set of obstacles. These interventions can be thwarted from the start by something as simple as scheduling the sessions. For example, scheduling in school settings can be particularly difficult because of the multitude of aspects that impact a school day; these include but are not limited to managing both the participants' and the leader(s)' availability, classroom content that might be missed during the group, prior tardiness or absenteeism that compounds the missed time for a group intervention, and other interventions provided for the student in or out of the school setting. Other barriers include buy-in from stakeholders such as teachers and administrators, parents, or the students themselves. Additionally, administrators and teachers strongly prefer that group interventions be run without students missing instructional time. In some instances, group sessions can be held before school, during lunch (time usually spent socializing or catching up on other work), or after school (when other important after-school activities or family responsibilities occur). While students benefit from not missing academic time, these choices may result in consequences associated with missed social, athletic, religious, and familial experiences.

To learn more about overcoming these challenges, the reader may wish to consider information found in Chapter 6 of this text.

Training

Another reason leading group interventions in schools is difficult appears to be the limited graduate counseling program focus on working with children and adolescents (Ohrt et al., 2014). Many group counselors working with children and adolescents are therefore left to draw upon their own personal experiences as youngsters and/or as students themselves. This suggests that they are likely to apply what was learned with adults to younger populations, which can result in missed opportunities to address the specific developmental needs of children and adolescents (Ohrt et al., 2014; Steen et al., 2014) Given the lack of supervision specific to group leadership development in graduate training (Springer et al., 2018), it is important for practicing school counselors to seek out continued clinical supervision and consultation related to small-group interventions in the school setting.

Advocacy for meaningful clinical supervision, both in training and in practice, must include supervisors and school counselors alike, acknowledging and distinguishing the developmental differences between the needs of children, adolescents, and adults participating in a group setting. Being familiar with these developmental differences as a group facilitator will ensure that groups run efficiently. It is important to have age-appropriate materials/topics and be cognizant of varying levels of attention spans. Children tend to have shorter attention spans, making it vital to avoid long, drawn-out activities or interventions (Busy Teacher, 2016). Games and storytelling are important tools for keeping children and adolescents engaged. In these cases, the size of the group space is of particular importance. The following best practice section focuses more specifically on the developmental needs of children and adolescent groups, and offers some important and practical leadership strategies for addressing these needs as they may appear in a small-group setting.

Group Leader Best Practices in Schools

School counselors must spend a great deal of time planning, implementing, and assessing a group's process and outcomes. When school counselors and other practitioners are actually facilitating group interventions, it is important for them as group leaders to use a few general strategies based on students' developmental needs in order to foster a safe and productive environment. The following highlights several key areas to consider when leading small groups in the school setting. Screening is a necessary component when putting together intervention groups. Screening can be done individually or as a group with the students during an initial session. It is recommended that the screening occur before the onset of the group to ensure appropriate member selection. One option is to observe potential group members in their classrooms as a form of screening. Classroom observation is a productive tool because observing how certain students interact with each other can be indicative of future group dynamics. In some cases, it can be helpful to observe classrooms with a potential group member present and absent to compare those dynamics and behaviors. Another option is to observe students during their lunchtimes, as this provides information about socialization patterns and behaviors—who is sitting together, alone, et cetera. When screening students for a specific group, it is essential to have an understanding of group goals and objectives, as well as specific topics and activities. This is particularly important given that certain group topics may impact students in different ways. During screening sessions, in combination with data from other stakeholders (e.g., teachers, parents), group leaders can learn members' interests or areas of need and help determine whether they may be a good fit for the group (Erford, 2016).

Group Design and Format

It is important that the space designated for group sessions is conducive to privacy and connection (Remley & Herlihy, 2020; Springer et al., 2019). A large classroom with windows and furniture wedged between members can often feel distant, potentially intrusive, or too academic. If logistically possible, using a comfortably sized smaller space can promote intimacy and safety, ultimately resulting in more member growth and development. In addition to examining the physical space and size of the room for any meeting, ground rules (e.g., norms, expectations, dos and don'ts) must be negotiated and agreed upon among group members at the onset of the group. This process can be co-constructed collectively, or the leader may ask group members to react to a list of expectations they generate before the group commences. Either way, privacy must be acknowledged and addressed, as there are sensitive issues that are likely to arise (American School Counselor Association, 2016, Section A.7.e) As with any group, leaders need to address the fact that confidentiality cannot be guaranteed; it is up to the members of the group to uphold this norm. This is especially challenging in a school setting, given that students interact with each other in and outside of the group on a regular basis. In addition to this ethical challenge, school counselors must also be aware of the specific legal and ethical considerations surrounding their work with minors, particularly as it relates to the "need to know" clause muddying the ethical boundaries surrounding adult confidentiality in the schools.

More information around the legal and ethical considerations for small-group work can be found in Chapter 1.

Effective Leader Attributes

Flexibility

Effective group leaders make spontaneous adjustments within sessions, regardless of the initial goals and objectives set forth from the beginning of the intervention. School counseling facilitators use their observation and conceptualization skills to understand the needs of each member and adapt the types of activities and leadership strategies based on how the group meeting or session is unfolding. For instance, leaders help to draw out the individual voices and strengths of each member by maintaining a present, moment-to-moment focus. This includes taking into consideration differences in the ways members communicate their feelings and experiences.

Just as teachers differentiate their instruction for students in the classroom, school counselors similarly recognize that some group members may respond better to talk therapy whereas others may communicate better in writing or through art, physical activities, or music (Roaten, 2011). This is also true regarding the speed at which members process information. While our society tends to reward quick and external processors, those who prefer to take time to process and do so internally have equally as much to offer the group. Group leaders must use this awareness, along with their assessment and critical-thinking skills, to differentiate their own leadership styles to accommodate individual member preferences. This approach not only benefits each individual group member but also provides optimal opportunities for the group as a whole to learn together and accomplish shared goals.

Congruence

An effective group counseling leader models what is expected of group members or colleagues participating in requisite groups (McMahon et al., 2014). Modeling behavior and exposure to different approaches and/or views in the group setting allows students and adults to observe appropriate or productive behaviors that may help to further facilitate meaningful discussions (Dougherty, 2013). When the here-and-now group process is managed appropriately, these discussions, even if they are difficult to engage in, can lead many of the group members to learn from one another and truly benefit from the overall group experience. Modeling self-disclosure concerning difficult and relevant experiences may be one way to facilitate trust and support deeper emotional connection (Henretty et al., 2014). For instance, racial and ethnic diversity must be acknowledged and broached to ensure members are aware that these topics can be examined or used as strengths to accomplish group goals. If a group member discusses a difficult topic, the leader can model appropriate vulnerability, empathy, reflection of feelings, and/or follow-up questions that can help others relate to their experience.

Readers can learn more about the infusion of cultural competencies into group work facilitation in Chapter 2 of this text.

Authenticity

Trust within any group is vital and considered the foundation of group cohesion (Corey et al., 2014; Yalom & Leszcz, 2005). Moreover, trust is especially important for groups with racially, ethnically, and culturally diverse students. Effective school counselors facilitating groups with racially and ethnically diverse members maintain a nonjudgmental disposition, willingness to use appropriate self-disclosure, and confidence when taking risks (Kottler & Englar-Carlson, 2014). One practice to achieve effective multicultural group leadership is to use authentic and appropriate self-disclosure (Bitar et al., 2014). For example, a new student might benefit from hearing the stories of the leader's own experiences with moving to a new country. By portraying self-awareness and insight, and by fostering this posture, school counselors will be able to modify their group by implementing culturally relevant techniques, skills, and strategies.

Conclusion

School counselors can use their group leadership knowledge and skills to offer support to others or to promote their school counseling programs. Given the evolving nature of the school counseling role, school counselors must demonstrate a commitment, enthusiasm, and professional vision that unites and encourages stakeholder buy-in. The successful group leader will likely need to demonstrate high levels of content expertise and/or partner with others to articulate and disseminate accurate information to the school community. Particularly when a school counselor is leading adult groups, they will need to remember that they likely have a deeper understanding of mental health than that of their educator peers. Therefore, they must be willing to use their voices to share their talents and expertise. For example, school counselors could be asked to be the point of contact for new and substitute teachers or act as a liaison between the school and other schools in the community. It is imperative for school counselors to be comfortable speaking in front of their colleagues, leading welcome presentations or icebreakers, and addressing others' concerns related to the health and wellness of members of the school community (i.e., students and adults) when possible. Many of these opportunities occur in a group fashion or in a manner that essentially fosters a collective environment conducive to growth and development for both faculty and students.

School counselors' willingness and openness to accept a leadership role in these initiatives often result in a reputation that fosters trust. Intentionally integrating group counseling leadership skills into a school counselor's role and providing detailed information for the community can help to clarify program goals and advocate for the overall importance of integrating and maintaining a comprehensive developmental school counseling program.

CONNECTING TO CHAPTER CONTENT

Personal Reflection Questions

- Now that you have read about how school counselors can use their group leadership knowledge and skills to support their population and promote their school counseling program, what do you perceive to be your group leadership strengths?
- What are your group leadership growth areas? What will you do to strengthen your areas for growth?
- After reading this chapter, how do you see yourself using group leadership skills beyond small-group interventions?
- Which of these group formats (e.g., consultation, parent-teacher conferences, tiered support, and progress monitoring) resonates with you the most?
- Which of these do you plan to use in your future school counseling programs?

Advice From the Expert/Author

It will be important to make a commitment to offering professional development to school administrations, teachers, staff, parents, and families that highlight the value of small-group counseling at the beginning of each year. Educating stakeholders on why you will run groups, how you will work with them to schedule and attempt to avoid conflicts, and the results you have seen when students are in small groups will help engender support for your small-group counseling program. Additionally, there are other ways to use group leadership beyond small-group interventions, so be sure to advocate for opportunities to utilize these skills within your programs.

References

American School Counselor Association. (2016). *ASCA ethical standards for school counselors*. https://www.schoolcounselor.org/getmedia/f041cbd0-7004-47a5-ba01-3a5d657c6743/Ethical-Standards.pdf

American School Counselor Association. (2020). *ASCA position statements*. https://www.schoolcounselor.org/About-ASCA/Position-Statements

Bitar, G. W., Kimball, T., Bermúdez, J. M., & Drew, C. (2014). Therapist self-disclosure and culturally competent care with Mexican-American court mandated clients: A phenomenological study. *Contemporary Family Therapy* 36(3), 417–425. https://doi.org/10.1007/s10591-014-9308-4

Busy Teacher. (2016). *Adults and children: The differences every teacher should know*. https://busyteacher.org/7935-adults-children-differences-every-teacher-should.html

Corey, M., Corey, G., & Corey, C. (2014). *Groups: Process and practice* (9th ed.). Cengage Learning.

Dougherty, A. M. (2013). *Psychological consultation and collaboration in school and community settings*. Cengage Learning.

Erford, B. T. (2016). *Group work in schools*. Routledge.

Gueldner, B. A., Feuerborn, L. L., & Merrell, K. W. (2020). *Social and emotional learning in the classroom: Promoting mental health and academic success*. Guilford Press.

Henretty, J. R., Currier, J. M., Berman, J. S., & Levitt, H. M. (2014). The impact of counselor self-disclosure on clients: A meta-analytic review of experimental and quasi-experimental research. *Journal of Counseling Psychology, 61*(2), 191–207. https://doi.org/10.1037/a0036189

Kottler, J. A., & Englar-Carlson, M. (2014). *Learning group leadership: An experiential approach*. Sage.

McMahon, H. G., Mason, E. C., Daluga-Guenther, N., & Ruiz, A. (2014). An ecological model of professional school counseling. *Journal of Counseling and Development, 92*(4), 459–471.

McGuire, L., Rutland, A., & Nesdale, D. (2015). Peer group norms and accountability moderate the effect of school norms on children's intergroup attitudes. *Child Development, 86*(4), 1290–1297.

Miller, F. G., Cohen, D., Chafouleas, S. M., Riley-Tillman, T. C., Welsh, M. E., & Fabiano, G. A. (2015). A comparison of measures to screen for social, emotional, and behavioral risk. *School Psychology Quarterly, 30*(2), 184–196. https://doi.org/10.1037/spq0000085

Ohrt, J. H., Ener, E., Porter, J., & Young, T. L. (2014). Group leader reflections on their training and experience: Implications for group counselor educators and supervisors. *Journal for Specialists in Group Work, 39*(2), 95–124.

Remley, T., & Herlihy, B. (2020). *Ethical, legal, and professional issues in counseling* (6th ed.). Pearson.

Roaten, G. K. (2011). Innovative and brain-friendly strategies for building a therapeutic alliance with adolescents. *Journal of Creativity in Mental Health, 6*(4), 298–314. https://doi.org/10.1080/15401383.2011.630306

Springer, S. I., Moss, L., Cinotti, D., & Land, C. (2018). Examining pre-service school counselors' site supervisory experiences specific to group work. *Journal for Specialists in Group Work, 43*(3), 250–273.

Springer, S. I., Peterson, J. S., Moss, L., & Vernon, A. (2019). The individual counseling process. In A. Vernon & C. J. Schimmel (Eds.), *Counseling children and adolescents* (5th ed., pp. 37–74). Cognella.

Steen, S., Vasserman-Stokes, E. A., & Vannatta, R. (2014). Group cohesion in experiential growth groups. *Journal for Specialists in Group Work, 39*(3), 236–256.

Yalom, I. D., & Leszcz, M. (2005). *The theory and practice of group psychotherapy* (5th ed.). Basic Books.

PART I

Foundation

Groups in Schools: Legal and Ethical Concerns

Carolyn Stone, EdD
University of North Florida

LEARNING OBJECTIVES

1. Apply legal principles as provided by the courts to group work with students in schools.
2. Provide students with safeguards for confidentiality in work with groups.
3. Practice ethically regarding informed consent, multicultural competence, skill level, and obligations to parents and guardians.

CONSIDER THIS SCENARIO

A school counselor colleague organized a small group of six students who wanted support for their struggles around sexual orientation issues. Now a student comes to you upset because she said the counselor berated the students for being gay instead of supporting them.

CONSIDER THESE QUESTIONS FOR DISCUSSION

- What is your reaction to the entirety of this scenario?
- Should you run a group for struggling students specific to sexual orientation?
- What precautions must be taken to protect the students?
- Do you have an obligation to address this issue with the offending counselor or her administration?

Introduction

The legal and ethical complexities of working with minors in schools require school counselors to remain vigilant about the rights and responsibilities of students and their parents or guardians, as well as the implications of those rights on their work (American School Counselor Association [ASCA], 2016). These ethical complications are acutely present in small-group delivery because small groups often involve social and emotional services in a setting designed for academic instruction (Corey et al., 2018; Gladding, 2019; Thompson & Henderson, 2016).

The *ASCA Ethical Standards for School Counselors* (2016) represents a year's worth of work by hundreds of school counseling professionals, which includes a complete overhaul of the section on group counseling to encourage group work that is

- brief and data-informed,
- appropriate for schools,
- evidence-based, and
- with measurable outcomes.

This chapter will highlight some of the basic principles of legal and ethical issues for small-group work with regard to confidentiality, informed consent, best practices, appropriate topics, skill level of the school counselor, parents/guardians' rights, multiculturalism, and obligations to administrators and teachers.

Informed Consent, Confidentiality, and Skill Level

A parent called the supervisor of school counselors to report that her daughter would not go back to her high school and needed a special assignment to another school. She explained that her daughter was in a group in school for incest survivors. The other group members breached her confidentiality, and her abuse is now being talked about all over the school.

There are alarming issues in this all-too-real case, which highlights many of the ethical principles that this chapter will address. Issues in this case include informed consent, confidentiality, appropriateness of school group topics, parental involvement, and the counselor's skill level.

Informed Consent

Small groups require that the school counselor provides informed consent, disclosing to group members the purpose, goals, techniques, and rules of procedure for the group. Informed consent is even more important for groups than individual counseling, as disclosing sensitive information happens in front of other students.

Informed consent is a fragile imperative to achieve, and it is the rare exception when school counselors actually achieve informed consent, not the rule. The construct in groups is pronounced since the emotional safety of all students is a primary concern (Stone, 2014). In the case of the incest group, students put their trust in the counselor with a level of confidence often unmatched with other educators. In many cases, students will assume that, "If the counselor is asking me to do this, then I will be safe and it must be okay."

School counselors are aware that even though attempts are made to obtain informed consent, it is not always possible. When needed, school counselors make counseling decisions on a student's behalf that promote their welfare (American School Counselor Association, 2016, Section A.2.c). School counselors have to be the guardians of informed consent by safeguarding, protecting, and proceeding on behalf of students who cannot actually act on their own behalf. Being the custodian or guardian of informed consent means the following:

- Recognizing and honoring that the current reality of informed consent in schools falls far short of its stated goals.
- Foregoing services when the potential risks outweigh the benefits.
- Honoring the elusiveness of informed consent while diligently trying to obtain it.
- Enhancing each student's ability to understand informed consent and providing many opportunities for students to ask questions and to check for understanding.
- Avoiding a mechanistic, routine approach and finding developmentally appropriate words and opportunities to explain informed consent.
- Protecting voluntariness. Schools by their nature are not voluntary for the overwhelming majority of students. If an educator or parent/guardian asks for services that a student does not want, avoid coercion and persuasion.
- Continuing to obtain written or oral permission from a parent or guardian for counseling services but still assuming the responsibility to protect the student. Repeating "This will

be in the hallways" with each student revelation will heighten your vigilance to monitor what students say in front of each other.

- Attending to the role that language, cultural background, and other elements of diversity play in the informed consent process.
- Reminding yourself often that informed consent is not an event but a process to help students move toward self-governance.
- Evaluating and considering other approaches to help students, such as giving groups generic titles—for example, "school success issues" (i.e., "stress management") to support students when a more precise theme or topic (i.e., "self-injury") may inherently render the group more susceptible to breaches in confidentiality or being the subject of gossip (Stone, 2014).

Confidentiality

The reality of working with minors in groups requires school counselors to come from the position that confidentiality will be breached (American School Counselor Association, 2016). A school counselor can never feel secure in the fact that a student understands all the nuances of informed consent. School counselors always remind themselves that whatever is said in the group can be tweeted, posted on social media, or discussed in the hallways within seconds or minutes. This awareness heightens school counselors' vigilance as to what they allow one student to talk about in front of other students. The ASCA codes specifically state that school counselors "communicate the aspiration of confidentiality as a group norm, while recognizing and working from the protective posture that confidentiality for minors in schools cannot be guaranteed" (American School Counselor Association, 2016, Section A.7.e). Before allowing students to discuss issues that explore family troubles, personal information, or painful situations, school counselors must ask themselves if the potential emotional cost to students and their families is worth the gains that could result from having allowed students to share in a setting where confidentiality might be breached.

Confidentiality is a problem in small groups in the brick-and-mortar setting because a school counselor can never feel secure in the fact that a student understands all the nuances of confidentiality and will abide by it. Confidentiality is exponentially more problematic in the virtual world, a place where counselors are more often finding themselves in their work. Small-group delivery is fragile. It is impossible to know who is listening in each student's household. A student might be powerless to seek a quiet, private place, have headphones, use a sound machine, or eliminate others from earshot. As discussed earlier, informed consent falls far short of its stated goals but in the virtual world of school counseling is even more problematic to obtain (Stone, 2014). When working with minors in groups, come from the posture that confidentiality will be breached and, therefore, highly sensitive topics that could harm a student if overheard are to be avoided. Helping students individually is a better choice, yet precautions in confidentiality are needed in this situation too (American School Counselor Association, 2020; Steen et al., 2014; DeLucia-Waack et al., 2014).

Counselors' Skill Level and Appropriate Topics

School counselors must practice within their competence level (American School Counselor Association, 2016, Section A.7.h). Sometimes teachers or administrators will request the use of topics or material that the counselor has not been trained to deliver. Topics for small groups in schools require careful consideration, as school is not the place for certain topics and/or the school counselor may need additional training to deliver particular information (American School

Counselor Association, 2016, Section A.7.f). School counselors cannot be expected to adequately address every issue that is presented to them, and certainly not the topic of incest.

Parental Involvement

Parental involvement does not necessarily mean written parental permission but can mean parental notification. The most current 2016 ASCA ethical standards moved from labeling parental notification for small groups as best practice to an ethical requirement. According to the *ASCA Ethical Standards for School Counselors*, "school counselors inform parent(s)/guardian(s) of student participation in a small group" (American School Counselor Association, 2016, Section A.7.b).

Parents sometimes question allowing their child to be included in small-group sessions for many reasons. One reason might be the fear that their child will be exposed to material they object to or that they will lose their place as the guiding voice in their child's lives (e.g., topics related to substance use or sexual activity). Some parents object to their child moving out of the academic realm into the social/emotional domain due to the inherent personal nature of topics in this domain. Savvy and alert school counselors educate themselves about the prevailing community standards and learn to predict and negotiate the political landscape.

For example, in 2006, two families in Lexington, Massachusetts, objected to their children's elementary school curriculum, which used a book depicting single-parent families, a family with two dads, and a family with two moms, and the book *King and King*, which depicts a wedding scene between two princes. In dismissing the ensuing lawsuit against the school district, district court judge Mark L. Wolf wrote, "parents do have a fundamental right to raise their children. The Parkers and Wirthlins may send their children to a private school. ... They may also educate their children at home. ... However, the Parkers and Wirthlins have chosen to send their children to the Lexington Public Schools with its current curriculum. The Constitution does not permit them to prescribe what those children will be taught" (*Parker v. Hurley*, 2007).

In this case, the dismissal was unanimously upheld by the First District Court of Appeals (*Parker v. Hurley*, 2008). The bottom line resulting from this decision for school counselors to keep in mind is that parents can refuse to have their child participate in a small group, but the counselor is free to decide the curriculum as long as the district is in support. School counselors implementing best practice work collaboratively with parents, as a child does not benefit when parents and school personnel are at odds.

Small Groups and the Counselor's Values

> You overheard your school counseling colleague encouraging a student to "reverse his choice to be gay." This counselor's behavior is unethical, but can she also be sued for negligence?

Counseling is not a platform to forward one's world views, prejudices, biases, or values rooted in one's religion, ethnicity, or culture. To impose one's religious beliefs on someone else's child is to invite punitive action.

In Hamilton v. Vallejo City Unified School District (2009), a school counselor required a student (Hamilton) to attend a special weekly support group for gay students. During the group, the counselor berated students for "choosing" to be gay and tried to convince them to change their sexual orientation or gender expression. This California school district reached a settlement to which they agreed to adopt a clear policy explicitly prohibiting discrimination and harassment based on sexual orientation or gender identity, develop a specific procedure for harassment and discrimination complaints, and provide mandatory training for all teachers and other staff who interact with students in how to identify antigay harassment and discrimination. Similar counselor values' conflicts are evidenced in Tennessee legislation (HB 1840/SB 1556). School counselors must remain mindful of their duty to bracket personal values that may conflict with client welfare. Counselors should remain especially dutiful around how this ethical posture informs group work.

Multicultural Considerations and Small-Group Sessions

The Association for Specialists in Group Work (ASGW) encourages finding ways to connect students to others that can help link them to the larger group. The ASGW 2012 guidelines (Singh et al., 2012) encourage school counselors to assess their group membership and expand or alter as needed to allow for a greater level of connection and support for group members who are isolated in the group due to one or more dimensions of multicultural identity or experience. School counselors ensure that a framework exists for members to feel supported for their diversity as group members (Ivers et al., 2016; Ratts et al., 2016). Ethical school counselors continually assess their own multicultural and social justice advocacy competence and strive for self-awareness of their own role as a systems and social change agent and identify issues of privilege and oppression that influence competency in group work (Ratts et al., 2016). Additional information related to the multicultural aspects of providing ethical group practice in school settings can be found in Chapter 2.

Conclusion

The *ASCA Ethical Standards for School Counselors* (2016) stresses confidentiality for students and the imperative that school counselors respect students' confidence while balancing minors' rights with parents or guardians' rights. Knowing when to invoke confidentiality at the exclusion of a parent's right to know provides a consistent tension for the ethical and responsive school counselor. They may find that by communicating the purpose and goals of their small-group sessions, they strengthen partnerships with parents. It is unrealistic for members of the school and larger community to expect that school counselors should have all the skills, knowledge, and time required for adequate knowledge of all topics. The astute counselor utilizes the rule of parsimony and delivers small-group sessions as a responsive intervention to reach as many students as possible but also maintains that it is not the best or only intervention to use with every student. Small groups are a critical tool and, when used with caution, can provide a supportive, productive, and safe environment for students to explore themselves and topics relevant to their growth and development.

CONNECTING TO CHAPTER CONTENT

Personal Reflection Questions
- Now that you have read the chapter, how does the *Hamilton v. Vallejo* court case summary inform your practice?
- Once you have read the *ASCA Ethical Standards for School Counselors,* what guidance did you receive regarding impaired or unethical colleagues?

- How will you ameliorate any harm done when during a small group a student brings up a highly personal and sensitive topic?
- How will you plan to support students in a variety of highly sensitive topics without causing them harm due to confidentiality breaches?

Advice From the Expert/Author

Groups are critical in helping school counselors attend to the needs of students, given the large caseloads. This essential service delivery method carries the extra need for vigilance due to the fact that not only is it impossible to protect confidentiality, it is best to come from the posture that it will be breached. Use groups but exercise great caution to guard what is said in the group to prevent students from harm due to a breach of confidentiality.

Check Out These Resources

- American School Counselor Association. (2020). *ASCA position statements*. https://www.schoolcounselor.org/About-ASCA/Position-Statements
- American School Counselor Association. (2020, August 10). *Legal and ethical FAQs*. https://www.schoolcounselor.org/About-School-Counseling/Ethical-Legal-Responsibilities/FAQs
- Berger, C. (2018). Bringing out the brilliance: A counseling intervention for underachieving students. *Professional School Counseling, 17*(1). https://doi.org/10.1177/2156759X0001700102
- Bore, S., Armstrong, S., & Womack, A. (2014). *School counselors' experiential training in group work*. http://jsc.montana.edu/articles/v8n26.pdf
- Steen, S., Liu, X., Shi, Q., Rose, J., & Merino, G. (2018). Promoting school adjustment for English-language learners through group work, *Professional School Counseling, 21*(1). https://doi.org/10.1177/2156759X18777096

References

American Civil Liberties Union. (2009, July 20). *Morrison v. Boyd Co. Board of Education: Case profile*. http://www.aclu.org/lgbt-rights_hiv-aids/morrison-v-boyd-co-board-education-case-profile

American School Counselor Association. (2016). *ASCA ethical standards for school counselors*. https://www.schoolcounselor.org/getmedia/f041cbd0-7004-47a5-ba01-3a5d657c6743/Ethical-Standards.pdf

American School Counselor Association. (2020, August 10). *Legal and ethical FAQs*. https://www.schoolcounselor.org/About-School-Counseling/Ethical-Legal-Responsibilities/FAQs

Corey, M., Corey, G., & Corey, C. (2018). *Groups: Process and practice* (10th ed.). Cengage Learning.

DeLucia-Waack, J., Kalodner, C. J., & Riva, M. T. (2014). *Handbook of group counseling and psychotherapy* (2nd ed.). Sage.

Gladding, S. T. (2019). *Groups: A counseling specialty* (7th ed.). Pearson.

Hamilton v. Vallejo City Unified School District. (2009). https://www.dgs.ca.gov/OAH/Case-Types/Special-Education/Services/-/media/Divisions/OAH/Special-Education/SE-Decisions/2009/2009—September/2009050182Acc.pdf

Ivers, N. N., Johnson, D. A., Clarke, P. B., Newsome, D. W., & Berry, R. A. (2016). The relationship between mindfulness and multicultural counseling competence. *Journal of Counseling and Development, 94*(1), 72–82. https://doi.org/10.1002/jcad.12063

Parker v. Hurley, 474 F. Supp. 2d 261 (2007).

Parker v. Hurley, 514 F. Supp. 3d 87 (2008).

Ratts, M. J., Singh, A. A., Butler, S. K., Nassar-McMillan, S., & McCullough, J. R. (2016, January 27). *Multicultural and social justice counseling competencies: Practical applications in counseling*. Counseling Today. https://ct.counseling.org/2016/01/multicultural-andsocial-justice-counseling-competencies-practicalapplications-in-counseling/

Singh, A. A., Merchant, N., Skudrzyk, B., Ingene, D., Hutchins, A. M., & Rubel, D. (2012). Association for Specialists in Group Work: Multicultural and social justice competence principles for group workers. *Journal for Specialists in Group Work, 37*(4), 312–325. https://doi.org/10.1080/01933922.2012.721482

Steen, S., Henfield, M., & Booker, B. (2014). The Achieving Success Everyday group counseling model: Implications for professional school counselors. *Journal for Specialists in Group Work, 39*(1), 29–46. https://doi.org/10.1080/01933922.2013.861886

Stone, C. (2014, September 1). *Informed consent: Is it attainable with students in schools?* ASCA School Counselor. https://www.schoolcounselor.org/Magazines/September-October-2014/Informed-Consent-Is-it-Attainable-With-Students-in

Stone, C. (2017). *School counseling principles: Ethics and law* (4th ed.). American School Counselor Association.

Thompson, C. L., & Henderson, D. A. (2016). *Counseling children* (9th ed.). Cengage Learning.

Utilizing Counseling Competencies to Design and Deliver Group Work in Schools

Raven K. Cokley, PhD, NCC
Johns Hopkins University

Zyer Beaty, PhD, NCC
Bard High School

Anneliese A. Singh, PhD, LPC
Tulane University

LEARNING OBJECTIVES

1. Explore the history of group work in schools as a social justice, school counseling practice.
2. Describe how various counseling competencies (ASCA, MCSJC, ALGBTIC, MRECC) inform group work in schools.

CONSIDER THIS SCENARIO

School counselor and social justice leader Chadwick wants to provide students with a small group to process and work through their feelings. Many of Chadwick's students reported feeling overwhelmed with the recent uprisings for racial justice across the country. Chadwick feels that he has the awareness, knowledge, and skills to run a racial trauma support group, but he is worried that the all-White administration at his school will not support it. He has received several emails from teachers and administrators asking him to remove the "Black Lives Matter" banner from his door, as it is too much of a "political statement for a school setting."

CONSIDER THESE QUESTIONS FOR DISCUSSION

- What is your general assessment of Chadwick's situation?
- What kind of attitudes, beliefs, knowledge, and skills might Chadwick need in order to successfully facilitate this group?
- What are some potential barriers for this group experience?
- Who are Chadwick's stakeholders? With whom can he collaborate to address some of these barriers?
- How can Chadwick advocate for himself and his students?

Introduction

School counselors have long been leaders in the field of group counseling, as their professional responsibilities naturally entail group facilitation (Steen et al., 2014). Given the multiple roles of school counselors in schools (e.g., educators, helpers, advocates), small-group counseling is a modality that allows for intentional relationship building, student support, and program evaluation. School counselors also use small groups for several reasons: (a) to tailor counseling interventions to certain populations (e.g., students of color, LGBTQ students, immigrant students, students preparing to be the first generation in their family to attend postsecondary education), (b) to help students achieve specific goals (e.g., college transition, leadership development), and (c) to help students develop various skill sets (e.g., study skills, time management). However, school counselors may easily overlook the power of small groups to address issues of race, racism, and social injustice, to cultivate cultural humility, to create affirming spaces, and to foster a sense of unity (Guth et al., 2018).

Across all types of group work, there are competencies that school counselors use to guide their facilitation. The *ASCA School Counselor Professional Standards and Competencies* (American School Counselor Association, 2019a; ASCA) specifically denotes group work as an important intervention in schools. There are several other competency documents within the American Counseling Association (ACA) that guide group interventions to ground school counselors in multicultural and social justice competencies, including the following:

- Multicultural and Social Justice Counseling Competencies: Guidelines for the Counseling Profession (Ratts et al., 2016).
- American Counseling Association Competencies for Counseling Transgender Clients (ALGBTIC Transgender Committee, 2010).
- Competencies for Counseling the Multiracial Population (MRECC Interest Network of the American Counseling Association Taskforce, 2015).
- Competencies for Counseling Lesbian, Gay, Bisexual, Queer, Questioning, Intersex and Ally Individuals (ALGBTIC LGBQQIA Competencies Taskforce, 2013).
- Association for Specialists in Group Work: Multicultural and Social Justice Competence Principles for Group Workers (Singh et al., 2012).

In this chapter, the use of counseling competencies to facilitate small-group work in schools is explored. Additionally, the history and current practice of group work as a culturally responsive practice in schools is discussed and an overview of the above competencies is provided.

History and Current Practices of Group Work in School Counseling

The foundation of group work in schools is rooted in multicultural and social justice concerns (Singh et al., 2012). Group work within schools was introduced to empower students to develop future social and career skills, which would help them to strengthen their communities (Steen et al., 2014). School counselors today continue the tradition of using group strategies to address multicultural and social justice issues within schools and within society. There has been a wealth of literature on multicultural and social justice group work in the last decade, including empowerment practices among Latino parents and families (Villalba et al., 2014); fostering resilience with LGBTQ students (Craig, 2013); college and career readiness among Black students with disabilities (Mayes, 2020); fostering a sense of belonging among Black boys (Challenger et al., 2020); and facilitating acculturation processes among refugee populations (Atiyeh et al., 2020). In addition, school counseling groups can target specific counseling issues such as emotional regulation, combating depression, academic anxiety, peer pressure, and other concerns common among marginalized student groups. For example, consider the following:

> Megan, a Latina woman and new middle school counselor, learned during her job interview that there is a large population of Latinx, first-generation college bound students at the school where she will start her school counseling career. To meet the needs of her students, Megan wants to facilitate a first-generation college readiness

group with high school juniors. She has some knowledge on the experiences of first-generation students, but she does not feel that she knows enough to facilitate the group on her own. She is also worried that she will not receive approval to facilitate the group during the school day, as teachers frown upon students missing instructional time. Megan has considered running an after-school group, but she knows that many of the students in her target demographic have family obligations or would need access to transportation.

Megan's circumstances are complex, but not unique. Megan and other school counselors in similar circumstances should consider how to best leverage competencies published by professional organizations to advocate for themselves, their program, and their students.

As the *ASCA School Counselor Professional Standards and Competencies* (2019a) and the *Multicultural and Social Justice Counseling Competencies* (Ratts et al., 2016) indicate, practicing school counselors, school counselor supervisors, and school counselor trainees keep in mind that they play an important role in developing the next generation of leaders who potentially cultivate a more positive, socially just school climate. In doing so, professional school counselors and school counselors-in-training are part of a long tradition of school counselors who continue to promote social justice change in schools.

ASCA School Counselor Competencies

The *ASCA School Counselor Professional Standards and Competencies* (2019a) provide school counselors with the fundamental rationale and justification for the design and implementation of group work in schools. These competencies require school counselors to have a solid foundation in group work theory and training, as well as a theoretical basis (e.g., relational-cultural theory, Adlerian, solution-focused therapy, reality therapy) to guide group interventions. School counselors are also asked to use group modalities to address the disparities that exist for distinct student groups by developing action plans to address identified educational gaps. Action plans often include using group counseling interventions to target and increase academic and personal achievement for all students (e.g., career development, college access, postsecondary preparedness, and social and emotional learning). Groups are also viewed as an important way to provide crisis response (American School Counselor Association, 2019b). As you contemplate what groups might be most impactful for students from a culturally responsive posture, consider the following:

> Shawn is a White male middle school counselor. Shawn's school demographics are mostly urban minority students whose families live below the poverty line. He knows and understands the importance of group work from his previous counseling experiences. Due to the global COVID-19 pandemic that began late last spring, students were forced to transition to virtual learning, leading to issues of access, familial strain, and student motivation to learn and be present in the "classroom." Shawn presented the idea of running a group for students who are having a challenging time with this transition to administration, but he was met with disapproval because it did not seem like a priority. Administration has concerns about holding groups virtually and the significance of holding groups during this time, because the most immediate issue was ensuring that students are attending class daily.

With the current COVID-19 pandemic forcing many schools into virtual and hybrid learning modalities, Shawn's case highlights an increasingly common one for school counselors, making it crucial for them to work creatively and collaboratively now more than ever. Leading small-group interventions provides school counselors with a way to meaningfully work with multiple students at a time, allowing them to make exponential use of their time with students. The *ASCA School Counselor Professional Standards and Competencies* also outline group facilitation skills that are requisite for running groups effectively, including promoting cohesion among group members and identifying and meeting shared goals (American School Counselor Association, 2019a). This approach is essential for the current nature of school counseling programs. In addition to the *ASCA School Counselor Professional Standards and Competencies*, the *ACA Multicultural and Social Justice Competencies* offer an additional lens for school counselors to consider when planning groups with a culturally responsive tone.

ACA Multicultural and Social Justice Competencies

In 2016, the ACA's Multicultural Counseling Competencies Revisions Committee provided an update of the original multicultural competencies developed by Sue, Arredondo, and McDavis (1992). These revised competencies describe the domains of multicultural development pertaining to counselor self-awareness, client world view, counseling relationship, and counseling and advocacy interventions. Each of these four domains is then broken down by counselor attitudes and beliefs, knowledge, skills, and actions.

The *Multicultural and Social Justice Counseling Competencies* (MSJCC; Ratts et al., 2016) help school counselors assess how they integrate the four domains into their group facilitation. For instance, if developing a small group for students with physical disabilities, school counselors evaluate if they have the attitudes and beliefs, knowledge, and skills required to effectively support this student group, while also questioning how to advocate for the accessibility and other needs of these students. Similarly, if there is a desire to create a group to process racial trauma at the school, the MSJCC allow school counselors to critically reflect on their own attitudes, beliefs, and knowledge around the issue. For example, consider the following:

> Naomi is a multiracial woman who is also a new high school counselor. She has had very little practice working with groups, but wants to run a trauma-informed group for teachers to support students who have experienced (lived or vicarious) trauma via police brutality and other forms of systemic violence. Naomi understands that group work can be impactful in helping to facilitate conversations around race and racism, while also providing psychoeducational support. She recognizes that several White teachers at her school have already shared feelings of dissent about the group, stating that "police brutality isn't real." Using the MSJCC, Naomi considers the attitudes of these teachers along with the needs of her students when planning how to move forward with her group intervention(s).

In addition to providing guidelines for counselor awareness and engagement, the revised MSJCC identifies four different counselor-client interactions related to privilege and oppression: the (a) privileged counselor-privileged client, (b) marginalized counselor-marginalized client, (c) privileged counselor-marginalized client, and (d) marginalized counselor-privileged client. School counselors use these interactions to explore the potential power dynamics that will influence their group facilitation and their students' potential perceptions of them. Being cognizant of how students perceive school counselors helps mitigate any tensions around differences in identity and experience, while also promoting a sense of safety and belonging between the school counselor and group members.

Competencies With LGBTQ Students

The *ACA Competencies for Counseling Transgender Clients* (ALGBTIC Transgender Committee, 2010) and the *Competencies for Counseling LGBQQIA Individuals* (ALGBTIC LGBQQIA Competencies Taskforce, 2013) are two documents that school counselors use in tandem. The Gay, Lesbian, and Straight Education Network (2015) reports that LGBTQ students experience disparities in academic, personal, and social achievement in schools (e.g., lower grades and skipping school due to bullying, high rates of verbal and physical harassment); therefore, school counselors are encouraged to use the aforementioned competencies to design and facilitate empowerment groups specific to LGBTQ students and to foster their success and feelings of safety in the school environment. Surveys have shown that school-based LGBTQ interventions and multicultural school leadership have helped to decrease bullying and violence toward sexual minority students (Gay, Lesbian, and Straight Education Network, 2015).

Both sets of competencies discuss group work and encourage facilitation skills that address the unique and intersecting identities of LGBTQ students. For instance, the competencies address common concerns among LGBTQ students, including experiences related to coming out, use of gender pronouns, sexual orientation and gender identity development, and family concerns; the competencies also address how counselors can navigate anti-LGBTQ issues that may arise within a group setting. Overall, school counselors use these competencies to both heighten their own awareness and train educators and school administrators on how to be inclusive of the diverse range of gender identities and sexual orientations.

ASGW Multicultural and Social Justice Competence Principles

The *ASGW Multicultural and Social Justice Competence Principles* (Singh et al., 2012) are aspirational in nature and provide specific examples of competencies related to group work facilitation, which are helpful to school counselors when facilitating small groups. The principles are presented in three sections: awareness of self and group members, strategies and skills, and social justice advocacy. In addition, this document provides case samples for school counselors.

Section I provides school counselors with guidelines on how to be aware of themselves and group members as they promote multicultural competence and advocate for social justice. Competencies in Section II examine the strategies and skills that are required of school counselors in order to promote effective planning and performance, and processing of leadership styles, techniques, and resources within the group setting. Section III outlines the steps that promote social justice and advocacy, which include utilizing opportunities for activism and community organization, experiencing consciousness-raising group participation, emphasizing how personal status shapes experiences of privilege and oppression, allocating resources to group members, and other pertinent issues.

Conclusion

Designing and facilitating group counseling experiences is a key responsibility for social justice-oriented school counselors. This expectation includes the specific use of small groups that promote educational access, equity, and academic success, helping to mitigate opportunity gaps among diverse groups of students. There are immense opportunities for school counselors to use competencies to guide and tailor their interventions to advance the multicultural and social justice competence and awareness of the entire school system. Although this work may be overwhelming at times, small-group work is incredibly rewarding, as students potentially have an immediate and powerful influence on each other. It is important to remember that these competency expectations help support school counselors in bringing to life the long traditions of advocacy and social justice, which are hallmarks of the school counseling profession.

CONNECTING TO CHAPTER CONTENT

Personal Reflection Questions

Attitudes and Beliefs
- How can critical self-reflection processes help you navigate dynamics of culture and power in small groups?
- How prepared are you to facilitate group work with marginalized groups at your school (e.g., first-gen students, students of color, LGBTQ+ students)?
- How can you foster cultural humility in group work? Consider the implications of doing this internally and within the small group.

Knowledge
- Who are the student groups at your school who are not being adequately and competently served? How can you address these opportunity gaps?
- What are some barriers related to group facilitation at your school?
- What kind of specialized training might you need in order to provide socially just group counseling services to marginalized students in schools?

Skills
- How can you ensure that small-group counseling spaces are affirming for all students?
- How might you advocate for students to have small-group experiences?
- How can small groups be used to address issues of multiculturalism, diversity, and social justice at your school?

Action
- In your personal life, what kind of social action can you engage in to help you learn more about the diverse needs of your students?
- How does understanding the critical need for groups in schools inform your perspective or practice?
- How will you use group work to advocate for your students and their academic, social, and emotional success?

Advice From the Expert/Author
- Identify stakeholders who support school counseling and small-group work early in the school year.
- Make doing professional development with teachers and staff on the value of small-group counseling a top priority at the beginning of each year. Educating stakeholders on why you will run groups, how you will work with them to schedule and attempt to avoid conflicts, and the results you have seen when students are in small groups will help engender support for your small-group counseling program.
- Collect data that highlights the ways that groups have helped your student population in previous years.
- Consider incorporating time for groups into the schedule (homeroom, advisory, etc.), which can also be used as a time for students to attend teacher office hours,

> recover previously failed courses, et cetera. Intentionally build groups into your counseling curriculum.

- Consider how incorporating the counseling competencies (ASCA, MCSJC, ALGBTIC, MRECC) can support small group work. This is especially important when responding to parents, students, teachers, and administrators who do not see the value in social justice-oriented counseling and small groups.

- Commit to critical processes of self-reflection and questioning as a personal and professional practice. Culture and power dynamics are always present in group work. Having the awareness, attitudes, beliefs, knowledge, and skills to competently and justly facilitate small groups is an ethical and professional requirement for school counselors.

- Consider your understanding of social justice, equity, access, anti-Blackness, anti-racism, homophobia, ability, and other issues. What do you believe to be true about these issues? What do you believe is your role as social justice-oriented school counselor in addressing these issues?

- Collaborate with community partners to run groups, serve as guest speakers, and build relationships with students' families. A lot of community organizations are looking to hold groups for students as well as provide them with resources along the way.

- Identify and attend professional development opportunities that will inform your practice of social justice-oriented school counseling (e.g., webinars, conference sessions, #AntiRacistSC Twitter chats, antiracism book lists curated by scholars of color). How can you put what you have learned into action?

- Be prepared to risk something. Advocating for students to have access to small-group experiences can be a professional and personal challenge. However, as school leaders, educators, and advocates, it is our job to ensure that all of our students have safe spaces in schools to build relationships with their peers, address interpersonal concerns, experience socioemotional growth, and succeed in all aspects of their lives.

Check Out These Resources

- American School Counselor Association. (n.d.). *The school counselor and group counseling.* https://www.schoolcounselor.org/Standards-Positions/Position-Statements/ASCA-Position-Statements/The-School-Counselor-and-Group-Counseling
- Day-Vines, N. L., Ammah, B. B., Steen, S., & Arnold, K. M. (2018). Getting comfortable with discomfort: Preparing counselor trainees to broach racial, ethnic, and cultural factors with clients during counseling. *International Journal for the Advancement of Counselling, 40*(2), 89–104. https://doi.org/10.1007/s10447-017-9308-9
- Hook, J. N., Davis, D., Owen, J., & DeBlaere, C. (2017). *Cultural humility: Engaging diverse identities in therapy.* American Psychological Association.
- Kinouani, G. (2020). Silencing, power and racial trauma in groups. *Group Analysis, 53*(2), 145–161. https://doi.org/10.1177%2F0533316420908974

References

ALGBTIC LGBQQIA Competencies Taskforce. (2013). Competencies for counseling lesbian, gay, bisexual, queer, questioning, intersex and ally individuals. *Journal of LGBT Issues in Counseling, 7,* 2–43.

ALGBTIC Transgender Committee. (2010). American Counseling Association competencies for counseling with transgender clients. *Journal of LGBT Issues in Counseling, 4*(3–4), 135–159. https://doi.org/10.1080/15538605.2010.524839

American School Counselor Association. (2019a). *ASCA school counselor professional standards and competencies.* https://www.schoolcounselor.org/getmedia/a8d59c2c-51de-4ec3-a565-a3235f3b93c3/SC-Competencies.pdf

American School Counselor Association. (2019b). *The ASCA national model: A framework for school counseling programs* (4th ed.).

Atiyeh, S., Choudhuri, D. D., & Dari, T. (2020): Considerations for facilitating refugee acculturation through groups. *Journal for Specialists in Group Work, 45*(4), 353–366. https://doi.org/10.1080/01933922.2020.1800879

Challenger, C. D., Duquette, K., & Pascasio, D. (2020). "Black boys: Invisible to visible": A psychoeducational group fostering self-efficacy, empowerment, and sense of belonging for African American boys. *Journal for Specialists in Group Work, 45*(3), 257–271.

Craig, S. (2013). Affirmative supportive safe and empowering talk (ASSET): Leveraging the strengths and resiliencies of sexual minority youth in school-based groups. *Journal of LGBT Issues in Counseling, 7*(4), 372–386.

Gay, Lesbian, and Straight Education Network. (2015). *The 2015 national school climate survey: Executive summary.* https://www.glsen.org/sites/default/files/GLSEN%202015%20National%20School%20Climate%20Survey%20%28NSCS%29%20-%20Executive%20Summary.pdf

Guth, L. J., Nitza, A., Pollard, B. L., Puig, A., Chan, C. D., Bailey, H., & Singh, A. A. (2018). *Ten strategies to intentionally use group work to transform hate, facilitate courageous conversations, and enhance community building.* Association for Specialists in Group Work. https://docs.wixstatic.com/ugd/513c96_fe59b76c04b040f8bb-17f653b3092b10.pdf

Mayes, R. D. (2020). College and career readiness groups for gifted Black students with disabilities. *Journal for Specialists in Group Work, 45*(3), 200–212.

MRECC Interest Network of the American Counseling Association Taskforce. (2015). *Competencies for counseling the multiracial population.* http://www.counseling.org/docs/default-source/competencies/competencies-for-counseling-the-multiracial-population-2-2-15-final.pdf?sfvrsn=6

Ratts, M. J., Singh, A. A., Nassar-McMillan, S., Butler, S. K., & McCullough, J. R. (2016). Multicultural and social justice counseling competencies: Guidelines for the counseling profession. *Journal of Multicultural Counseling and Development, 44*(1), 28–48. https://doi.org/10.1002/jmcd.12035

Singh, A. A., Merchant, N., Skudryzk, B., & Ingene, D. (2012). Association for specialists in group work: Multicultural and social justice competence principles for group workers. *Journal of Specialists in Group Work, 37*(4), 312–325. https://doi.org/10.1080/01933922.2012.721482

Steen, S., Henfield, M. S., & Booker, B. (2014). The achieving success everyday group counseling model: Implications for professional school counselors. *Journal for Specialists in Group Work, 39*(1), 29–46.

Sue, D. W., Arredondo, P., & McDavis, R. (1992). Multicultural counseling competencies and standards: A call to the profession. *Journal of Counseling Development, 70*(4), 477–486.

Villalba, J. A., Gonzalez, L. M., Hines, E. M., & Borders, L. D. (2014). The Latino parents-learning about college (LaP-LAC) program: Educational empowerment of Latino families through psychoeducational group work. *Journal of Specialists in Group Work, 39*, 47–70.

PART II

Best Practices

Using Data to Inform and Advocate for Small-Group Counseling Practice

Trish Hatch, PhD
San Diego State University, Chief Executive Officer & President of Hatching Results, LLC

Ashley Kruger
San Diego State University & Team Member at Hatching Results, LLC

Nicole Pablo
San Diego State University & Team Member at Hatching Results, LLC

LEARNING OBJECTIVES

1. Justify why all students deserve to receive data-driven school counseling interventions (as opposed to random acts of interventions).
2. Discuss the importance of developing consistent school-wide data elements that trigger the appropriate intervention.
3. Differentiate between the different types of data and uses of data as they pertain to Tier 2 interventions and group counseling.
4. Articulate an example of aligning small-group curriculum with data elements used to determine need and measure impact.
5. Propose an action plan that describes how group counseling can impact perception and outcome data.

CONSIDER THIS SCENARIO

Cecelia is an experienced elementary school counselor. She has been running groups based on teachers' recommendations for 10 years. Each quarter, she would put a list with titles of group topics on the wall in the teacher's lounge and ask teachers to write the names of students they thought might benefit from these groups. In her recent district training, however, Cecelia learned the value and benefits of evidence-based practices and committed to Tier 2 interventions based on data-driven needs. Further, she agreed to measure the impact of her group on the students she served. Unfortunately, when she returned to her school, she struggled to find the data she needed. When she asked teachers for their "data," she felt like she was bothering them. She wasn't sure where to look for or how to gain access to the student information system on her own, since she wasn't given access and wasn't included in the teacher training.

CONSIDER THESE QUESTIONS FOR DISCUSSION

- What are your initial thoughts about Cecelia's situation?
- If you were Cecelia, what would you do to gain access to the student information system?
- Once access is gained, what data elements would you review?
- How would you use data to determine which students to invite to group counseling?

Introduction

This chapter focuses on the use of data when running Tier 2 small-group interventions in K–8 schools. Tier 2 activities are designed for students who:

- exhibit barriers to learning,
- are struggling to achieve academic success, or
- are identified as deserving of instruction and/or supports in addition to Tier 1 activities (e.g., foster youth, students experiencing homelessness).

Similar to how teachers identify and provide additional support to students struggling with specific academic issues, the school counselor utilizes data to identify students who may benefit most from Tier 2 interventions. For example, schools implementing multitiered interventions may identify students who are far below grade level in reading ability and determine additional supports needed to improve their proficiency. Similarly, students who are struggling behaviorally or with particular academic skills, such as time management or organization, require multitiered interventions to teach strategies for self-control, problem solving, and organization— skills possibly best taught in a small-group setting. If implemented intentionally, such groups are prescheduled and predetermined through the use of data, utilizing screening elements. While all students are serviced through Tier 1 activities, 15% to 20% of these may need this type of Tier 2 support or the even more intensive Tier 3 supports (Belser et al., 2016).

If a school counselor determines that a particular student or group of students require additional support after looking at the data, how does the school counselor determine what they need? How can the counselor decide *who* needs *what?* This can be a tricky part of their role—how to meet the needs of all referred students while ensuring students who may not have been referred for intervention do not fall through the cracks. Although promoted heavily in texts and by the American School Counselor Association (ASCA), the field of school counseling has not consistently trained school counselors in ways to utilize data to drive intervention-based decisions (Hatch et al., 2015; Young & Kaffenberger, 2011). Instead, many counselors inconsistently pick and choose interventions for referred students, allowing subjectivity to affect access and efficacy of our school counseling programs and services.

Looking at past practices, it was not uncommon for school counselors to create groups by sorting the tall stack of teacher referrals into common areas of concern or to create group topics and ask teachers to sign up their students for a particular group. Some counselors ran groups on topics not suitable for school, such as incest, cutting, and abuse. However, as the field has continued to embrace a paradigm shift in the preventive work of school counseling, the support the school counselor provides is increasingly intentional, equitable, and subsequently, ethical.

The *ASCA Ethical Standards for School Counselors* (American School Counselor Association, 2016) revised their recommendation on small-group counseling to include a stronger focus on collecting data, selecting topics appropriate for school counselors, facilitating an evidence-based approach, and measuring outcomes to improve programs and services for students. Rather than wait for teachers to refer students to the school counselor, the school counselor is called to utilize a proactive approach. Today's school counselor recognizes that best practices for small-group interventions

- are driven by data (e.g., attendance, behavior, work/study habits),
- are predetermined and agreed upon,
- are prescheduled and calendared,
- utilize screening elements,
- are conducted on a short-term basis,
- are content-specific, aligning with data-driven need,

- include ongoing progress monitoring,
- measure results and impact, and
- empower them to make systemic change.

Data-Driven Small Groups

Using data to drive decision-making begins with determining which students are in need of the intervention and then determining which intervention is most appropriate. When deciding which short-term small-group interventions to offer to students, school counselors are encouraged to collect and analyze consistent data elements throughout the year. The third edition of *The ASCA National Model* includes a data profile tool with recommendations for the types of data school counselors may want to consider (American School Counselor Association, 2012). The fourth edition calls for a data program summary sheet under the category of program planning (American School Counselor Association, 2019). The types of data most commonly used in targeting small-group interventions align with the following:

- Attendance.
- Discipline referrals or suspensions.
- Course/homework completion.
- Course failure.

Attendance, behaviors, citizenship marks, and study habits represent early warning signs of students at risk for dropping out (Balfanz et al., 2010). Students often begin exhibiting behaviors that lead to dropping out as early as elementary school (National Forum on Education Statistics, 2018).

Recognizing the early warning signs of dropout behavior and intervening to teach the knowledge, attitudes, and skills that students need can help prevent future student failure (Jobs for the Future, 2014). Successful student habits, which are developed in the formative years, build the foundation for academic success in later years. School counselors are encouraged to utilize data to identify those students who receive moderate grades but may lack sufficient study and organizational skills. Intervening early may help students gain the skills they need to succeed as the academic curriculum increases in its rigor (Hatch, 2014; Hatch et al., 2019).

Study habits data align with research on noncognitive skills and academic mindsets (Farrington et al., 2012; Dweck et al., 2014). These data are typically located in elementary and some middle schools in the work skills, study habits, and citizenship areas of the report card. This often underutilized data element provides early insight into which students are struggling in the classroom and serves as an excellent screening tool for small-group interventions (Duarte & Hatch, 2014; Hatch et al., 2019).

Predetermined Data Elements

Collaborating with stakeholders is recommended when data will be consistently utilized to drive group counseling interventions. This requires communication and leadership on the part of the school counselor to garner support within the school and district. To gather and utilize meaningful data, teachers must be consistent when filling out ratings in report cards in the area of citizenship and work habits to ensure what they are reporting accurately represents the students' needs. For example, without thoughtful rubrics to help facilitate the use of qualitative report card marks, one teacher may give many students an "N" citing that every student *needs improvement*, while another teacher may give an "N" for a certain percent of missing assignments. Consistency is important, and school counselors will benefit from partnering with teachers to create rubrics in order to clarify what each of the ratings signifies.

Once school counselors have agreed upon which data elements will be used to target small-group interventions, it is recommended that they preschedule their annual calendar, including when small groups will occur throughout the year. Calendaring and marketing small-group interventions serve to inform stakeholders that interventions are guaranteed for all students who meet the identified data-driven criteria. Therefore, at the end of the agreed-upon timeline (e.g., first progress report, end of the quarter), the counselor queries the data, gathers names of students meeting the predetermined criteria, and screens them for an appropriate intervention. Prescheduling time on the calendar each grading period to disaggregate data, screen potential group members, and notify parents (as appropriate), as well as coordinate times for holding the small group, provides assurance that this process is followed in a timely manner.

Utilizing Data Systems as Screening Elements

Student database systems are the most efficient and effective way to query which students meet the identified need. Regardless of the student database system that a school uses, school counselors should establish systems and procedures to ensure that information is collected at regular, predetermined intervals. For instance, attendance and discipline rates may be queried on a monthly basis. Rather than having a teacher refer a student for discipline or study skills interventions, the school counselor proactively queries students at the end of the month or quarter or sets up a system to be notified when students receive the identified number of discipline referrals. After identification, the counselor meets with the student to interview them on contributing factors to behavior and determines the student's eligibility for small-group intervention.

Another example might be a school counselor who schedules time to review progress report data of students, then queries coursework completion and intentionally recruits students missing a specific percentage of assignments (e.g., 60% or less). Once the information is disaggregated, the counselor then assesses the students' appropriateness for group or other interventions. When student database systems are inaccessible or nonexistent, school counselors are encouraged to advocate for access to or the purchase of such a system or to utilize a form—such as those provided in the Resources section at the end of this chapter—to identify the need, monitor progress, and measure impact.

In *The Use of Data in School Counseling*, Hatch (2014) recommends surveying students to gain their perspectives as to why they are struggling with coursework completion, attendance, or appropriate behavior and gain insight into their commitment to attend a group intervention prior to assigning them to a small group. For example, a student may be failing a course, but this does not necessarily mean they need a study skills group; perhaps an academic mindsets group (e.g., perseverance, grit) is more appropriate. The American School Counselor Association (2016) recommends school counselors facilitate groups that are short term in nature and aligned with evidence-based practices, and address students' academic, career, and social/emotional issues. One example of how to align small-group topics in schools with data is seen in Table 3.1.

TABLE 3.1 Sample Data Elements for Group Counseling

Group Topic	Data Element	Example
Academic skills, academic mindsets, study skills, or goal setting	Report card data (study habits Ns)	3 or more Ns
	Course work completion	< 60% completion
	Grades	2 or more Fs
Conflict resolution, emotion management, peer relationships, or social skills	Office discipline referrals	3 or more Ns
	Report card data (citizenship Ns)	

Note: N = Needs improvement

An evidence-based approach is recommended when designing a small-group curriculum. For example (see Table 3.2), an elementary school counselor formulated her group counseling content by aligning the topics to the report card "Work Habits/Social Skills" markings. The chart below indicates the number of students in her third and fourth grade classes who received Ns (Needs Improvement) and Us (Unsatisfactory) in these areas. After disaggregating her data, she designed her small-group content to align with their data-driven need.

TABLE 3.2 Sample Number of Students with Ns and Us

Work Habit/Social Skill Data Element	Number of Students With Ns and Us
Completes homework consistently	18
Completes classwork consistently	16
Listens and follows directions	7
Organizes self and materials for learning	20
Uses materials appropriately	5
Follows school and classroom rules	2

Note: N = Needs improvement
    U = Unsatisfactory

Recognizing that the majority of her students needed more support in completing homework and classwork and in organizing self and materials, she created group content (see Table 3.3) that is aligned with this data-driven need.

TABLE 3.3 Sample Small-Group Curriculum

Week Number	Session Topic
1	Introduction/Purpose of Group
2	Goal Setting/Self-Assessment
3	Organizing Myself
4	Organizing Materials for Learning
5	Strategies for Completing Classwork
6	Strategies for Completing Homework
7	Goal Setting/Self-Assessment Review
8	Closure

Progress Monitoring During Group

Ensuring students benefit from the group intervention they receive requires collecting data before, during, and after the small-group intervention. Progress monitoring is an effective way to improve group outcomes by obtaining intermittent feedback from the teacher during the small-group intervention. In this method, the school counselor can assess teacher-reported improvements or challenges regarding student behaviors.

For example, an elementary school counselor is running a small group with fourth grade students who received multiple "Needs Improvement" (*N*) marks in the areas of homework completion and organization. During the small group, students will learn various skills on how to stay more organized, and systems will be put into place in order to improve the rate of homework completion. Rather than waiting until the six-to-eight-week intervention ends, it may be helpful to assess how the students in the small group are progressing throughout the intervention by utilizing a monitoring tool (see Table 3.4).

TABLE 3.4 **Progress Monitoring Tool**

Please rate the level the student demonstrated this week:				
Work Habit/Social Skill Data Element	**(U)**	**(N)**	**(S)**	**(O)**
Completes homework consistently	☐	☐	☐	☐
Completes classwork consistently	☐	☐	☐	☐
Organizes self and materials for learning	☐	☐	☐	☐

Note: U = Unsatisfactory
    N = Needs improvement
    S = Satisfactory
    O = Outstanding

Creating a form (or Google Doc) for teachers to fill out quickly before each small-group session provides valuable information, which allows for continuous feedback in order to determine the rate at which students' behaviors are shifting—increasing, decreasing, or staying the same. Based on this feedback, adjustments to the group intervention can be made in a timely manner. By doing this, the school counselor can manage the small-group curriculum responsively. Additionally, data should be collected and interpreted if additional or more intensive interventions are required.

Evaluation and Sharing Group Results With Stakeholders

There are multiple ways to use data to evaluate the impact that small-group interventions have, which includes participation data, mindsets and behaviors data, and outcome data.

Participation Data

Previously, *process data* was the terminology used in the first three editions (2003, 2005, and 2012) of the ASCA National Model to describe the activities that school counselors implement to support student needs. The fourth edition renamed process data *participation data* (American School Counselor Association, 2019); however, the terms are synonymous. Process or participation data provide evidence that an event occurred.

Participation data (formerly process data) refers to collecting information on the number of students served, the curriculum delivered, and other descriptions of the who, what, where, and when of the specific intervention, as in this example:

Who: 13 third and fourth grade students (92% group attendance rate)
What: Eight-week goal-setting and organization group
Where: School counseling office
When: Mondays from 12:50 p.m. to 1:30 p.m. beginning January 13, 2021

Mindsets and Behaviors Data

The term *perception data* has historically been used to measure the standards and competencies students are expected to master as a result of a school counseling lesson or intervention. In the fourth edition of the ASCA National Model, this is now called "mindsets and behaviors" data and answers the question, What did students learn through participation in the school counseling activities? (American School Counselor Association, 2019, p. 35).

Mindsets and behaviors data (formerly perception data) refers to measuring improvements or shifts in students' attitudes, knowledge, and skills as a result of the small-group intervention. The school counselor measures this by giving students in the small group a pretest to determine what they already know, believe, and can do. The posttest allows counselors to determine if students' attitudes, knowledge, and skills have improved as a result of the small-group intervention. School counselors are reminded to ensure that the content of the session aligns with the content of the assessment. For example, as suggested in Table 3.5, to measure the impact of a goal-setting session, a pretest and posttest assessment of a student's knowledge, attitude, and skills may include the following:

TABLE 3.5 Sample Mindsets and Behaviors Data for Content

Content	Mindsets and Behaviors Data
Goal Setting	The percentage of students who believe that goalsetting matters
	The percentage of students who can define what a goal is
	The percentage of students who can define the difference between a short- and long-term goal
	The percentage of students who can write a SMART goal

For more information on helping students develop SMART goals, see https://www.projectschoolwellness.com/teaching-middle-schoolers-how-to-write-smart-goals/

Outcome Data

Outcome data refers to measuring change in student behavior, particularly as related to the data-driven element. The Every Student Succeeds Act in 2015 revised data requirements collected and shared publicly on state-level data reporting systems. States now collect achievement-related data elements like parent and family engagement, school climate ratings, attendance, office referrals, et cetera. Achievement data elements include, for example, a reduction in failing grades or improved GPA.

In the previous example, the school counselor compared the first-semester report card data and looked for improvement on the second-semester report card. While this example has been specific to work skills and study habits, this technique can also be used with similar topics. As a reminder, change takes time. Shifts in data resulting in a reduction of Ns reported for students' work skills and study habits may align with improvements in classwork and homework completion but may not immediately affect large changes in grades or other achievement data. Utilizing progress monitoring, however, may allow for counselors and teachers to assess smaller increments of forward progress.

Conclusion

Measuring the impact of small groups is essential for many reasons. First, group counseling often interrupts instructional learning time. Demonstrating the effectiveness of small-group interventions can go a long way in gaining stakeholder support for future Tier 2 interventions. Secondly, results can also be used to help school counselors improve their instructional techniques when implementing small-group curricula. If no results are seen, they are encouraged to reevaluate and improve their evidence-based techniques. Finally, counselors are encouraged to share their results data and student outcomes with appropriate stakeholders to demonstrate successes, to learn and grow, and to inform future best practice.

CONNECTING TO CHAPTER CONTENT

Personal Reflection Questions

- Now that you have read the various logistical challenges that face school counselors when establishing their small-group counseling program, what do you perceive to be the challenges you will face?
- How can you plan to overcome some of the logistical challenges involved in garnering access to data, disaggregating data, and measuring data to evaluate impact when running small groups in a school setting?

Advice From the Expert/Author

Pay attention to the training the teachers attend. Even if you are not invited, if the training will help you in your work, attend! Advocate with the central office for similar training designed to support school counselors as they utilize the students' information system. Educating stakeholders on why collecting and analyzing data matters, how you use data to run groups, and how you will evaluate the impact and use what is learned to improve practices will help shift perspectives and ensure school counselors are part of all data-based decision-making teams, as well as provide support for your small-group counseling program.

Check Out These Resources

- Hatching Results LLC—MTMDSS: https://vimeo.com/304246315
- Hatching Results MTMDSS Planning Worksheet: https://static1.squarespace.com/static/5532b947e4b0edee99477d27/t/5a6fb6bb8165f5354fdeaff7/1517270716709/MTMDSS+Planning+Worksheet+2017.pdf
- Hatching Results Tier 2 and 3 Online Appendix, Hatching Results Tier 2 Action Plan Template, and Hatching Results Tier 2 and 3 Flow Chart: https://www.hatchingresults.com/elementary-t2-3-online-appendix
- Hatch, T. (2014). *The use of data in school counseling: Hatching results for students, programs and the profession.* Corwin Press.
- Hatch, T., Kruger, A., Pablo, N., & Triplett, W. (2019). *Hatching tier two and three interventions in your elementary school counseling program.* Corwin Press.

References

American School Counselor Association. (2012). *The ASCA National Model: A framework for school counseling programs* (3rd ed.).

American School Counselor Association. (2016). *Ethical standards for school counselors.* https://www.school-counselor.org/asca/media/asca/Ethics/EthicalStandards2016.pdf

American School Counselor Association. (2019). *The ASCA national model: A framework for school counseling programs* (4th ed.).

Balfanz, R., Bridgeland, J. M., Fox, J. H., & Moore, L. A. (2010). *Building a grad nation: Progress and challenge in ending the high school dropout epidemic (ED517690).* ERIC. https://eric.ed.gov/?id=ED517690

Belser, C. T., Shillingford, M. A., & Joe, J. R. (2016). The ASCA model and a multi-tiered system of supports: A framework to support students of color with problem behaviors. *Professional Counselor, 6*(3), 251–262.

Duarte, D., & Hatch, T. (2014). Successful implementation of a federally funded violence prevention elementary school counseling program: Results bring sustainability. *Professional School Counseling, 18(1)*, 71–81. https://doi.org/10.1177%2F2156759X0001800106

Dweck, C. S., Walton, G. M., & Cohen, G. L. (2014). *Academic tenacity: Mindsets and skills that promote long-term learning.* Gates Foundation.

Farrington, C. A., Roderick, M., Allensworth, E., Nagaoka, J., Keyes, T. S., Johnson, D. W., & Beechum, N. O. (2012). *Teaching adolescents to become learners. The role of noncognitive factors in shaping school performance: A critical literature review.* University of Chicago Consortium on Chicago School Research.

Hatch, T. (2014). *The use of data in school counseling: Hatching results for students, programs and the profession.* Corwin Press.

Hatch, T., Poynton, T., & Perusse, R. (2015). Comparison findings of school counselor beliefs about ASCA national model school counseling program components using the SCPSC. *SAGE Open, 5*(2). https://doi.org/10.1177%2F2158244015579071

Hatch, T., Kruger, A., Pablo, N., & Triplett, W. (2019). *Hatching tier two and three interventions in your elementary school counseling program.* Corwin Press.

Jobs for the Future. (2014). *Early warning indicators and segmentation analysis: A technical guide on data studies that inform dropout prevention and recovery.* U.S. Department of Education. https://www2.ed.gov/programs/dropout/earlywarningindicators.pdf

National Forum on Education Statistics. (2018). *Forum guide to early warning systems* (NFES2019035). U.S. Department of Education, National Center for Education Statistics.

Young, A., & Kaffenberger, C. (2011). The beliefs and practices of school counselors who use data to implement comprehensive school counseling programs. *Professional School Counseling, 15*(2), 67–76. https://doi.org/10.1177%2F2156759X1101500204

Utilizing Group Facilitation Skills to Enhance the Multitiered Systems of Support (MTSS) Process

Carol Dahir, EdD
New York Institute of Technology

Megyn Shea, PhD
New York Institute of Technology

LEARNING OBJECTIVES

1. Explain how MTSS is integral to whole child development.
2. Understand the relationship between comprehensive school counseling and MTSS.
3. Utilize the three-tier system to plan, implement, and evaluate interventions.

CONSIDER THIS SCENARIO

You are a school counselor in a large urban high school. You were fortunate to be selected to attend the state school counselor association conference this year. The expectation is that you would bring back the latest in innovative ideas, new information, and effective data-driven activities, and share these with your colleagues. At the next department meeting after the conference, you shared the concept of multitiered systems of support (MTSS). Everything you learned at the conference showed how utilizing MTSS complements the ASCA National Model. Your colleagues' reaction was not positive. They reminded you that the graduation rate and postsecondary going rate is the second highest in the city, and they believe that they have a comprehensive program in place. So why change?

CONSIDER THESE QUESTIONS FOR DISCUSSION

- Why is the thought of change so challenging, especially when student results show success?
- How can you show your colleagues that the delivery system they use for counseling services and activities already aligns with a MTSS system?
- How can you describe the benefits for students when utilizing MTSS?

Introduction

As the American School Counselor Association (ASCA) reminds us:

School counselors address all students' academic, career and college, and social/emotional development needs by designing, implementing, evaluating and enhancing a comprehensive school counseling program that promotes and enhances student success. (American School Counselor Association, 2020).

Some students struggle with academic achievement while others struggle with behavioral challenges. There are students who are challenged by both. School personnel must respond to all students who struggle in their abilities to learn. All educators should be sensitive to the time and resources students need to learn, especially for those who struggle to achieve a level of minimum proficiency.

School counselors ascribe to the belief that all children can learn and all children can achieve. Additionally, they have an ethical responsibility to collaborate with all school personnel, especially teachers, administrators, and student services professionals (American School Counselor Association, 2016a, Section B.2.q) to ensure that students with learning and instructional differences are treated with the same respect and are given the same opportunities as those considered part of the general student population. School counselors accomplish this by incorporating a variety of interventions (e.g., classroom delivery, individual and group counseling) that support the diverse needs of students receiving both regular and special education services. This requires counselors to work within a social justice framework to advocate for and appropriately utilize differentiated systems of support that deliver services, programs, and opportunities in a manner that addresses equity and fairness.

Supporting Students' Individual Needs

Multitiered systems of support (MTSS) is a framework that helps educators provide academic and behavioral strategies for students with various needs. MTSS grew out of the integration of two other intervention-based frameworks: response to intervention (RTI) and positive behavior intervention supports (PBIS). MTSS is culturally responsive and evidence-based, and uses data-based problem solving to integrate academic and behavioral instruction and intervention at tiered intensities to improve the learning and social/emotional functioning of all students (Sink, 2016). School counselors are critical players in the development and implementation of multitiered systems of supports in their schools as they assume collaborative and leadership roles through comprehensive school counseling and within MTSS to effectively and efficiently support all students (American School Counselor Association, 2018).

Districts may differ in how they use MTSS; some continue to use RTI and MTSS interchangeably. MTSS incorporates RTI and culturally responsive PBIS. However, school districts have largely adopted the MTSS framework as a schoolwide improvement process because of its focus on the whole child, which includes improving overall instruction, making decisions based on data, and providing behavioral support (Samuels, 2016). School counselors, as social justice advocates, play an important leadership role in MTSS with respect to supporting the early identification of students who will benefit from varying levels of intervention, both academic and behavioral. Whether by choice or by assumption in a leadership capacity, school counselors often have opportunities to both advocate for small-group interventions and utilize their group leadership skills to provide students with specific supports to address their needs.

The Evolution of MTSS

RTI resulted from federal education initiatives after the 2004 reauthorization of the Individuals With Disabilities Education Improvement Act (IDEA) and was considered an instructional framework that focused on assessment and early intervention. PBIS predates RTI in its inclusion in federal law; it was first introduced in the 1997 reauthorization of IDEA as a research-based framework for supporting children with behavioral concerns. Similar to the RTI process, PBIS utilizes three tiers. All students are initially taught certain behavioral expectations and rewarded for following them; select students exhibiting more needs are provided with increasingly intensive interventions based on their challenges. Aligned with the ASCA National Model, PBIS utilizes classroom lessons, group counseling, and individual counseling as an example of applying Tier 1, 2, and 3 interventions.

By implementing MTSS, schools make an effort to tackle both behavioral and academic concerns, concurrently recognizing that they often go hand in hand, as a student who can't follow what's going on in the classroom is more likely to act out, and a student who is grappling with behavior problems is not going to be able to focus on academics (Samuels, 2016).

> MTSS is a potentially powerful framework for assessing, organizing, allocating, and evaluating educational resources to meet the instructional and behavioral needs of all students and to prevent long-term school failure (Samuels, 2016).

MTSS teams identify students at risk for poor learning outcomes, monitor student progress, provide evidence-based interventions, adjust the intensity and nature of those interventions depending on students' responsiveness, and identify students with learning disabilities or other disabilities (National Center on Response to Intervention, 2010). This is accomplished effectively when team leaders understand the systems that influence students' academic, behavioral, and social/emotional development and are able to facilitate cohesive teams by managing multiple layers of group dynamics.

School Counselors as Facilitators of the MTSS Process

School counselors align their work with MTSS through the implementation of a comprehensive school counseling program designed to effect student development in the academic domain (achievement), the career and college domain (career exploration and postsecondary opportunities), and the social/emotional domain (behavior). Comprehensive school counseling and MTSS have much in common: a culturally responsive focus, whole child development, data-driven practices, equity and access, and the utilization of differentiated delivery systems (Goodman-Scott et al., 2019). MTSS offers school counselors opportunities to have a lasting impact on student academic success and behavior development while integrating the framework within the comprehensive school counseling program (Ziomek-Daigle et al., 2016). Who better than the school counselor to help manage these group dynamics to ensure that each student receives a quality and appropriate education? School counselors recognize the critical importance of early intervention for struggling students and can use their leadership skills to facilitate groups of stakeholders (e.g., teachers, other student services professionals, and families) throughout the assessment process. In doing so, they can work collaboratively with other educators to remove systemic barriers and help to implement specific learning supports that assist every student in achieving academic and behavioral success.

Facilitating groups of educators throughout this process, however, can be a challenging task, particularly given that group members may approach student learning and the change process in a variety of ways based on their individualized expertise. Understanding how member roles (e.g., monopolists and silent members) affect group dynamics and using whole-group process skills (e.g., "It seems like we all have a similar goal for this student but have different ideas about how to integrate the family into this process") to help the group address "the elephant in the room" are important ways that school counselors use their knowledge and expertise specific to group process to help facilitate MTSS teams in meaningful ways. In order for this process to work effectively, it is important to identify the role teachers and school counselors collaboratively play in the delivery of Tier 1, 2, and 3 interventions. Table 4.1 provides an overview of the roles that both the classroom teacher and the school counselor play in the delivery of tiered interventions.

TABLE 4.1 **Differentiated Delivery**

	From Classroom Teacher	From School Counselor
Tier 1 ——————▶ All Students Receive	Subject Classroom Lesson	School Counseling Curriculum (Large-Group Classroom)
Tier 2 ——————▶ Some Students Receive	Small-Group Remediation	Small-Group Counseling
Tier 3 ——————▶ A Few Students Receive	Individual Extra Help	Individual Counseling, Crisis Counseling, External Referral

Looking at Tier 1 And Tier 2 School Counseling Interventions

The school counseling core curriculum (Tier 1) is a sequence of learning activities and strategies that addresses the academic, career, and social/emotional development of every student (Gysbers & Henderson, 2012). It is planned and ongoing, has a scope and sequence, and is systematic with units of instruction aligned with the ASCA mindsets and behaviors along with input from school and community stakeholders. Large-group and classroom lessons (Tier 1) represent a common example of how school counselors deliver support. During these lessons, must initiate their group leadership skills to promote group cohesion and universality. As counselors link members' experiences, students begin to recognize more commonalities in their social/emotional, academic, and career interests and trajectories. Effective school counselors can utilize large-group interventions as a way to plant seeds for shared language across the school and future small-group interventions.

Small-group counseling (Tier 2) is an effective and developmentally appropriate school-based intervention (DeLucia-Waack, 2000; Erford, 2018; Sink, 2016) used to target specific student needs.

School counselors provide counseling sessions in small-group settings that:

- help students overcome issues impeding achievement or success,
- assist students to identify problems, causes, alternatives, and possible consequences so they can make decisions and take appropriate action, and
- are planned, goal-focused, evidence-based and short-term in nature. (American School Counselor Association, 2020).

Utilizing group counseling as a Tier 2 intervention affords students opportunities to learn from each other and develop important academic and relational skills. Within these groups, students share ideas, give and receive feedback, increase their awareness, gain new knowledge, practice skills, and think about their goals and actions (Sink et al., 2012). Small-group counseling may be integrated as part of an MTSS or PBIS intervention, a 504 plan, or as part of a student's individualized education plan to engage students in behavioral analysis, change, and adjustment (Quigney & Studer, 2016). Critical to the success of any intervention is the need to collaborate with teachers to set up groups for students receiving regular and special education services. The following offers two examples of how school counselors can utilize their group facilitation skills to support MTSS teams while using these skills to design, implement, and collect data around their small-group counseling (Tier 2) interventions.

Best Practice: Real Life MTSS Teams in Action

Case #1

Third grade marks the transition from the lower elementary school to the upper elementary setting in one particular school district. A third-grade counselor has noticed a need to support transitioning students and uses her role to address these needs in her building. This scenario offers a detailed progression of tiered interventions as they apply to the specific students at this respective school.

The school counselor operating from an MTSS (and ASCA best-practice) model would first plan preventatively regarding Tier 1 interventions. For example, the school counselor might structure a core curriculum lesson focused on the importance of peer–peer interactions, teamwork, and/or friendship in all third-grade homeroom classes. In this Tier 1 intervention, the school counselor ensures that all third-grade students receive the same developmental counseling lesson and, therefore, aligns comparable mindsets and behaviors for students' social/emotional transition to third grade. Whole-group process comments such as "I am noticing that the majority of us are feeling anxious about our changing friendship groups" may be utilized to highlight therapeutic factors (e.g., universality, cohesion) that can help individuals feel more connected to each other. Subgroup-level linking skills might further support students who benefit from observing appropriate social skills and imitative behaviors (e.g., "Kareem and Anna are both using 'I' statements with their respective partners to communicate how they are feeling about the drawing activity we are doing now").

Even though all students receive access to the school counselor's core curriculum third-grade transition lesson, she remains aware that some students (typically 10% to 20% of the total population targeted with the initial curriculum intervention) will not acquire the minimum competence proposed by the lesson's learning objectives (e.g., mindsets and behaviors). Therefore, she will rely on assessment measures (e.g., pretests and posttests, behavior observations, teacher feedback) to determine which specific students are in need of subsequent Tier 2 interventions to reinforce, reteach, and/or remediate the learning outcomes identified by the initial (Tier 1) intervention. For example, in the case of the third-grade transition/friendship topic, after providing the initial developmental counseling lesson to each third-grade homeroom, the school counselor could identify students who maintain deficits in their abilities to adjust to a new school, and make social connections accordingly. Once this cohort of students has been identified, the counselor can structure an appropriate Tier 2 intervention to support them.

In this case, a "social skills" small group focused on friendship or cooperation might provide just the right level of direct instruction and support to help students master the mindsets and behaviors necessary for them to have a successful upper-elementary school transition. In fact, typically (for all but about 1% to 10% of students) Tier 2 interventions provide the perfectly placed redirection to get students back on track. Just as in Tier 1 interventions, it is important for school counselors to collect useful, informative data to decide which students have recouped the skills and abilities needed for success versus the students who continue to struggle and will need additional support. For the few students who do not respond to Tier 2 interventions as anticipated, the school counselor will need to construct interventions that are even more intentional and individualized. These, known in the MTSS and RTI models as Tier 3 interventions, often involve individual counseling, crisis counseling, and referrals to supports provided externally (e.g., special education services, specialized support programs, alternative school settings). To further extend the third-grade transition example, the school counselor would select a targeted Tier 3 intervention for each student who did not respond as anticipated to the (Tier 2) small-group intervention. For one student, that might mean inviting them to eat lunch in the counselor's office with a peer or to an even more focused small group until social and transition progress is noted. For another student, it might mean a referral for more intense mental health counseling. Whatever the intervention selected, it is important to remember that school personnel must work intentionally and skillfully at this stage of a multitiered intervention process to ensure that each student receives what they need.

Case #2

The process outlined below describes a second example of the role of the school counselor. This time, the counselor is facilitating the adult MTSS team. This example highlights how the counselor's group facilitation skills are key to the success of each meeting and several of the recommended interventions. Understanding the stage and dynamics of this group's process helps the school counselor to appropriately intervene at various levels (individual, subgroup, and group as a whole), ensuring that members are working in the best interest of students and that group goals are met.

MTSS Team Background

The middle school MTSS team facilitated by you, the school counselor, includes a building administrator, two regular education teachers, a special education teacher, a reading specialist, and a math specialist. This group meets bimonthly to examine student data reports (e.g., test scores, attendance records) and discuss individual students in need of academic, behavioral, and social/emotional support. Your agenda for the December meeting includes the examination of data specific to school climate initiatives. As the leader of the team, you are tasked with the goal of ensuring that the school is meeting its mission to provide a safe educational environment for all students.

Scenario

Your building conducts annual climate surveys for students, teachers, and parents. The surveys include questions about support from teachers/staff/counselors/administration, student peer relations, perception of school safety, and the learning environment. As the MTSS team analyzes this survey data, they notice a spike in concerns involving peer relations and the learning environment. The MTSS team also collects teacher referral data. Similarly, they identify an increase in referrals related to student bullying behaviors. In addition to this information, you provide school counseling referral data that shows an increase in student self-referrals regarding bullying concerns. With this information, the MTSS team identifies bullying as a problem that needs to be addressed by the entire school community.

You, as the school counselor, are charged with leading the development of a systemic plan that will help the climate become a safer learning environment for all students. Considering the steps needed to address these goals, you are aware that the success of this adult group can be greatly enhanced by your ability to manage group dynamics, draw out their perspectives, challenge assumptions, and validate each member's experiences. This is particularly important, as each of the group members has identified different areas of concern based on their independent experiences in the school. It will therefore be important to address members' perspectives individually, in subgroups, and in the group as a whole. This will include making group process comments (group as a whole) if the group appears to be stuck or at a point of contention, connecting members' experiences to each other (subgroup level), and where appropriate, drawing out feedback and perspectives from each individual member. To begin, the group discusses ways to address the issues of bullying and assertiveness as a Tier 1 intervention.

Tier 1

The MTSS team decides that the most appropriate Tier 1 intervention is for the school counselors to conduct anti-bullying lessons for all students in the middle school. Each school counselor uses their group facilitation skills to conduct the large-group classroom lessons. These focus on identifying bullying, empathy for others, strategies for bystanders to intervene, and reporting procedures to utilize when instances of bullying occur.

The MTSS reconvenes to look at post-Tier 1 intervention data. The hope was to see a decrease in bullying incidents, but based on the data, the team notes an even larger increase in reports of bullying in the seventh grade. Although increased reporting was not what your MTSS group hoped to see, they determine it may not be that bullying has increased but rather students now understand what to look for and who to talk to when something occurs. Although the data can be framed in a positive manner, the large-group intervention was not enough to decrease seventh-grade bullying incidents. The team decides a Tier 2 intervention is necessary to address the problem at a more targeted level.

Tiers 2 and 3

The team agrees that school counselor-led groups serve as an appropriate Tier 2 intervention and plan accordingly. The small groups will consist of six to eight students and target approximately 15% of the seventh-grade population. The Tier 2 intervention will be for students who are having difficulty asserting themselves with others. Students are identified through teacher, counselor, and administrator referral. Once the list of students is gathered, you take a closer look at data related to each one. You notice a pattern emerge; many of those identified for the Tier 2 assertiveness intervention are also underperforming in the classroom. You and the rest of the MTSS members believe assertiveness related to learning needs as well as relationships with peers should be included in the small-group intervention.

You decide to collect data related to the effectiveness of the group throughout the Tier 2 small-group intervention. You want to make sure the group is gaining the information and skills you want them to know and be able to do. For example, does each member know what assertiveness looks like when talking with peers and teachers? Are they able to demonstrate appropriate assertiveness skills learned after each group session?

Upon completion of the small groups, you also collect data from teachers related to each student's use of assertiveness skills and their respective grades. You reconvene the MTSS team once again to look at all the data, including teacher perceptions, student perceptions, student skill demonstration, student grades, and bullying incident reports. Based on the data collected, the MTSS team determines that the majority of the participating students have improved their assertiveness skills. In addition, bullying reports have decreased and several students improved their grades. However, a few students are still struggling and appear to need even more support. These students will move to Tier 3 and receive individual interventions. The MTSS team will continue to monitor the Tier 3 student data to determine the needs and effectiveness of the interventions.

Reflection

In this situation, the school counselor facilitated a small group of teachers and administrators throughout the MTSS process. Using assessment and group facilitation skills, the school counselor drew out the voices of each group member and helped to complete the goals set forth by this task group. This was especially challenging at certain times, particularly in the storming stage of the group, as a certain member (e.g., seventh-grade teacher) felt as though her perspective was more valuable than others. By attending to this process and providing a group-as-a-whole intervention, the school counselor drew out more silent members who shared differing perspectives that contributed to a more systemic view of the presenting problem.

In addition to using facilitation skills as part of the MTSS group itself, the school counselor also utilized group leadership skills with students while providing classroom guidance lessons (Tier 1) and designing and facilitating assertiveness small groups (Tier 2) for struggling seventh-grade students. Implementing these groups helped to address students' needs more intensely and to provide the MTSS team with data in which to progress monitor individual students. Each of these contributions ultimately helped to ensure that students were feeling safe and supported throughout the school day.

Conclusion

The shift to MTSS offers school counselors opportunities to bring many of their skills to the table and facilitate conversations that support whole child development by simultaneously addressing academic support (Tiers 1, 2, 3) and behavioral support (classroom, group, individual) as depicted in the differentiated delivery chart (Table 4.1). Operating within the MTSS system can feel complex for emerging school counselors or overwhelming for veteran counselors who do not have experience with this model. The reality is that school counselors have delivered the MTSS model without even realizing it. However, when they leverage MTSS in a manner that highlights group work in schools, students benefit greatly. School counselors are then able to combine their knowledge of group dynamics and group process with their group counseling facilitation skills to develop small groups for students or lead task groups consisting of school faculty (e.g., MTSS task groups) on behalf of students. Students in today's schools have diverse academic and behavioral needs (Lopez & Bursztyn, 2013; Vincent et al., 2011), and comprehensive school counseling program and MTSS implementation play a critical role in meeting these needs (Lapan, 2012; Wilkerson et al., 2013). In these applications, school counselors provide invaluable expertise that contributes to safe, secure, and equitable educational learning environments.

CONNECTING TO CHAPTER CONTENT

Personal Reflection Questions
- How can I use my training in group facilitation skills to bring a new level of understanding to my colleagues to utilize MTSS?
- How can I use my group facilitation skills to help the counseling department improve collaboration and teaming with teachers?
- Equally important, how will shifting this mindset create positive student outcomes?

Advice From the Expert/Author

After reading the chapter, you have a better understanding of MTSS and how it aligns with the ASCA National Model. School counselors recognize the critical importance of early identification and early intervention for struggling students. They can use their leadership skills to facilitate groups of stakeholders (e.g., teachers, other student services professionals, and families) to implement specific learning supports that assist every student achieve academic and behavioral success. School counselors can utilize the MTSS three-tier system to plan, implement, and evaluate interventions.

Check Out These Resources

- American School Counselor Association. (2018). *The school counselor and multitiered system of supports* [Position statement]. https://www.schoolcounselor. org/Standards-Positions/Position-Statements/ASCA-Position-Statements/ The-School-Counselor-and-Multitiered-System-of-Sup
- American School Counselor Association. (2020). *Making MTSS work* [Webinar]. https://videos.schoolcounselor.org/making-mtss-work
- Goodman-Scott, E., Betters-Bubon, J., & Donohue, P. (2019). *The school counselor's guide to multi-tiered systems of support.* Routledge.
- Goodman-Scott, E., Betters-Bubon, J., Olsen, J., & Donohue, P. (2020). *Making MTSS work.* American School Counselor Association.
- Olsen, J., Parikh-Foxx, S., Flowers, C., & Algozzine, B. (2017). An examination of factors that relate to school counselors' knowledge and skills in multi-tiered systems of support. *Professional School Counseling, 20*(1), 159–171. https://doi.org/10.5330 %2F1096-2409-20.1.159

References

American School Counselor Association. (2014). *ASCA mindsets & and behaviors for student success: K–12 college- and career-readiness standards for every student.* https://www.schoolcounselor.org/getmedia/7428a787-a452-4abb-afec-d78ec77870cd/Mindsets-Behaviors.pdf

American School Counselor Association. (2016a). *ASCA ethical standards for school counselors.* https://www.schoolcounselor.org/getmedia/f041cbd0-7004-47a5-ba01-3a5d657c6743/Ethical-Standards.pdf

American School Counselor Association. (2016b). *The school counselor and students with disabilities* [Position statement]. https://www.schoolcounselor.org/Standards-Positions/Position-Statements/ASCA-Position-Statements/The-School-Counselor-and-Students-with-Disabilitie

American School Counselor Association. (2018). *The school counselor and multitiered system of supports* [Position statement]. https://www.schoolcounselor.org/Standards-Positions/Position-Statements/ASCA-Position-Statements/The-School-Counselor-and-Multitiered-System-of-Sup

American School Counselor Association. (2019). *ASCA National Model: A framework for school counseling programs* (4th ed.).

American School Counselor Association. (2020). *The school counselor and group counseling.* [Position statement]. https://www.schoolcounselor.org/Standards-Positions/Position-Statements/ASCA-Position-Statements/The-School-Counselor-and-Group-Counseling

DeLucia-Waack, J. (2000). Effective group work in schools. *Journal for Specialists in Group Work, 25*(2), 131–132. https://doi.org/10.1080/01933920008411456

Erford, B. T. (2018). *Group work: Processes and applications* (2nd ed.). Routledge.

Goodman-Scott, E., Betters-Bubon, J., & Donohue, P. (Eds.). (2019). *The school counselor's guide to multi-tiered systems of support.* Routledge.

Gysbers, N. C., & Henderson, P. (2012). *Developing and managing your school guidance program* (5th ed.). American Counseling Association.

Lapan, R. T. (2012). Comprehensive school counseling programs: In some schools for some but not in all schools for all students. *Professional School Counseling, 16*(2), 84–88. https://doi.org/10.1177%2F2156759X1201600201

Lopez, E. C., & Bursztyn, A. M. (2013). Future challenges and opportunities: Toward culturally responsive training in school psychology. *Psychology in the Schools, 50*(3), 212–228. https://doi.org/10.1002/pits.21674

National Center on Response to Intervention. (2010). *Essential components of RTI: A closer look at response to intervention.* American Institutes for Research, Center on Multi-Tier System of Supports. https://mtss4success.org/sites/default/files/2020-07/rtiessentialcomponents_042710.pdf

Quigney, T., & Studer, J. (2016). *Working with students with disabilities.* Routledge.

Samuels, C. (2016, December 13). *What are multi-tiered systems of support?* Education Week. https://www.edweek.org/policy-politics/what-are-multitiered-systems-of-supports/2016/12

Sink, C. A., Edwards, C. N., & Eppler, C. (2012). *School based group counseling.* Cengage Learning.

Sink, C. (2016). Incorporating a multi-tiered system of supports into school counselor preparation. *Professional Counselor, 6*(3), 203–219. https://tpcjournal.nbcc.org/wp-content/uploads/2016/09/Pages203-219-Sink.pdf

Vincent, C. G., Randall, C., Cartledge, G., Tobin, T. J., & Swain-Bradway, J. (2011). Toward a conceptual integration of cultural responsiveness and schoolwide positive behavior support. *Journal of Positive Behavior Interventions, 13*(4), 219–229. https://doi.org/10.1177%2F1098300711399765

Wilkerson, K., Perusse, R., & Hughes, A. (2013). Comprehensive school counseling programs and student achievement outcomes: A comparative analysis of RAMP versus non-RAMP schools. *Professional School Counseling, 16*(3), 172–184. https://doi.org/10.1177%2F2156759X1701600302

Ziomek-Daigle, J., Goodman-Scott, E., Cavin, J., & Donohue, P. (2016). Integrating a multi-tiered system of supports with comprehensive school counseling programs. *Professional Counselor, 6*(3), 220–232. https://tpcjournal.nbcc.org/wp-content/uploads/2016/09/Pages220-232-Ziomek-Daigle.pdf

The Importance of Stakeholder Collaboration

Clare Merlin-Knoblich, PhD
University of North Carolina at Charlotte

LEARNING OBJECTIVES

1. Explain the importance of collaboration with school stakeholders when running groups.
2. Identify how groups can inform and be informed by school stakeholders.
3. Generate ideas for groups designed or cofacilitated with community members.

CONSIDER THIS SCENARIO

Andre is an elementary school counselor. After 5 years of working collaboratively with parents, community leaders, and his co-counselor at Arnold Elementary School, he begins a new job at Draper Elementary School, where he is the only school counselor. After getting to know his administrators and speaking with his predecessor, Andre concludes that minimal collaboration occurs at the school with stakeholders. His predecessor reports no relationships with community organizations or leaders, and teachers indicate to Andre that they did not previously work with the school counselors in any collaborative ways. After settling into his school during the first half of the year, Andre decides that he wants to make a plan for collaborating with stakeholders in the second half of the year. He sets a specific goal to involve stakeholders in the groups he plans to run.

CONSIDER THESE QUESTIONS FOR DISCUSSION

- If you could describe Andre's plan in three steps, what would those steps be?
- How do you think Andre will know if he meets his goal?
- What do you think will be the biggest hurdles Andre will face in executing his plan?

Introduction

As a school counselor educator, I savor the time my school counseling students have in our program, carefully learning techniques, discussing best practices, and embracing the supervision support of their peers and professors. These efforts sometimes feel as though they are all in preparation for the moment they graduate, get hired, and are "out on their own," working as paid school counselors in the field. But the truth is, these students will never actually be "out on their own," and it is a misnomer to label them as such. Even once the newest school counselor leaves their training program and begins work independently, they should not work independently at all. This is because school counselors are called to work collaboratively with school stakeholders. Engaging in group work is no exception.

Collaboration in School Counseling

Collaborating with stakeholders is an essential part of comprehensive school counseling programs. Gone are the days of "guidance counselors" working independently in their offices to support only the highest and lowest achieving students in a school building. Instead, professional school counselors work actively with others to support the needs of students (American School Counselor Association [ASCA], 2019; Foxx et al., 2017). In fact, *collaboration* was one of four themes emphasized in the original ASCA National Model framework (American School Counselor Association, 2003). Although these themes no longer appear around the border of the National Model diamond, the fourth edition of the ASCA National Model weaves all of them, including collaboration, throughout the model (American School Counselor Association, 2019).

Collaboration is a process in which individuals work together toward the same goal (American School Counselor Association, 2019). In comprehensive school counseling programs, collaboration occurs in a number of ways and with a variety of different people. School counselors often partner with families, colleagues, and community organizations to support students (American School Counselor Association, 2019; Foxx et al., 2017). This work is sometimes in the form of crisis response when immediate emergencies arise, or it can be planned and scheduled in anticipation of student needs (American School Counselor Association, 2019). School counselors also serve on school committees, teaming up with others to plan school programs, as well as collaborate with families and caregivers to support student success (American School Counselor Association, 2019).

Stakeholders

Merriam-Webster (n.d.) defines the term *stakeholder* as "one that has a stake in an enterprise" or "one who is involved in or affected by a course of action." Given this definition, all of society is arguably a stakeholder for K–12 schools, as all people will be affected by the actions of our future generations. More specifically, school stakeholders typically refer to those with a vested interest in supporting student outcomes. These include teachers, parents and caregivers, business owners, community members, local leaders, neighbors, family members, and administrators.

Collaboration With Stakeholders

Collaborating with stakeholders is key in building and maintaining a school counseling program that effectively supports students (American School Counselor Association, 2019; Nelson et al., 2020). Researchers have found that when school counselors partner with teachers to plan counseling programs, their collaborative efforts improve teachers' perceptions about the work (Villares et al., 2020). Researchers have also found that parent and community member collaboration in schools is positively correlated with student academic achievement and attendance (Bryan et al., 2016; Henry et al., 2017; Nelson et al., 2020). When school counselors build collaborations with community members, those collaborations result in improved advocacy and empowerment for youth and their families, in addition to building assets that allow families to thrive (Bryan & Henry, 2012; Bryan et al., 2020; Nelson et al., 2020).

Although all schools exist within communities of some kind, are often distanced from the businesses and neighbors in their communities (Epstein, 2011; Nelson et al., 2020). When school counselors reach out to community members and form partnerships, they bridge this gap, increasing community support and gaining valuable resources that help students (Kladifko, 2013; Nelson et al., 2020). Such efforts make meaningful differences to a school and its students.

School counselors communicate with stakeholders to both inform and be informed. For example, counselors work to understand the needs of their students in order to design a school counseling program that best meets those needs. If a school counselor built their program off their perception of student needs, their program would be limited in scope by their inherent world view and bias. Moreover, if this perspective only represents views in majority groups, such as White people, straight people, and/or U.S. citizens, it lacks important views that may uniquely characterize marginalized groups, such as people of color, LGBTQ people, and non-U.S. citizens or immigrants. Instead, when school counselors poll students' teachers, family members, and neighbors, they glean a more comprehensive understanding of students' needs that represents a variety of diverse viewpoints. Building a comprehensive school counseling program from such comprehensive information provides a more accurate view of what students need; and thus, the program is more effective, once implemented.

In addition to being informed by stakeholders, school counselors are well-positioned to inform and educate stakeholders. It is important to regularly share information with parents and caregivers, administrators, and community members regarding the opportunities students receive from their school counseling program (American School Counselor Association, 2019). For example, if a school counselor is planning a series of parent workshops on identifying and reducing anxiety in adolescents, they can expand their advertising of these workshops not only by informing parents and caregivers about them but also by asking local leaders, business owners, and community organizations to promote the events. School counselors consult with local community organizations, such as the Boys and Girls Club or YMCA to ensure that community members are aware of the workshops and that the organizations are not already planning similar programs to support families. Such collaboration enhances a school, its school counseling program, and the community itself (American School Counselor Association, 2019).

School counselors are expected to collaborate with school stakeholders throughout their comprehensive programs, and group work is a key area in which collaboration occurs. Stakeholders support school counselors in a number of ways when planning, leading, and assessing the small groups in their programs. By familiarizing yourself with each of these steps in the group work process and with how school stakeholders collaborate in them, you can implement group interventions that are meaningful and extend beyond your own world view.

Planning

When planning groups, needs assessments are a key tool to determining student needs, whether in social/emotional, academic, or career development. In a needs assessment, school counselors ask stakeholders to evaluate the biggest needs of students so that they can plan corresponding services (including groups) that address those needs (Merlin & Knoblich, 2016). Needs assessments may indicate that students struggle in a particular area, and by distributing needs assessments to parents and caregivers, teachers, and community members in addition to students, school counselors gain a comprehensive understanding of student needs. When planning groups, the information gathered will indicate what kinds of groups a counselor should lead in order to address student needs, and which types of students they should invite to participate in the group. For example, a needs assessment in which most parents and caregivers indicate that transition anxiety is a concern could prompt an elementary school counselor to plan a small counseling group for fifth-grade students preparing to move to middle school. A needs assessment in which high school teachers indicate that students are unaware of how to apply to college could prompt a counselor to plan a psychoeducational group for 11th-grade students about the college application and matriculation processes.

Needs assessments also highlight areas in which students are not lacking services, thus directing a school counselor's attention elsewhere, where it is more valuable. (Merlin & Knoblich, 2016).

When I was a high school counselor, I had two students seek my support because they identified as having eating disorders. I suspected that this concern might be widespread in the school and therefore warrant a group for students. However, when I surveyed parents, teachers, and students about 20 different potential needs, eating disorders were the least-frequently indicated need by participants. I was guilty of assuming that just because a topic was presenting at my office door, it was pervasive throughout the school. Through the needs assessment, I learned that instead of concerns about widespread eating disorders, nearly all teachers and parents who participated were concerned that students lacked career development support. I collaborated with colleagues to determine which students seemed most in need of career planning support, then created and led a group for eight students over the course of 6 weeks. I also learned an important reality about collaborating with school stakeholders: by basing groups on specific data collected from stakeholders rather than just hunches, school counselors ensure that their groups help students in the areas they need it most.

Leading

Stakeholder collaboration is not only useful when planning groups. When coordinating and leading groups, partnering with school stakeholders can elevate the content and value of those groups. There are two ways in which school counselors involve stakeholders in executing groups. First, they utilize school stakeholders as resources in piecemeal ways when needed. For instance, a group leader might invite a local business owner to serve as a guest speaker for a single session about owning a small business in a group for exploring career interests. The guest speaker would not be present for the other group sessions and only contribute when needed for the specific session about owning a business. Similarly, when planning a small group about study skills, a school counselor could consult one time with a school media specialist about recommendations for students to use the media center while studying.

Additionally, counselors can use school stakeholders in more expansive, consistent ways to coplan and cofacilitate full groups together. This is a useful approach when a they need additional expertise about a particular topic for which they are leading a group. For example, in my community, school counselors often cofacilitate groups with counselors from Kinder-Mourn, a nonprofit organization that supports children experiencing grief. Although school counselors are experts in leading groups and their own students (American School Counselor Association, 2019), KinderMourn counselors bring extensive expertise in death, dying, and grief to support students in grief groups at local schools. School counselors may also benefit from cofacilitating groups supporting LGBTQ students with local community members who are experts in LGBTQ identity development. School counselors could explore holding a support group for immigrant students and partner with local immigrant advocacy organizations to plan the group. Lastly, they could consider partnering with a school nurse to cofacilitate a group for pregnant teenagers.

Assessing

Whether a school counselor leads a group on their own or with stakeholders, it is important that they review their school counseling program, including its groups, with stakeholders. They can actively engage stakeholders by reviewing data from group work to collaboratively assess how the data may or may not reveal impacts on students. In particular, school counselors review data with their program advisory council. This council is a group of representative stakeholders that ideally includes several teachers, community members, parents, and an administrator (American School Counselor Association, 2019).

This idea is best illustrated in an example about an academic motivation group a school counselor led with 8th-grade students. After the group ended, the counselor asked her school counseling program advisory council to collaboratively examine mindsets and behaviors data and outcome data (American School Counselor Association, 2019) related to the group, without revealing any participant or teacher names. The mindsets and behavior data showed that the students in the group enjoyed the experience. Students reported that they learned about the importance of doing well in school. On a scale of 1 ("I learned nothing") to 5 ("I learned a lot"), the eight students in the group reported an average learning perception of 4.5. However, the outcome data revealed that on average, the group participants' grades were lower after the group compared to before. When discussing this discrepancy with the advisory council, members suggested valuable explanations for the data. One teacher suggested that students may have increased their academic motivation after the group, but that not enough time had passed for the improvement to be evident in their grades. A parent mentioned that perhaps the students' motivation had increased but that they were in need of additional academic support to improve their grades. Like in this example, by reviewing the data and discussing group work ideas with the advisory council, school counselors learn from their efforts and make informed plans to improve or replicate them in the future.

Lastly, when school counselors have a clear idea of how groups are impacting students, it is important that they share such information with school stakeholders to keep them informed (American School Counselor Association, 2019). They can communicate their findings in counseling department brochures, newsletters, or via their website. School counselors also benefit from providing a summary of their work to faculty and staff members at the end of each school year so colleagues understand the services that school counselors offer to students and how those services, including group work, support student development (American School Counselor Association, 2019; Foxx et al., 2017).

Confidentiality

Whether school counselors collaborate with stakeholders by cofacilitating groups or sharing updates at meetings, it is important to keep student confidentiality in mind. Although confidentiality cannot be guaranteed to group members, as indicated in this text's chapter on ethics, it is best practice to request that members keep group content to themselves and do not disclose it to others outside the group. When partnering with a community member to cofacilitate a group, school counselors inform their coleaders of this expectation, in case they do not come from a counseling background and are not already familiar with it. When informing stakeholders about groups they have held, school counselors should not disclose any names or other details that might reveal student identities or information that ought to be kept confidential. For example, when sharing an update about a recently held group for 9th-grade boys failing algebra, a school counselor should avoid naming students in the group or mentioning details like "most of the participants came from Mrs. Green's class." They should de-identify any data shared with stakeholders when engaging in collaborative assessment.

Conclusion

Despite extensive growth in the school counseling profession in the last 100 years, school counselors are still outnumbered by teachers, administrators, and parents in a school community (American School Counselor Association, 2019). Thus, it is tempting for school counselors to work independently, siloed from their colleagues and community—because after all, they are perhaps the only school counselor in the building. Yet, given that school counselors work toward the same goal as other educators and parents—supporting student success—it is most beneficial for them to work collaboratively with school stakeholders (Nelson et al., 2020). Such collaboration does not apply to merely some of a school counselor's tasks. Collaboration should, instead, be woven throughout a comprehensive school counseling program, including group work (American School Counselor Association, 2019). By teaming with teachers, administrators, community members, business leaders, and families, school counselors improve the planning, delivery, and assessment of their group work. As a result, students will be all the better for it.

CONNECTING TO CHAPTER CONTENT

Personal Reflection Questions

Some people are more comfortable engaging with parents/caregivers, teachers, and community members than others. Naturally, some school counselors feel more comfortable doing so, whereas others do not.

- What personality characteristics do you think are more associated with ease when partnering with school stakeholders? Which of these are strengths of yours? Which are not strengths for you?
- Of the three primary steps in group work (planning, leading, assessing), in which step do you feel most comfortable collaborating with stakeholders? In which step do you feel least comfortable collaborating with stakeholders?
- What would make you more comfortable when initiating collaborations with school stakeholders?

Advice From the Expert/Author

Just like new school counselors are sometimes told "we don't run groups here," they can also be told "we don't involve the community much here." In these situations, school counselors would be best to think they heard "we don't involve the community much here ... yet." Collaboration with stakeholders, especially community members and families, can be challenging work. Some community members have past experiences feeling excluded by school systems, and indeed, many educators have a history of marginalizing certain populations and neighbors. But meaningful partnerships need to begin somewhere, and school counselors would benefit from viewing this work as a marathon, not a sprint. I encourage you to set small goals each year to gradually build relationships with neighbors, community members, and local leaders. Consider inviting one new person to join your school counseling advisory council each semester. Or partner with one new cofacilitator to run a group each year. By gradually building collaborations with your community, you are more likely to gain trust, be successful, and not burn out in the process.

Check Out These Resources

- Bryan, J., Williams, J., & Griffin, D. (2020). Fostering educational resilience and opportunities in urban schools through equity-focused school-family-community partnerships. *Professional School Counseling, 23*(1, Pt.2). https://doi.org/10.1177/2156759X19899179
- Henry, L. M., Bryant, J., & Zalaquett, C. P. (2017). The effects of a counselor-led, faith-based, school-family-community partnership on student achievement in a high-poverty urban elementary school. *Journal of Multicultural Counseling and Development, 45*(3), 162–182. https://doi.org/10.1002/jmcd.12072

- Nelson, K. L., Morris, J. R., Brinson, J., & Stahl, M. A. (2020). School-community group model: Collaborating for the empowerment of adolescent African American male students. *Journal for Specialists in Group Work, 45*(2), 113–128. https://doi.org/10.1080/01933922.2020.1740848

References

American School Counselor Association. (2003). *The ASCA National Model: A framework for school counseling programs.*

American School Counselor Association. (2019). *The ASCA National Model: A framework for school counseling programs* (4th ed.).

Bryan, J., & Henry, L. (2012). A model for building school-family-community partnerships: Principles and process. *Journal of Counseling and Development, 90*(4), 408–420. https://doi.org/10.1002/j.1556-6676.2012.00052.x

Bryan, J., Williams, J., & Griffin, D. (2016). Closing achievement gaps for Black male students through school-family-community partnerships. In M. S. Henfield & A. R. Washington (Eds.), *School counseling for Black male student success in 21st century urban schools* (pp. 75–97). Information Age.

Bryan, J., Williams, J., & Griffin, D. (2020). Fostering educational resilience and opportunities in urban schools through equity-focused school-family-community partnerships. *Professional School Counseling, 23*(1, Pt.2). https://doi.org/10.1177/2156759X19899179

Epstein, J. L. (2011). *School, family, and community partnerships: Preparing educators and improving schools* (2nd ed.). Westview Press.

Foxx, S. P., Baker, S. B., & Gerler, E. R., Jr. (2017). *School counseling in the 21st century* (6th ed.). Routledge.

Henry, L. M., Bryant, J., & Zalaquett, C. P. (2017). The effects of a counselor-led, faith-based, school–family–community partnership on student achievement in a high-poverty urban elementary school. *Journal of Multicultural Counseling and Development, 45*(3), 162–182. https://doi.org/10.1002/jmcd.12072

Kladifko, R. E. (2013). *Practical school community partnership leading to successful educational leaders* (EJ1013145). ERIC. https://eric.ed.gov/?id=EJ1013145

Merlin, C., & Knoblich, A. J. (2016). Needs assessment and unit/lesson design. In J. Z. Daigle (Ed.), *Classroom guidance for prevention, accountability, and outcomes* (pp. 118–152). Sage.

Nelson, K. L., Morris, J. R., Brinson, J., & Stahl, M. A. (2020). School-community group model: Collaborating for the empowerment of adolescent African American male students. *Journal for Specialists in Group Work, 45*(2), 113–128. https://doi.org/10.1080/01933922.2020.1740848

Merriam-Webster. (n.d.). Stakeholder. In *Merriam-Webster.com dictionary*. Retrieved March 15, 2020, from https://www.merriam-webster.com/dictionary/stakeholder

Villares, E., Brigman, G., Webb, L., Carey, J., & Harrington, K. (2020). A randomized control trial of elementary teachers' perceptions of school counselor impact. *Counseling Outcome Research and Evaluation.* https://doi.org/10.1080/21501378.2020.1788929

Uniquely School Counseling: Overcoming Challenges to Group Work

Christine J. Schimmel, EdD, NCC, LPC
West Virginia University

Ed Jacobs, PhD, LPC
West Virginia University

LEARNING OBJECTIVES

1. Recognize at least four unique challenges that school counselors face when planning the logistics of running small groups.
2. Discuss solutions for addressing logistical challenges to running small groups in schools.
3. Identify the unique challenges of running small groups in schools that may cause you, the reader, the most difficulty.

CONSIDER THIS SCENARIO

Kyra is a new elementary school counselor. She learned in her master's program that running small groups is one of the most effective and efficient Tier 2 interventions that school counselors can offer students, so she is excited to get her small-group counseling program up and running. In her first meeting with her new principal, she learns that the former school counselor didn't run groups and that it doesn't seem like there is much understanding about their value. The principal goes on to say that she is not sure when Kyra could even access students to be in small groups; there is too much classroom instruction that needs to occur during the day to pull students out of class. The principal also expresses concerns about parents consenting to allow students to participate.

CONSIDER THESE QUESTIONS FOR DISCUSSION

- What are your initial thoughts about Kyra's situation?
- If you were Kyra, what would be the first thing you might do in this situation?

Introduction

The literature surrounding group counseling in schools is rich with evidence that supports the value of running groups in school settings (Steen et al., 2008; Swank et al., 2018; Bowers et al., 2015). Conducting group counseling in a school setting, whether it is elementary, middle, or high school, has many unique challenges. Those challenges include identifying the best times to run groups, the limited number of times that are available to conduct groups, dealing with heavy caseloads that can lead to a crisis or other distractions that interfere with group times, and the pressure from teachers and administrators to include students in groups who are not suitable for group work. However, with experience and practice, these challenges can be overcome or dealt with so that this kind of counseling can become the integral piece of the comprehensive school counseling program (CSCP) that it should be. In this chapter, there will be a brief discussion regarding the ways in which school counselors can manage the challenges they face when establishing small groups in schools.

Challenge 1: Finding Time to Conduct Group Counseling

In our many years of supervising school counseling students and providing group leadership training to practicing school counselors, this challenge is expressed time and time again. Unfortunately, there is no perfect time to pull students for conducting group counseling. Having said that, counselors must be very aware of the fact that they must work in tandem with classroom teachers and students to find a compromise for students missing valuable class time. A few suggestions seem warranted to address this challenge. First, school counselors should alternate group meeting times throughout the school schedule. A third-grade friendship group should not meet, for example, every Monday at 9:00 a.m. Instead, consider alternating the time or day in which the group meets. For example, the first meeting could be held Monday at 9:00 a.m., while the second meeting occurs Monday at 1:00 p.m. or Tuesday at 10:00 a.m. Alternating the time or day prevents students from missing the same classroom content each week. Teachers appreciate their involvement in determining the best mutual time for students to be out of class. Additionally, it is recommended that groups do not meet for extended periods of time. A typical school group should theoretically only last 30 to 40 minutes, depending on the developmental ages of the children or adolescents in the group. This approach honors the level of the students' maturational development as well as serves to respect teachers' time by minimizing student time out of class.

Let us be clear, some teachers will never be happy that students are missing any amount of classroom time, yet this should not discourage school counselors from leading groups. It is strongly encouraged that counselors do everything possible to engender support from teachers. This includes developing a schedule that is palatable for both counselor and teacher. It should not be forgotten that group counseling is a vital piece of the CSCP (American School Counselor Association, 2019), and collaborating with teachers to impress this upon them is vital. Some states have begun to highlight the importance of group counseling in policy. In West Virginia, for example, it is specifically listed as an integral piece of a CSCP—it is noted that group counseling is short term in nature and will only minimally impact classroom time (West Virginia Department of Education, 2017). In states where there are no policies for or little acknowledgment of the necessity of group work, school counselors consider various advocacy efforts to implement policies to support it. For example, by connecting with local or state professional organizations, school counselors may be able to make gains toward systematic inclusion of group practices in the school setting.

Many school counselors avoid the interference with classroom time by only running groups during student lunch times. While this may be a viable option, counselors give thought to the challenges this creates. Primarily holding groups during student lunch likely interferes with one of the few times they have to socialize during the school day. This can cause mild to moderate resistance from students who do not want to give up their limited social time. Meeting during lunch also creates the dilemma of when students can eat. Do school counselors let them eat during group? This promises to be quite distracting! Should the counselor decide that lunch is the only viable time in which you can run groups, we offer this thought: devote the first 10 to 15 minutes to allowing students to focus on eating and socializing. After that time, the school counselor can begin to lead the group. While this provides a briefer group counseling experience, the time may be more productive if students are not trying to balance group interactions with eating and managing the ketchup for their fries!

Moreover, school counselors often inquire about leading groups before the day begins or after the school day has ended. This often proves to be a wonderful option for preventing groups from interfering with class time; however, before- or after-school groups create specific logistical issues that require thought and planning. Primarily, transportation must be a top concern. How will group members get to school early or how will they get home after wards? Additionally, school counselors are aware that when students arrive at their early or stay late, it may compromise their right to confidentiality for group membership. Again, while this option may be the best for scheduling purposes, effective counselors think through the implications of groups that meet outside of the traditional school day and thus develop creative strategies to address such issues.

Finally, school counselors often report a lack of support from administrators in assisting or supporting them in designating time to lead groups, a challenge that is rarely encountered by counselors in clinical settings. To gain support from school administrators, school counselors must highlight the impact of running groups, ideally in the form of data collection. According to the American School Counselor Association's (ASCA) *ASCA Ethical Standards for School Counselors* (2016), school counselors "measure the outcomes of group participation (participation, Mindsets & Behaviors, and outcome data)" (2016, Section A.7.i.), but beyond the ethical requirement, data allow school counselors to show the number of students served by the group counseling component of the program (participation data), students' thoughts about what they are learning in group (mindsets and behaviors), and most importantly, the impact that groups are having on student attendance, behavior, and academics (outcome data) (Kaffenberger & Young, 2018).

Most administrators lack an understanding as to why school counselors run groups and how groups affect those student members. Data provide administrators with the kind of solid proof needed to assist them in understanding how critical group counseling is to the overall mission of the school and how it is tied to their school's goals and improvement plans. To summarize, school counselors collaborate with stakeholders in finding the best times to run groups. They use data to demonstrate the effectiveness of groups and highlight the fact that group counseling is essential as part of the school counseling program and to the overall mission of the school.

Challenge 2: Acquiring Parent Permission

Mental health workers who practice in clinical settings rarely face the challenge of acquiring parental permission; clients who are minors are typically accompanied by and encouraged to participate in the clinical process by parents who desire their child to be involved in a therapeutic relationship, which often includes being involved in groups—this, however, is not the case with schools. While the group counseling experience is and should be viewed as a vital piece of a child's total educational process, school counselors also balance involvement in groups where sensitive and personal material can be discussed with the parent's right to be the guiding voice in a child's life. The *ASCA Ethical Standards for School Counselors* (American School Counselor Association, 2016) states that "school counselors inform parents and guardians of student participation in a small group" (Section A.7.b.), which underscores the importance of parental consent.

School counselors attempt to gain parental permission in a timely manner so that lack of consent does not delay the start of the group. One strategy that counselors employ is to distribute blanket permission forms to all parents and guardians at the beginning of the school year.

Blanket permission forms can go home with students within the first few weeks of school and outline all the activities that they may be involved in as a student who is receiving services from the school counseling program, including participation in groups. These forms often outline the kinds of groups that the school counselor intends to offer during the year and even allows parents and guardians to indicate a desire for their child to be in a particular one. Finally, these types of forms encourage caregivers to contact the school counselor should they have questions or concerns about their child's participation in any of the activities associated with the school counseling program.

Challenge 3: Achieving the Correct Membership

Mental health counselors have the luxury of selecting members for their groups based on their clients' personalities and the specific needs of each individual. School counselors are passionate about allowing *all* students access to the school counseling program services, which often includes finding a place for students in groups. However, it is imperative that counselors recognize that not all students are appropriate for group counseling. Some students do not work well in groups and, in fact, may sabotage or ruin what has the potential to be a good group experience. Additionally, school counselors are constantly faced with the question of whether to run mixed gender groups or not. Mixed gender groups can have positive benefits for students; however, some topics may be better suited for same gender groups (i.e., not all students who identify as girls may feel comfortable sharing about their fear of math or issues about friendship in a group with students who identify as boys). Therefore, in order to find the best mix for school groups, best practice calls upon school counselors to screen members ahead of running their groups. Further, the *ASCA Ethical Standards for School Counselors* (American School Counselor Association, 2016) states that "school counselors screen students for group membership" (Section A.7.c.). However, even when screening is done with great care, it is not uncommon for cliques and alliances to form within the group. When this happens, school counselors get creative about how to address this issue. For example, the group leader can simply label seats prior to the group members entering the room. This will serve to separate members who are forming alliances or being too "chatty" with one another during group. Encouraging members to sit in a different place in the room will create a different energy in the room, which can often be desirable (Jacobs et al., 2016).

Challenge 4: Nonvolunteer Groups

When working in a mental health setting or an inpatient setting, rarely are group members required to participate in a group because of behavior; participation may be required as a part of involvement in the program but not as a behavioral consequence. In the schools, counselors are often expected to place a student in a group due to some violation of rules or an inability to behave appropriately in class. We cannot emphasize this enough: participation in group counseling in schools should not be used as a consequence for inappropriate behavior. However, when administrators exercise their authority and mandate inclusion of certain students in the group, school counselors are again called upon to be creative in order to make groups productive for these students.

To address this issue, school counselors should consider running groups where the membership is composed of students who are all mandated to be in the group (i.e., a group for students who have all been reported for skipping school) as opposed to infusing those students in groups alongside others who requested to participate with the purpose of helping them to improve their academics. A group where the membership is composed only of students who are required to attend likely makes the group more difficult to run, but it prevents students who may not want to take part from ruining the experience for those who do want to be in the group. In a group with all nonvolunteer members, school counselors should be very clear that the purpose of the group is to market the idea of change to these members—that is, to sell the idea that participating can be fun and engaging, and offer students some alternative to always getting into trouble. This group will require that the school counselor be exceptionally creative and engaging in using activities such as movement, writing, drawing, and the use of strong redirecting skills to make the group productive. Schimmel and Jacobs (2011) offer many creative ideas and strategies, such as doing the unexpected, for dealing with challenging members in groups.

Challenge 5: Confidentiality Issues

Confidentially in school groups is a unique challenge due to the very nature of work in schools. When school counselors begin to consider issues of confidentiality, they must again refer to the *ASCA Ethical Standards for School Counselors* (2016), which state that school counselors "communicate the aspiration of confidentiality as a group norm, while recognizing and working from the protective posture that confidentiality for minors in schools cannot be guaranteed" (Section A.7.e; for more discussion on confidentiality, see Chapter 1 of this text). More succinctly put, school counselors cannot guarantee confidentiality in groups but should work to promote the idea of keeping what is said in the group, in the group.

Due to the tricky nature of confidentiality, school counselors think carefully about the kinds of groups that are run in the school setting. It is recommended that most small groups be based on topics that do not require the sharing of highly sensitive material (e.g., sexual/physical abuse). Students are best served by groups that focus on academic success and school-related issues. However, running groups on divorce, friendships, and anger management are certainly helpful to students, yet promoting and encouraging confidentiality are very important.

Jacobs et al. (2016) promote the use of creative techniques to make concepts more concrete in groups. One creative way to help students understand confidentiality in groups is presented in *My Secret Technique* (original technique by Laurie Witherow, and revised for group counseling and shared by Virginia Dansby, both of Middle Tennessee State University). Group leaders ask each group member to take a small piece of paper and write "my secret" on it and fold it in half. Students then pass the piece of paper to another student in the group. The leader then initiates a discussion about how it feels to know that someone now has control of your private information. This can lead to a productive conversation with students about how they would like their fellow group members to handle their private information.

In summary, school counselors recognize that confidentiality among students in school groups does not exist but that the counselor's responsibility is to work hard to encourage and promote it. As such, school counselors must give great thought to the kinds of groups they run and the various creative ways to teach students about the concept of confidentiality. This is often accomplished by helping students understand the consequences of talking about group topics outside of the group.

Challenge 6: Training Issues

One final, unique challenge deserves mention: For school counselors to feel competent enough to lead groups, training programs must address these and other challenges that counselors face when leading groups. Steen et al. (2008) note that the school counselors they interviewed made special mention of their perceived lack of specific training for counselors in group leading. Springer and Schimmel (2016) note that many training programs do not address the unique needs of pre-service school counselors, such as the ability to observe groups with children and adolescents in their programs. Many school counseling training programs are home to clinical mental health programs as well and tend to focus training experiences on topics that primarily affect adults and situations where groups are prevalent in mental health settings. As pointed out in this chapter, school counselors who lead groups with children and adolescents in schools face a unique set of challenges. School counselors who do not feel competent leading groups due to a lack of focus on school-aged groups in their training programs should seek opportunities to engage in professional development, consultation, and supervision in an effort to increase their group-leading self-efficacy. For more on this topic, see Chapter 9 in this text.

Conclusion

In closing, it is hoped that the reader has been provided with an overview of the many unique challenges that school counselors face in their efforts to lead groups in schools. Additionally, suggestions on how effective school counselors overcome those challenges have been provided. When counselors make a strong commitment to overcome the challenges outlined in this chapter, they achieve the primary goal of all school counselors—the ability to make a positive impact on a greater number of students they serve. Group counseling is not simply a best practice for school counselors; group counseling is an essential practice of school counselors and a vital piece of an effective, comprehensive school counseling program (American School Counselor Association, 2019).

CONNECTING TO CHAPTER CONTENT

Personal Reflection Questions
- Now that you have read the various logistical challenges that face school counselors when establishing their small-group counseling program, what do you perceive to be the challenges you will face?
- How will you plan to overcome some of the logistical challenges involved in running small groups in a school setting?

Advice From the Expert/Author
Here is a tip from the author—make doing professional development with teachers and staff on the value of small-group counseling a top priority at the beginning of each year. Educating stakeholders on why you will run groups, how you will work with them to schedule and attempt to avoid conflicts, and the results you have seen when students are in small groups will help engender support for your small-group counseling program.

Check Out These Resources
- Confident Counselors: 16 Tips for Organizing & Running Small Group Counseling. http://confidentcounselors.com/2016/09/15/small-group-counseling-organize-and-run-successful-groups
- Counselor Clique: 7 Tips for Running Small Groups at the High School Level. http://www.counselorclique.com/2019/08/how-to-run-small-groups-at-high-school.html
- Heart & Mind Teaching: 7 Steps to Starting Small Group Counseling. https://heartandmindteaching.com/2019/04/starting_small_group_counseling.html

Other Readings

Jacobs, E., Schimmel, C. J., Mason, R., & Harvill, R. (2016). *Group counseling: Strategies & skills* (8th ed.). Cengage.

Sink, C., Edwards, C. N., & Eppler, C. (2012). *School based group counseling* (3rd ed.). Cengage.

References

American School Counselor Association. (2014). *ASCA mindsets & behaviors for student success: K–12 college- and career-readiness standards for every student.* https://www.schoolcounselor.org/getmedia/7428a787-a452-4abb-afec-d78ec77870cd/Mindsets-Behaviors.pdf

American School Counselor Association. (2016). *ASCA ethical standards for school counselors.* https://www.schoolcounselor.org/getmedia/f041cbd0-7004-47a5-ba01-3a5d657c6743/Ethical-Standards.pdf

American School Counselor Association. (2019). *The ASCA national model: A framework for school counseling programs* (4th ed.).

Bowers, H., Lemberger, M., Jones, M., & Rogers, J. (2015). The influence of repeated exposure to the student success skills program on middle school students' feelings of connectedness, behavioral and metacognitive skills, and reading achievement. *Journal for Specialists in Group Work, 40*(4), 344–364. https://doi.org/10.1080/01933922.2015.1090511

Jacobs, E. E., Schimmel, C. J., Masson, R. L., & Harvill, R. L. (2016). *Group counseling: Strategies and skills* (8th ed.). Cengage.

Kaffenberger, C., & Young, A. (2018). *Making DATA work* (4th ed.). American School Counselor Association.

Schimmel, C. J., & Jacobs, E. E. (2011). When leaders are challenged: Dealing with involuntary members in groups. *Journal for Specialists in Group Work, 36*(2), 144–158. https://doi.org/10.1080/01933922.2011.562345

Springer, S. I., & Schimmel, C. J. (2016). Creative strategies to foster pre-service school counselor group leader self-efficacy. *Journal for Specialists in Group Work, 41*(1), 2–18. https://doi.org/10.1080/01933922.2015.1111486

Steen, S., Bauman, S., & Smith, J. (2008). The preparation of professional school counselors for group work. *Journal for Specialists in Group Work, 33*(3), 253–269. https://doi.org/10.1080/01933920802196120

Swank, J. M., Cheung, C., & Williams, S. A. (2018). Play therapy and psychoeducational school-based group interventions: A comparison of treatment effectiveness. *Journal for Specialists in Group Work, 43*(3), 230–249. https://doi.org/10.1080/01933922.2018.1485801

West Virginia Department of Education. (2017). *Comprehensive school counseling program (2315).* http://apps.sos.wv.gov/adlaw/csr/readfile.aspx?DocId=49580&Format=PDF

PART III
Skills

Essential Skills for Leading Small Groups in Schools

Ed Jacobs, PhD, LPC
West Virginia University

Wilson Harvey, MA, Provisionally
Licensed Counselor
Buckhannon-Upshur High School

LEARNING OBJECTIVES

1. Describe the difference between an active approach to group leadership and a more passive approach to group leadership and why school counselors often choose a more active approach.
2. Name at least three skills that school counselors use *before* they begin leading small groups.
3. Name at least three skills that school counselors use *during* their small groups.

CONSIDER THIS SCENARIO

Velma is a school counselor who is leading a group of middle schoolers on bullying. One member, Eric, tends to take over each session by telling stories not relevant to the purpose of the group. During the first two sessions, Velma has not been able to keep the group on topic due to Eric's domination. Eric is known to be a student who bullies others, and members seem to be afraid to speak up. Two members, Char and Toby, went to see Velma after the second session and they said they were not sure they would come back because Eric is always talking, and they don't seem to be talking about bullying.

CONSIDER THESE QUESTIONS FOR DISCUSSION

- What does Velma need to do to have a good third session?
- What skills might Velma use in the next sessions that she likely did not use during the first two?

Introduction

Many books have been written about group counseling but most do not approach the topic with a specific focus on small groups in schools and the unique skills needed for leading groups in that setting (Corey, 2016; Gladding, 2020; Jacobs et al., 2016; Yalom & Leszcz, 2021). Additionally, there is discussion in the field of group counseling around leadership styles and specifically how active the leader should be (Capuzzi et al., 2010; Corey et al., 2014). Should the leader be more facilitative or more directive? Should the leader let the members dictate the flow of the session or should the leader direct the flow? Historically, a common term used in group counseling is *group facilitation*; this often refers to a more "group-directed" approach to group counseling (Jacobs et al., 2016), the implications of which being that the group members play the primary role in determining the direction and content of the group. But consider a contrasting position, *group leadership*, referring to a more "leader-directed" approach. In this approach, group leaders are clear about their responsibilities to make the group productive and helpful for all members. This topic is of special importance when planning and presiding over a school group. In school groups, we assert that the approach to leadership is less debatable. Given that students are still in the early stages of their emotional and neurological development (Cozolino, 2020), in most groups of this type, the leader should be in charge and direct the flow when needed in accordance with developmentally appropriate practice. The school counselor often needs to approach groups proactively to avoid sessions becoming chaotic and unproductive. Furthermore, given the time constraints of school counseling—groups are often 45 minutes or less—and the idea that traditional group facilitation takes a long time, a leader-based and directive model is most appropriate in school groups.

It is not lost on us as authors that facilitation is a popular method of group leadership, even among some school counselors. Facilitation done well has benefits for group members. Facilitation allows for many of Yalom and Leszcz's (2021) curative factors to develop over time and therefore is a valuable skill for school counselors to include in their toolboxes. This is especially true for certain types of counseling groups, such as grief or support groups. However, experience has taught us that many groups, especially with young students, require a more direct leadership approach. To be clear, leadership does not imply that the school counselors are free to impose their values on group members or the process. Effective group leaders run groups on topics that meet areas of student need (often identified in school data), adapt as needs present themselves, and consistently empower group members throughout the process by giving them a stake in the group's purpose (American School Counselor Association, 2020).

As leaders of school counseling groups, it is the school counselor's responsibility to keep the group both engaging and relevant for the members. A group leader who comes to sessions with a flexible plan, a willingness to steer the conversation when necessary, and a knowledge of how to take the group session to a meaningful level will be able to make a significant impact. In this chapter, we offer essential group leadership skills that school counselors need when leading groups. For a more detailed discussion of these skills, we encourage you to read other texts such as *Group Counseling: Strategies and Skills* (Jacobs et al., 2016) and *School Based Group Counseling* (Sink et al., 2012) that focus on group leadership skills.

"Before" the Group

It is imperative that school counselors begin the planning phase of their small group counseling program by examining relevant school data (i.e., a survey of students' stress levels; a survey of staff to inquire who they perceive could benefit from a small-group intervention; an examination of school data such as attendance, academics, or discipline referrals) (American School Counselor Association, 2020). By beginning the group process here, the school counselor ensures that the content and group topics will be relevant for all members. Then the leader can begin to craft sessions to the specific needs of the members. Using data to select student group members offers the counselor an opportunity to work with students who have specific needs (attendance, behavior, academics) and allows the school counseling program to reach more students.

Purpose

First and foremost, we teach in our classes and group workshops that establishing a clear purpose is the most important skill for leaders to understand and master. Awareness of the group's purpose is vital because the clarity of purpose keeps the leader on track and in turn helps members stay on track. Given its importance to the group success, it is surprising how often currently practicing school counselors report feeling unclear as to the kind of group they are leading (e.g., counseling group, psychoeducation group, or a skills group) and what they hope to accomplish in their meetings. We explain to them that when the leader lacks clarity of purpose, members are more likely to share irrelevant stories and bring up random topics unrelated to the group's purpose (e.g., students in a "Getting Ready for College" group discussing their plans for the prom for any length of time), and leaders struggle to redirect the members back to the group's intent when members veer too far off topic. For example, if the purpose of a psychoeducation group is to improve study skills, when members start complaining about their teachers, the leader might skillfully redirect students to the topic of how to better use their time when studying, saying something such as:

> I know that discussing teachers can be very interesting for each of you, but when we started this group, we said that we wanted to work to improve our study skills. I want to make sure that you get the most of your time today; if necessary, in the coming weeks we can talk more about how to interact with difficult teachers and difficult people.

Screening

Once the purpose and specific needs of students and group topics have been identified, the next step is screening potential members. As previously mentioned in the introduction chapter of this text, screening is a necessary step in developing groups in a school setting. The *ASCA Ethical Standards for School Counselors* clearly states that school counselors "screen students for group membership" (American School Counselor Association, 2016, Section A.7.c). As such, carefully choosing members is as important as any leadership skill because without careful screening, groups can have members who are not appropriate for one reason or another (e.g., lack developmental maturity, struggle with attention issues, conflicts with other members, lack desire to be in a group), which in turn leads to unproductive groups. Leaders should continually assess member selection. For students who initially pass the first round of screening but then create difficult dynamics that prevent the group from productive dialogue moving forward, additional screening and boundary setting may be necessary. The school counselor should be prepared to provide individual counseling and/or other services that would meet the needs of that student. An example of this might be an academically gifted student who wants to join a test-taking skills psychoeducation group for children experiencing anxiety but whose social skills may present below grade level. If a leader notices that this student is becoming behaviorally disruptive when interacting with peers, the leader must make some decisions about this student's readiness for this modality. Some individual work with this student might be needed before they can be an appropriate member of this type of group.

Screening students often involves meeting with them individually to share the group's purpose and discuss the student's level of interest in participating in the group. School counselors often seek to answer questions related to potential group members' abilities to work well in groups, their capability of understanding the group material, and whether the purpose of the group aligns with the students' needs. Screening can also occur by briefly meeting with teachers to assess a student's ability to focus and get along well with peers. Additionally, as mentioned in the introduction chapter of this text, classroom observation of students is helpful in determining a student's ability to work with peers and interact in appropriate ways (Kolbert et al., 2016).

Intentional Leadership

With regard to group leadership, students don't mind being led when they are led well. (Jacobs et al., 2016). In fact, many will expect you to lead, just as teachers do in their classrooms. For small groups in schools, we suggest taking an active leadership (leader-directed) role rather than predominantly being an observer (group-directed). Making this clear from the outset is crucial. The leader should explain what leadership of the group will look like (e.g., that they may cut off students while they are talking at times, or redirect the conversation to help to keep it relevant or to explore a topic in more depth). This will help the members to feel safer and increase the predictability of the group sessions. Readers can learn more overall group-specific leadership styles in the Yalom and Leszcz (2005) and Gladding (2020) texts. It is important for school counselors to be clear about their role within the group and to lead in a way that meets the developmental needs of its particular population. For instance, kindergarten students will need a very different type of leadership than high school seniors. Transparency as far as expectations, boundaries, and intent of leadership skills can aid in the productivity of the group's process.

Session Planning

One of the most important macro skills of a counseling group leader is the ability to plan engaging, relevant, and productive sessions. In school counseling, every minute counts. Often, groups may only last 20 minutes in elementary schools or 40–50 minutes in middle and high schools. A strong plan helps the counselor ensure they make the most of that limited time. Planning should be conducted for all three phases of the session: the warm-up, the middle/working phase, and the closing phase. Groups should not be improvised. Often leaders do not plan and simply "go with the flow," which leads to members jumping from topic to topic and straying from the group's purpose. This can be prevented with good, thoughtful planning.

Even the best-laid plans can be disrupted. Especially in school groups, much can change, and quickly. Even so, leaders benefit greatly from having an idea of what to do during each phase of the session. Planning the warm-up phase is especially important. Often in education, the "hook," or opening, of the lesson is mentioned as the most imperative (Marzano, 2017). The beginning of a group, just as the beginning of a lesson, sets the tone for the session. If the warm-up/opening is not planned, it can end up lasting too long and focusing on irrelevant topics. The warm-up should typically last no more than 5 to 8 minutes and should be used to get members present and focused on the topic(s) of the session. The first session may have a warm-up phase that takes 10 to 12 minutes. Examples of effective, engaging warm-ups typically include asking students to share their names and one piece of information about the members relevant to the group. In an anger management group, students could share one time in which they got mad and then suffered a negative consequence ("Say your name and one time your anger caused you to get in trouble"). In the warm-up for a leadership group, members might be asked to share one personal goal they have for their school ("Say your name and share one change you would like to see in our school").

Other elements that are commonly included in effective group plans include specific activities for the middle or working phase of the group as well as thought-provoking questions to ask following the activity. Group plans should include specific instructions for the closing phase of each session as well as the closing for the group as a whole to ensure that adequate time is devoted to wrapping up any issues that arise. Finally, the ASCA mindsets and behaviors (American School Counselor Association, 2014) that the group will address should always be included in group plans.

Leadership Skills

Setting the Tone

Due in part to the nature of the educational setting, school counselors can be prone to setting a group tone that is not conducive to foster sharing and openness among members. This often occurs when counselors run groups like a class with strict rules and structure, which leads to little sharing or no growth. On the other hand, some leaders go too far in the opposite direction and set a tone that promotes fun and enjoyment at the expense of encouraging a space where students are learning and growing. For example, a school counselor might decide to use a fun arts and crafts activity using glitter and glue in an anger management group; without intentionality in how this activity connects with the purpose of the group, this may result in fun and laughter but lack depth in group sharing and processing. Skilled leaders are always conscious of the tone—they strive to make it serious, caring, and interactive so that students feel free to share and connect with other members. The tone may, of course, vary based upon the subject matter and to some extent the members of the group—a group on grief and loss, for example, requires a very different tone than one whose purpose is to discuss postsecondary planning. Effective leaders recognize the intentional, skillful use of one's voice to assist and model the tone required. Strong leaders consider how the pacing of their voices impacts the function and progress of the group.

Generating and Building Interest and Energy

An important skill often overlooked is the leader's ability to continually monitor the energy of the group and, when the energy begins to lag, generate and build interest for a topic or an activity. One way to generate energy is to vary the format; in other words, to change what is happening. For instance, if energy is low (e.g., students are not sharing, their nonverbals indicate boredom, or they begin to bring up topics unrelated to the group purpose), the leader can shift to something different like a written activity, a movement exercise, having students share in dyads (pairs), or asking a good, thought-provoking question. One of the most important reasons for active leadership (as opposed to facilitation) is that leaders can vary the format to continually meet the changing needs and energy levels of members. The effective leader is continually attending to the verbal and nonverbal cues that might suggest progress or stagnation.

Scanning the Room (Using Your Eyes)

Many know this skill, but don't use it effectively in groups. While simple to explain, scanning the room can be difficult to implement in the group setting. When individuals are talking, they frequently fixate on or talk toward the leader and risk losing the interest of the rest of the group. The leader can address this without interrupting the flow of the discussion by glancing around or scanning the other students so that the person talking connects with other listening members. By scanning the room, the leader can assess the reactions of other individuals, identify those who resonate with what the speaker is saying, and determine who might want to share next. In order to continue to build predictability into the group, we advocate that leaders explain that they will often be looking around for this purpose and encourage other members to do so as well. This can build cohesion and a greater sense of community within the group.

Drawing Out

Two essential skills for leading effective groups in schools are drawing out and cutting off. First, we discuss drawing out. Membership in a school counseling group is a unique opportunity for students to practice using their voices in a space where they feel safe and supported. However, some members may be less comfortable speaking up than others. Many students begin group shy or afraid to speak up for various reasons. Skilled leaders come prepared with many ways to draw out students and to make them feel more comfortable with sharing their thoughts and ideas. Primarily, group leaders skillfully call on members in gentle ways to encourage sharing. Activities that encourage members to share include written exercises (e.g., asking students to create a list of things they like about school, asking students to complete a fill-in-the-blank about a group-related topic), group rounds ("Let's go around the room and say one word about how you are feeling about being in the group"), and movement exercises such as asking students to move to a specific place in the room to represent a certain relevant group concept (e.g., "Move to the label on the wall that best 'fits' how you feel about school: I hate school, I love school") (Schimmel & Jacobs, 2014).

Another important reason for mastering the skill of drawing out is that it prevents one or two students from monopolizing the talking in group, which can decrease the engagement/buy-in of other members. A third reason for drawing out members is to promote the curative factor of universality (Yalom & Leszcz, 2021). Feeling alone is a common occurrence among young clients; when individuals are encouraged to share experiences in a safe and supportive setting, they realize that they are not alone in their struggle or situation. Skillful drawing out ensures more sharing. Before drawing out, effective leaders must consider that there may be reasons, whether cultural, trauma-based, or otherwise, that a member does not feel comfortable sharing. In such situations, the leader should work with that student to discover ways of sharing that best honor their experience, and then incorporate those naturally into the group structure.

Cutting Off

Students may tell stories, ramble, or act out to gain attention as per their developmental stage. In groups with leaders who are not comfortable cutting off or redirecting, these members will dominate the group. Cutting off can be done effectively with a kind but firm redirect, as in these examples:

- "Juan, I appreciate your input, and now I think it's important that we hear what other members have to say on this subject"
- "Desersa, I appreciate your enthusiasm for the game tonight. I want to make sure that we make the most of these 40 minutes, and I think we want to stay focused on the purpose of the group in terms of how we can deal with our anger."

Cutting off is crucial when members are making hurtful or inaccurate comments that stand to disrupt the safe and supportive nature of the group. Knowing how and when to cut off individuals when they are talking is an imperative skill used to ensure that the leader can control the group when needed and make it as productive as possible (Gladding, 2020; Jacobs et al., 2016).

Focusing Skills

Focusing the session is an essential skill. It is the leader's responsibility to acquire, hold, shift, and deepen the focus in line with the purpose of the group. During a session, the focus is either on a topic, a person, or an activity. The skilled leader pays careful attention, focusing the group by bringing up relevant topics or activities or by attending to individuals who want to share. Once the sharing starts, the leader then pays close attention and decides whether to hold the focus on the topic and/or the person, to shift the focus to another topic, or to deepen the focus to achieve more meaningful interactions. Leaders determine which is necessary based on how the information connects with the purpose of the group and the members themselves. For instance, if a leader running a conflict resolution group notices that students regularly change the subject when asked to talk about a time when they had a fight with someone, this could be an appropriate time to revisit the purpose of the group and shift the focus to discussing things that make it difficult to talk about conflict in this setting. Holding the focus in this area can help the leader to assess the safety of the group and can support shared experiences and deeper feelings. Holding and shifting the focus takes practice, and timing is crucial. Far too often, leaders who do not understand how or when to employ these skills let members tell stories or jump from topic to topic, often leading to more surface-level discussions (Jacobs et al., 2016).

Asking Effective Questions

One difference between the skilled and unskilled leader is the ability to ask effective questions. The unskilled leader asks questions that elicit stories or short answers. Conversely, the skilled leader asks thought-provoking questions that are relevant to the purpose of the group and are meant to focus and/or deepen sharing among members.

Consider the following examples of effective and less effective questions:

- Less effective: How was your week? (This could lead to many irrelevant stories that take the group far off-topic.)
  More effective: How did you use what you have learned in this group during the past week? (Focused question tied to the purpose.)
- Less effective: How was studying this week?
  More effective: What, if anything, has been different about your studying habits this past week?
- Less effective: Any thoughts from the week?
  More effective: What did you notice this week about how people's behaviors toward each other impacted your classroom climate?

Process Skills

Knowing Your Allies in the Group

A skill seldom highlighted in textbooks about group work but invaluable in school groups is knowing your allies. By this, we mean recognizing a member or members the leader can count on to assist in bringing the focus back to the purpose. Members will get off track, so being able to call on an ally who is typically tuned in is a helpful skill to master and allows the leader to share accountability for the group's progress. Group allies, when called upon, answer in ways that align with the group purpose or the activity just completed. Group leaders recognize allies by their abilities to provide comments that are helpful to their own growth as well as the growth of other members. Leaders must be mindful, however, of not overly relying on these members as the only ones to support group accountability. This could lead to a subgrouping of the leader and ally members, creating a dynamic that hinders the progress of the group or could result in other participants relying on the "good groupers" to take the majority of the responsibility for the group's process.

Utilizing Counseling Theories

In school groups that focus on personal issues such as parents divorcing, parents who have substance use issues, shyness, anger, stress, or other similar topics, effective leaders are able to actively apply one or more evidence-based counseling theories. We advocate for the use of theories that can be taught easily to students so that they in turn can use the theories to help themselves and the other members of the group. Common evidenced-based counseling theories often used in small groups include rational emotive behavior therapy (REBT)/cognitive behavior therapy (CBT) (Vernon, 2019); reality therapy/WDEP (Wubbolding, 2019); solution-focused brief counseling (SFBC; Sabella, 2019); and transactional analysis (Schimmel & Jacobs, 2014). Consider the following application of using theory in school groups:

- Leaders recognize the impact of teaching students with anger issues that their thoughts have a relationship to their feelings (REBT/CBT).
- Leaders can teach students to creatively problem solve by using the WDEP approach (reality therapy).
- Leaders can work with group members to identify strengths that have worked for them in the past to help resolve current issues (SFBC).

Theories such as these are easily understood by students from ages nine through eighteen (Corey, 2017; Sommers-Flanagan & Sommers-Flanagan, 2018).

Conclusion

Prior to the implementation of any group, effective leaders use data to inform the kinds of groups they will run and are clear about the leadership role they will utilize with members. While facilitation can be a popular approach to group counseling, an active leadership approach offers a model more effective for use in the school setting (Capuzzi et al., 2010; Gladding, 2020). Screening group members for appropriateness is essential and can help to promote the established purpose of the group. During each session, effective leaders maintain boundaries and support progress by using skills such as drawing out, cutting off, and varying the format in order to create interest and energy among members. Effective leaders ensure that the group, whatever its purpose, is impactful for students rather than leaving the effectiveness of the group to chance.

CONNECTING TO CHAPTER CONTENT

Personal Reflection Questions

Here are some questions to ask yourself that can help you assess your leadership comfort:

- How comfortable are you with taking charge?
- When it is obvious you need to do so, how difficult will it be to cut off a rambling member?
- Do you know one or more counseling theories well enough to teach it to your group members?

Advice From the Expert/Author

Leading groups is one of the most difficult tasks that school counselors are asked to do. If you were not trained heavily in the skills of leadership, you may shy away from groups. Perhaps your group course, like many at the master's level, focused more on group dynamics and personal participation as a member, and when you finished the course, you did not feel confident in group-leading skills. You can enjoy leading groups. You can learn the essential skills of group leading, and you can practice those skills until you become an effective leader.

Check Out These Resources

- Greenberg, K. R. (2020). *Group counseling in K–12 schools: A handbook for school counselors*. Pearson.
- Mason, E. C. M., & McMahon, H. G. (2009). Leadership practices of school counselors. *Professional School Counseling, 13*(2), 107–115. https://doi.org/10.1177%2F2156759X0901300206
- Schimmel, C. J., & Jacobs, E. (2014). How to select and apply change strategies in groups. In R. Conyne (Ed.), *Group work practice kit: Improving the everyday practice of group work*. Sage.

References

American School Counselor Association. (2014). *ASCA mindsets & behaviors for student success: K–12 college-and career-readiness standards for every student*. https://www.schoolcounselor.org/getmedia/7428a787-a452-4abb-afec-d78ec77870cd/Mindsets-Behaviors.pdf

American School Counselor Association. (2016). *ASCA ethical standards for school counselors*. https://www.schoolcounselor.org/getmedia/f041cbd0-7004-47a5-ba01-3a5d657c6743/Ethical-Standards.pdf

American School Counselor Association. (2020). *The school counselor and group counseling* [Position statement]. https://www.schoolcounselor.org/Standards-Positions/Position-Statements/ASCA-Position-Statements/The-School-Counselor-and-Group-Counseling

Capuzzi, D., Gross, D. R., & Stauffer, M. D. (2010). *Group work*. Love.

Corey, G. (2016). *The theory and practice of group counseling* (9th ed.). Cengage Learning.

Corey, G. (2017). *The theory and practice of counseling and psychotherapy* (10th ed.). Cengage Learning.

Corey, M. S., Corey, G., & Corey, C. (2014). *Groups: Process and practice* (9th ed.). Cengage Learning.

Cozolino, L. (2020). *The pocket guide to neuroscience for clinicians*. Norton.

Gladding, S. T. (2020). *Groups: A counseling specialty* (8th ed.). Pearson.

Jacobs, E., Schimmel, C. J., Masson, R., & Harvill, R. (2016). *Group counseling: Strategies and skills* (8th ed.). Cengage Learning.

Kolbert, J. B., Williams, R. L., Morgan, L. M., Crothers, L. M., & Hughes, T. L. (2016). *Introduction to professional school counseling*. Routledge.

Marzano, R. J. (2017). *The new art and science of teaching*. Solution Tree Press.

Sabella, R. (2019). Solutions-focused brief counseling. In A. Vernon & C. J. Schimmel (Eds.), *Counseling children and adolescents* (5th ed., pp. 147–184). Cognella.

Schimmel, C. J., & Jacobs, E. (2014). *How to select and apply change strategies in groups*. In R. Conyne (Ed.), *Group work practice kit: Improving the everyday practice of group work*. Sage.

Sink, C. A., Edwards, C., & Eppler, C. (2012). *School based group counseling*. Cengage Learning.

Sommers-Flanagan, R., & Sommers-Flanagan, J. (2018). *Counseling and psychotherapy theories* (3rd ed.). Wiley.

Vernon, A. (2019). *Rational emotive behavior therapy*. In A. Vernon & C. J. Schimmel (Eds.), *Counseling children and adolescents* (5th ed., pp. 222–257). Cognella.

Wubbolding, R. (2019). Reality therapy. In A. Vernon & C. J. Schimmel (Eds.), *Counseling children and adolescents* (5th ed., pp. 185–221). Cognella.

Yalom, I. D., & Leszcz, M. (2005). *The theory and practice of group psychotherapy* (5th ed.). Basic Books.

Yalom, I. D., & Leszcz, M. (2021). *The theory and practice of group psychotherapy* (6th ed.). Basic Books.

Creative Strategies (Improvisation and Gaming) With School Counseling Small Groups

Matthew B. Tolliver, MA, LPC, NCC, ALPS
University of the Cumberlands

Carla Smith, M.Ed, LPC-S
University of the Cumberlands

LEARNING OBJECTIVES

1. Summarize the main concepts of improvisation and gaming as used in small-group counseling.
2. Identify various small-group activities arising out of improvisation that can be used to build cohesion in small-group counseling.
3. Associate multiple small-group counseling creative activities that teach social skills with various concepts from the world of gaming.

CONSIDER THIS SCENARIO

You are starting a group for fourth graders focused on building social/emotional skills. Through referrals from teachers, assessment data, and personal experiences, you have screened and selected ten students to include in your group. Key areas of focus for the group include emotional regulation, focus/attention, and working with others collaboratively. Knowing the needs of these students, consistent engagement during your sessions is imperative.

CONSIDER THESE QUESTIONS FOR DISCUSSION

- How would you go about planning the initial session (and subsequent sessions) to make them creative and engaging for students?
- In what ways will you work to ensure the needs of all participants are met?
- How could you adapt the activities for older students?

Introduction

The American School Counselor Association (ASCA) adheres to the belief that small-group counseling effectively supports students' positive academic, career, and social/emotional skills development (American School Counselor Association, 2020). As a staple of comprehensive school counseling programs across the United States, small-group counseling is an excellent avenue for implementing creative approaches for developing those skills. Due to school counselors' time constraints, group work is typically brief and allows for innovative and solution-focused techniques to meet multiple students' needs. School counselors have unique opportunities to integrate creative counseling techniques (specifically in obtaining necessary materials) through collaboration and consultation with related arts teachers (art, music, PE, etc.) and classroom teachers.

Children naturally engage in creativity through play, art, and singing. According to Vernon (2019), certain moments during the counseling process offer school counselors opportunities to use those natural tendencies by incorporating creative interventions to help alter thoughts, feelings, and behaviors. When students get "stuck" in certain thinking patterns, engaging in creative activities allows for a shift in perspective and flexibility in thinking (Duffey & Trepal, 2016). Gladding (2016) asserts that the creative arts (e.g., drama, humor, and movement) help provide students with developmentally appropriate activities that support therapeutic change when outside of the counseling environment. Creative techniques in small-group school counseling may increase member engagement and willingness to participate by celebrating the feelings of connectedness, integration, and purpose (Atkins et al., 2003; Gladding, 2016).

The purpose of this chapter is to discuss two emerging creative interventions that are gaining empirical support for their use with small groups: improvisation and gaming. Additionally, this chapter focuses on how these interventions can be applied within small-group school counseling sessions.

Improvisation

If you have ever seen the television show *Whose Line Is It Anyway?*, what you watched is known as "short-form" improvisation. The performers' high-paced action and turbo-speed wit on *Whose Line* convey an almost superhuman level of thinking. The root of improvisational theater can be traced back to the 16th–18th centuries, where it thrived throughout European countries as Commedia Dell'arte, or "comedy of the profession." DeMichele (2019) notes the later impact of theater director Viola Spolin in the 1950s in Chicago with classifying improvisational theater as an art form in and of itself.

While the importance of physicality and comedic timing are crucial skills with this type of entertainment, the truth is that there are also specific guidelines or "rules" of improvisation that performers use to help guide their scenes. These same "rules" are now being integrated across multiple disciplines, including medicine, law, business, education, the military, and mental health for developing both personal and professional skills (DeMichele, 2019; Joseph, 2017; Farley, 2017). There is emerging evidence that supports school counselors looking to improvisation to build skills in the students with whom they work.

Applied Improvisation

In a Delphi Study completed by the Applied Improvisation Network (AIN), Tint and Froerer (2014) defined applied improvisation as "the use of principles, tools, practices, skills, and mindsets of improvisational theater in non-theatrical settings, that may result in personal development, team building, creativity, innovation, and/or meaning" (p. 2). In small-group counseling, improvisation techniques are not intended for entertainment but rather skill development (though humor is most often a byproduct). Also, applied improvisation exercises are not solely "icebreakers" or "getting to know you" activities per se, although some exercises are appropriate for group norming. Multiple behaviors from the *ASCA Mindsets and Behaviors* (American School Counselor Association, 2014) are inherent in improvisation. Skills like active listening (B-SS 1), understanding tone of voice and reading body language (B-SS 1), intentional physical movement (B-SMS 2), growth mindsets and resiliency building (B-SMS 6 and B-SMS 7), empathy (B-SS 4), creative exploration (B-LS 2), and teamwork (B-SS 2 and B-SS 6) are all developed through applied improv (American School Counselor Association, 2014; Applied Improvisation Network, 2016). Corey (2016) also suggests that specific approaches to multicultural counseling are found in improvisation: encouraging open dialogue among diverse populations, exercises for either individual or group needs, personalization for group needs, use of nonverbal communication, and supporting clients who may not usually freely express their feelings.

The "Rules" of Improv

The "Rules of Improvisation," adapted from the AIN Adelphi Study, are listed in Table 8.1 (Tint & Froerer, 2014). While there are variations in the "rules" according to different practitioners, the first rule is universal: say "yes, and ..." The adherence to "yes, and ..." means that players accept the reality of their partners, or for our conversation, the other group members. Acceptance may not necessarily mean *agreeing* with a partner's perspective but that one *accepts* what is real to their partners. As ethical school counselors, we do this by bracketing our own "personal values and beliefs" (American School Counselor Association, 2016, p. 3) to respect our students' autonomy. The idea of complete acceptance through both "yes, and ..." and Rule 6, "be supportive with complete acceptance" (aka unconditional positive regard in person-centered counseling), center on empathic and active listening—to be fully integrated into the other person's reality, no matter how radical or impossible it seems. These tenets have clear implications for fostering cohesion and universality in group counseling.

TABLE 8.1 The "Rules" of Improvisation

1. Say yes, and ...

2. Always take care of your partner(s)

3. Create an atmosphere of play

4. Play at the top of your intelligence

5. Be in the moment, "here and now"

6. Be supportive with complete acceptance

7. Take risks and commit to them

Note. Based on Tint and Froerer (2014)

Say "yes, and ..." is not the only improv "rule" with inherent application to small-group counseling. Table 8.2 represents a crosswalk between each of the seven "rules of improvisation" with relevant counseling theories and techniques. Specifically, the overlap between person-centered, behaviorism, and Gestalt approaches to counseling are highlighted.

Training and Resources

While specialized training is not a requirement to use applied improvisation exercises, school counselors do have an ethical responsibility to "practice within their competence level and develop professional competence through training and supervision" (American School Counselor Association, 2016, Section A.7.h.). We suggest that readers seek out opportunities for participation in improv training groups, either in-person or virtually. Several applied improvisation Facebook groups (globally, nationally, regionally, and even content-specific) often promote upcoming training opportunities and numerous resources. There are also multiple videos available through YouTube with exercise explanations and demonstrations (see Check Out These Resources below).

TABLE 8.2 **Crosswalk of the "Rules" of Improvisation**

The "Rules" of Improvisation (Tint & Froerer, 2014)	Crosswalk With Counseling Theory and Techniques (Wedding & Corsini, 2018; Corey, 2016)		
	Person-Centered	**Behaviorism**	**Gestalt**
Say "yes, and …"	unconditional positive regard; empathic and active listening	radical acceptance	empathy development
Always take care of your partners; be supportive with complete acceptance.	unconditional positive regard; group support; an environment of trust	social learning theory; social skills training	empathy development; group support
Atmosphere of play	balance of freedom and structure	balance of freedom and structure	spontaneity and creative expression
Play at the top of your intelligence	clients push themselves to explore	clients are challenged to grow, not maintain	encourages growth and enhancement
Be in the moment, "here and now"	active participation	continual assessment of experiences	direct experiences
Take risks and commit to them	failure is nonthreatening due to the supportive environment	clients are pushed to make changes	"stay with it" when faced with certain feelings or ideas resiliency building

Sample Improv Exercises

The following are sample exercises that can be used with school counseling small groups. It is crucial that, after participation in improv exercises, the school counselor devotes time to debriefing with participants to help process their experience.

Charades

A classic party game, charades challenges participants to use pantomime, sounds, and non-verbals to convey clues to other group members. The school counselor creates clues based on relevant concepts for the group topic. For example, in a group whose purpose is to teach healthy coping skills (e.g., deep breathing, mindfulness/yoga, go for a walk, listen to music, call a friend on the phone, talk to a trusted adult, exercise), the school counselor would develop clues that lead the members to guess these specific skills. If developmentally appropriate, group members themselves could create the clues to be used in the game. Group members could work in dyads or teams to create the clues and act out the healthy coping skills for the other dyads or teams to guess.

One Word/One Line Story

To begin, group members form a circle. The school counselor starts by saying "once upon a time" followed by a topical sentence relevant to the group purpose. For example, in a group for students whose families are going through divorce, the school counselor might say, "Once upon a time there was a boy named Michael. One evening, Michael's parents asked him to join them in the living room and told him that they were getting a divorce/separating." After giving the initial prompt, each group member can contribute either one word or one sentence to create a group story. The story could go around once or continue around the circle multiple times.

Cross the Room

Group members are asked to stand on one side of the room. The school counselor then asks the group members (either collectively or individually) to "cross the room" as or like something. The one rule of this exercise is that the members must fully commit to, even exaggerate, their choice. The "something" can be any noun, including concepts. The "something" should be topical to the group discussion or purpose. For example, in a friendship group, the school counselor may instruct the members to "cross the room like you want to talk to someone new but are nervous." Going further, members could create an alter ego who would behave opposite to how they would typically respond. Through this experience, students explore their typical emotional and physical responses to situations and what it feels like to behave in ways they would not normally.

Polar Opposites

The focus of this exercise is on empathy building and perspective taking. It is excellent for conflict resolution. Two group members are selected and given an irrelevant topic to debate (e.g., "toilet paper, over or under," or "glass half full or half empty," or "dogs versus cats."). Players take opposite viewpoints, give their arguments, not caring if they make sense, but are wholly committed to their side. After a minute or two, they switch places and take the opposing view.

For separation/divorce, students often take the side of going to one parent's house over the other. Often, students may side with one parent over the other. In a group for high school students who are at risk of dropping out of school, members could take sides on the debate about whether to drop out or not. This exercise forces them to consider the positives within each environment. If students cannot think of positives, prompt them to make it how they wish it is.

Small Talk

As a more advanced exercise in larger groups (8–10 members), the focus of "small talk" (Phillips et al., 2016) is to help group members practice social initiation skills previously taught by the school counselor (e.g., listening and finding a jump-in point, asking questions, sharing a story or joke, commenting on something said). It also introduces the concept of "strategic improv," or the need to change one's response based on particular situations. To begin, one or two members leave the room. The remaining group members break into smaller groups of two to three. The school counselor then assigns each smaller group a different "difficulty level," meaning how difficult it will be for the outsiders to join their conversation. When the outsider participants reenter the room, their goal is to join the group's discussion. After a few minutes, the school counselor instructs the participants to move to a new group. When processing this exercise, students need to verbalize any feelings of embarrassment or shame and how they might have had similar past experiences. The counselor leading the processing stage of "small talk" could prompt students to answer questions such as "What feelings did you experience when trying to enter the groups and make a connection?" or "Were there any scary moments when you tried to join your groups?" or "What did you learn that can help you perform better in uncomfortable situations?"

Final Thoughts on Improvisation

This is not a definitive list of all improvisational exercises that can be applied to small-group settings. Activities vary from building trust and group cohesion, rhyming and creating songs, to more advanced guessing games requiring higher-level skills like interpretation and innuendo. We hope this section has provided a foundational understanding of improvisation and practical suggestions to guide you toward improvisation with school counseling small groups.

Social Skills Training Through Gaming

A study report completed by the Gallup-NewSchools Venture Fund in 2019 found that 65% of teachers reported using digital learning tools to teach every day. Many teachers (53%) said that their students use these types of tools every day, and 57% of students (63% high, 64% middle, and 45% elementary) said that they use digital learning tools every day (Gallup, 2019). Gallup defined "digital learning tools" as "websites, apps, online tutorials, online games, and videos or programs used to teach and support student learning and schoolwork" (p. 5). The Gallup survey was conducted before the global pandemic of COVID-19, which forced millions of educators and students to switch to a virtual education format. Even before COVID-19, many public school districts in the United States began providing one-to-one technology (e.g., Chromebooks, iPads, and smart notebooks) for individual students. With such availability, integrating digital learning tools into school counseling groups will continue to grow in popularity and can be an excellent asset for school counselors.

One growing area is gaming technology for adaptive social skills training (SST), which adjusts to individual players' needs. Centervention, a technology company based in Durham, North Carolina, has been creating evidence- and research-driven SST programs to address these needs (Centervention, 2020). Centervention has developed partnerships with both the ASCA and the National Association of School Psychologists in supporting their programs. Zoo U, one of their games for older elementary students, focuses on six different skill areas (impulse control, communication, cooperation, social initiation, empathy, and emotional regulation). From the multiple "skill builder" games provided in Zoo U, nearly every one of the ASCA mindsets and behaviors (American School Counselor Association, 2014) are addressed in some manner. Within the game, student-created avatars are placed into various social situations and asked to select the most socially appropriate responses for the situation—a "choose your own adventure," if you will. One of the Zoo U program's biggest bonuses includes pre/post and ongoing assessment data to help progress monitor students.

So how do these games, which were designed for individual intervention, apply to groups? Grounded in social learning theory and modeling, Zoo U, and similar SST programs in group settings, allow for discussion among the participants regarding why individual choices may be more appropriate. The gameplay also allows for small-group discussions focused on tone of voice and body language when responding to others in real life as represented in making choices in the game. Initially, the school counselor serves as the leader and facilitator of the group discussions. Over time, once students learn how to navigate the program, they can take turns leading the group as they play through the game together; the school counselor's role becomes one of supervisor and facilitator as needed.

Students can also continue to play the game individually, outside of their group, to continue building their skills. The biggest bonus to programs like Zoo U is that there is zero preparation time for school counselors! There is no lesson planning involved, and there is no abundance of supplies to gather—just a laptop connected to a media projector or television with speakers.

It is important to note that student licenses for Centervention are not free. However, do not let this hinder you from pursuing this intervention. One could start with a few free promotional licenses that target just a few students. Once success can be shown through data collection to administrators, school counselors might request additional funding to support licenses for more students. To help, we have provided a list of potential funding sources in Table 8.3. Be advised that funding sources may be limited based on your location and availability of funds. As similar technology grows in the coming years, opportunities for free programs may also begin to emerge.

TABLE 8.3 Potential Funding Sources

School district education foundation
Local or state counselor association
Nonprofit agencies (grants)
Colleges and universities
Professional sports teams (items for auction)
Faculty Senate money
Parent/Teacher Association Phoebe Apperson Hearst Award
Dollar General Family Literacy Grants
Target Education Grant
Office Depot Community Involvement Grant
Walmart Local Community Support Grant
Lowe's Toolbox for Education Grant
State Farm Better Educated Communities Grant
Best Buy Community Grant
W. K. Kellogg Foundation

Breakout Boxes and Escape Games

According to data compiled by the professional networking site LinkedIn, the top five "most in-demand 'soft skills'" for 2020 included creativity, persuasion, collaboration, adaptability, and emotional intelligence (Pate, 2020). Time management was mentioned as a highly sought-after task-oriented "soft skill" (Pate, 2020). LinkedIn defines "soft skills" as "the essential interpersonal skills that make or break our ability to get things done in our current jobs and take on new opportunities ahead" (Pate, 2020). These same skills are once again reflected in the *ASCA Mindsets and Behaviors* (American School Counselor Association, 2014).

Breakout boxes and escape games (BBEG) are creative, small-group strategies to help students build and further hone their "soft skills," mindsets, and success behaviors. With a primary focus on teamwork, BBEGs have gained popularity in recent years in the United States. Kelly O'Brien Weaver, an elementary school counselor in Maine, presented on the use of BBEGs during the 2019 American School Counselor Conference in Boston, Massachusetts. According to Weaver (2019), the inquiry and experiential learning experiences innate to BBEGs keep students engaged and excited about their group sessions. Weaver (2019) posited that BBEGs stimulate student engagement with high energy, the desire to find missing information, the examination of self, the use of mild pressure, and encouragement of more favorable competition. During the experience, participants search for clues and solve multiple smaller puzzles or tasks (either individually, in a smaller group, or as a whole team), leading to a final puzzle or overarching goal (Escape the Room, 2019). Time limits for task completion can help participants focus on their time management and encourage friendly competition.

During BBEG experiences, the school counselor serves as a supervisor and facilitator by encouraging equal participation, allowing members to struggle, and helping participants navigate mild conflicts (Weaver, 2019). The school counselor also provides small "nudges" by pointing out missing information, clarifying goals, and reaffirming/restating relevant information presented by members (Weaver, 2019). Most importantly, the school counselor also helps facilitate debriefing discussions with participants after their experience. Weaver (2019) identifies three different types of debriefing with BBEGs. Natural debriefing is an organic conversation that transpires without prompting; process debriefing includes what things should stay the same and what things could be improved; content debriefing focuses on the skills or knowledge intended for the experience (Weaver, 2019). Debriefing with participants helps the school counselor reflect upon the experience for future planning and preparation.

The topics and themes for which school counselors can use BBEGs with small groups are limitless. While the preparation and planning may seem overwhelming, a quick internet search offers various resources and planning suggestions. Teacherspayteachers.com, for example, provides a variety of different BBEGs (free and for purchase) for both in-person and virtual experiences. Once created, resources can be used for multiple groups over time. From academic standards to targeted mindsets and behaviors, BBEGs are a fun and engaging approach to small-group school counseling.

Conclusion

The inclusion of creative strategies such as improvisation and gaming in school counseling groups provides opportunities for even greater benefits. Creative interventions including these two approaches help address the ASCA mindsets and behaviors for student success, supporting the use of a standards-driven comprehensive school counseling program. Creative techniques have been shown to help students deescalate and better regulate their emotions. Improvisation and gaming are two emerging approaches that support school counselors in their work to assist students with self-regulation. Other benefits of creative strategies in small-group school counseling include enhanced student engagement and participation, thus increasing social learning opportunities for the application of group skills outside of the counseling environment.

CONNECTING TO CHAPTER CONTENT

Personal Reflection Questions
- Which of the strategies that were discussed do you feel competent in using today?
- Which of the strategies will require you to undergo further professional development (e.g., additional reading, attending workshops, supervision, consultation from seasoned practitioners)?
- Some of the strategies discussed in the chapter require financial support. Not all school counselors have access to the same resources. Which of the suggested financial resources are you comfortable seeking on your own and which ones will require help from others? (Are you secure in asking people for money? Do you have experience with grant writing? Are you comfortable advocating for your program with administrators, outside businesses, and other stakeholders?)

Advice From the Expert/Author
Using creative techniques such as improvisation and gaming requires vulnerability on the part of the school counselor. This vulnerability includes taking risks when asking for financial support knowing that "no" is highly probable. When being creative with students, one must convey a

sense of play and imagination to establish a supportive and nonjudgmental small-group atmosphere. If we expect our students to tap into the creative parts of their brain, we, as the adults in the room, must agree to do the same. In the words of Dr. Suess, "You'll never be bored when you try something new, there's really no limit to what you can do."

Check Out These Resources

- Applied Improvisation Network: http://www.appliedimprovisation.network
- Centervention: http://www.centervention.com
- Escape the Room: https://escapetheroom.com/blog/what-is-an-escape-room/
- Responsive Classroom: https://www.responsiveclassroom.org/wp-content/uploads/2017/10/Responsive-Classroom-for Special-Area-Teachers.pdf
- Teachers Pay Teachers: https://www.teacherspayteachers.com/Browse/Search:escape%20rooms

Additional Readings

- Farley, N. (2017). Improvisation as a meta-counseling skill. *Journal of Creativity in Mental Health, 12*(1), 115–128. https://doi.org/10.1080/15401383.2016.1191402
- DeMichele, M. (2019). *One rule improv: The fast, easy, no fear approach to teaching, learning, and applying improv.* Academic Play.
- Fey, T. (2011). *Bossypants.* Reagan Arthur Books.
- Joseph, G. (2017). *The act resilient method: From trauma to transformation.* Eve Publishing.

References

American School Counselor Association. (2014). *ASCA mindsets & behaviors for student success: K–12 college-and career-readiness standards for every student.* https://www.schoolcounselor.org/getmedia/7428a787-a452-4abb-afec-d78ec77870cd/Mindsets-Behaviors.pdf

American School Counselor Association. (2016). *ASCA ethical standards for school counselors.* https://www.schoolcounselor.org/getmedia/f041cbd0-7004-47a5-ba01-3a5d657c6743/Ethical-Standards.pdf

American School Counselor Association. (2019). *The ASCA national model: A framework for school counseling programs* (4th ed).

American School Counselor Association. (2020). *The school counselor and group counseling* [Position statement]. https://www.schoolcounselor.org/Standards-Positions/Position-Statements/ASCA-Position-Statements/The-School-Counselor-and-Group-Counseling

Applied Improvisation Network. (2016). *About applied improvisation.* http://www.appliedimprovisation.network/about-applied-improvisation/

Atkins, S., Adams, M., McKinney, C., McKinney, H., Rose, L., Wentworth, J., & Wentworth, J. (2003). *Expressive arts therapy.* Parkway.

Centervention. (2020). *Supporting research.* Centervention®. https://www.centervention.com/social-emotional-learning-research-studies/

Corey, G. (2016). *Theory and practice of counseling and psychotherapy.* Cengage.

DeMichele, M. (2019). *One rule improv: The fast, easy, no fear approach to teaching, learning, and applying improv.* Academic Play.

Duffey, T., & Trepal, H. (2016). Introduction to the special section on relational-cultural theory. *Journal of Counseling and Development, 94*(4), 379–383.

Escape the Room. (2019, July 24). *What is an escape room.* https://escapetheroom.com/blog/what-is-an-escape-room/

Farley, N. (2017). Improvisation as a meta-counseling skill. *Journal of Creativity in Mental Health, 12*(1), 115–128. https://doi.org/10.1080/15401383.2016.1191402

Gallup. (2019). *Education technology use in schools: Student and educator perspectives.* https://www.newschools.org/wp-content/uploads/2019/09/Gallup-Ed-Tech-Use-in-Schools-2.pdf

Gladding, S. T. (2016). *The creative arts in counseling* (5th ed.). American Counseling Association.

Joseph, G. (2017). *The act resilient method: From trauma to transformation*. Eve Publishing.

Pate, D. L. (2020, January 13). The top skills companies need most in 2020—and how to learn them. *LinkedIn Learning Blog*. https://www.linkedin.com/business/learning/blog/top-skills-and-courses/the-skills-companies-need-most-in-2020and-how-to-learn-them

Tint, B., & Froerer, A. (2014). *Delphi summary study*. Applied Improvisation Network. http://appliedimprovisation.network/wp-content/uploads/2015/11/Delphi-Study-Summary.pdf

Vernon, A. (2019). Creative arts interventions. In A. Vernon & C. J. Schimmel (Eds.), *Counseling children and adolescents* (5th ed., pp. 75–110). Cognella.

Weaver, K. O. (2019, June 29–July 2). *Enhance your comprehensive program with breakout boxes and escape games* [PowerPoint]. ASCA Annual Conference 2019, Boston, Massachusetts, United States.

Wedding, D., & Corsini, R. J. (2018). *Current psychotherapies*. Cengage.

PART IV

Advancement of Practice

Sharpening Your Group Leadership Skills: Advocating for Supervision, Peer Consultation, and Professional Development

Jason Duffy, PhD
SUNY Oswego

Sean Finnerty, PhD
SUNY Oswego

LEARNING OBJECTIVES

1. Distinguish between administrative supervision and clinical supervision, specifically in relation to the school context.
2. Learn strategies to advocate for school counselor peer consultation.
3. Discuss why professional development, including clinical supervision and peer consultation, is necessary for school counselor growth as group leaders.

CONSIDER THIS SCENARIO

Shanise is a new high school counselor in an urban school district. Having just finished her master's degree several months ago, she is excited to get various small groups started with her students. As she begins to run the groups during her students' lunch blocks, she realizes that some of the skills she needs (e.g., behavior management in adolescent-level groups) could use development in order to enhance the group outcomes as well as her own confidence. Currently, there is not an official director of counseling or lead counselor in her department, so she is unsure how she might polish her skills and raise her confidence.

CONSIDER THESE QUESTIONS FOR DISCUSSION

- What are your initial reactions to Shanise's situation?
- If you were Shanise, what would be the first thing you might do in this situation to advocate for more skill acquisition?

Introduction

As discussed in Chapter 5, school counselors regularly work with a variety of stakeholders to support student growth. Additionally, it remains crucial for school counselors to continually expand their own uniquely positioned knowledge and skill sets. Unfortunately, it is typical for counselors to be evaluated by school administrators and/or directors who do not have school counseling experience nor training related to how school counselors can be leveraged to best support student success (Cleveland & Hartline, 2017). This has potential implications for clinical practice, as the relationship between school counselors and district administration, while supporting educational initiatives, does not typically promote counseling skill development and conceptualization.

Additionally, school counselors are required by state departments of education to obtain professional development in order to maintain certification. In many cases, it is not uncommon for district and state-wide professional development options to be teacher, rather than school counselor, focused (DeKruyf et al., 2013; Splete & Grisdale, 1992). It is therefore important for school counselors to advocate for supervision, consultation, and professional development with supervisors and colleagues who understand the appropriate roles of the school counselor. It is also necessary for school counselors to lean on professional organizations (e.g., American School Counselor Association [ASCA], American Counseling Association, Association for Specialists in Group Work) to continue to develop their professional identity and practice through participation in conferences and continuing education programming (e.g., Evidenced-Based School Counseling Conference, American School Counselor Association continuing education offerings).

Maintaining a clear professional posture and related skill set may be especially important for areas that may not be emphasized in graduate school counselor education programs (i.e., group counseling) in order to help school counselors avoid falling into ineffective or unethical practices. Accordingly, this chapter provides readers with a foundational framework for approaching supervision, peer consultation, and professional development as these constructs apply to group leader development and practice.

Supervision

According to Bernard and Goodyear (2014), supervision is defined as "an intervention provided by a more senior member of a profession to a more junior colleague to colleagues who typically (but not always) are members of that same profession" (p. 9). The supervisory relationship extends over time and has several simultaneous purposes, which include enhancing the skills of the more junior person(s), overseeing the quality of the services provided by the supervisee to clients, and gatekeeping for the particular profession to which the supervisee hopes to become a part. Additionally, supervision is evaluative in nature, and for school counselors, may include a focus on administrative, programmatic, and clinical support.

Clinical supervision specifically is an integral part of school counselor training programs (Krell & Donohue, 2018; Luke & Goodrich, 2019) and is considered a foundational component of school counselor development (American School Counselor Association, 2019; CACREP, 2016). Despite its importance, many school counselors do not receive clinical supervision once employed (Luke & Bernard, 2006). This incongruence creates unfortunate circumstances, as many school counselors strongly desire and need the continuation of clinical supervision to address issues related to professional isolation, emotional support, accountability, interventions, service delivery, resources, debriefing, and professional development, as well as issues related to client welfare (Luke & Goodrich, 2019). Additionally, with the increase in school districts implementing comprehensive school counseling programs, counselors are now tasked with the huge job of developing a wide range of preventative programming (e.g., leading more small groups) to meet the educational needs and goals of all students (American School Counselor Association, 2016). These expectations often overwhelm even the most seasoned professional. As such, it is no surprise school counselors who receive regular clinical supervision report an increased sense of comfort on the job, self-efficacy, and professionalism (Ladany & Bradley, 2011).

Clinical supervision should include a focus on counselors' skill development across different modalities (e.g., individual, small-group, large-group, classroom). Unfortunately, it is common, beginning even in graduate training, that the focus of clinical supervision centers more on individual rather than group counseling skills (Yalom & Leszcz, 2020). This often has implications for the development and maintenance of group leader self-efficacy and group counseling advocacy in the schools (Springer, 2016). Facilitating small groups requires skills not typically utilized by school teachers, school administrators, and other school-based stakeholders. For example, the focus on group-level processes and small-group membership related to age, gender, sexual orientation, developmental readiness, et cetera are typically different than those encountered by the average teacher or school administrator. Based on their education, training, and experience, school counselors run groups that specifically target psychoeducation- and counseling-related concerns. This is why clinical supervision from a counseling professional is particularly important. The basic skills required to lead these groups are typically taught and practiced during a preservice school counselor's time in graduate school; however, this should be viewed as the beginning of the professional school counselor's group leader developmental journey and reinforced through clinical supervision in practice. More information specific to the development of preservice group leadership supervision is provided in Chapter 10.

Referring again to Bernard and Goodyear (2014), the clinical supervision process may include pairing experienced counselors with nonexperienced counselors to provide support, instruction, and feedback as they evaluate the implementation of clinical services. Unfortunately, of the three documented types of school counselor supervision (i.e., clinical, administrative, and programmatic), clinical supervision appears to be the most needed ethically, yet the least provided in school systems (Cinotti & Springer, 2016). The administrative supervision that is frequently provided in schools is often evaluative and involves a power differential between the supervisor and supervisee(s). This typically comes in the form of an administrator serving as a supervisor for a school counselor. Some school counselors receive supervision that, at first, appears to be appropriately aligned with practice—that is, they are assigned supervision under a director of school counseling or an individual who is designated as "lead counselor." While this initially seems like a good fit for clinical supervision, it must be recognized that in some cases, that supervisor has no background or training in school counseling but nonetheless contributes to the counselor's evaluation. In such cases, it is important for school counselors to collaborate with these supervisors to ensure that they are evaluated accurately based on the appropriate role of the school counselor rather than as a teacher. The need for practicing school counselors to advocate for clinical supervision and effective evaluation in the schools is high, especially specific to skill sets (e.g., group leadership) that are less reinforced in graduate training.

Peer Consultation

When school counselors do not receive clinical supervision with regularity, they must rely on consultation with other school counseling colleagues (e.g., peer consultation) or, when available, skilled counselors outside of the school setting. In contrast to supervision, peer consultation is typically collegial in nature and does not include an evaluative component, nor does it obligate consultees to do anything different based on the feedback and information received. According to Thompson and Henderson (2011), consultation is "a process in which the consultant works with the consultee with the goal of bringing about positive change" (p. 529). Consultation in the school counseling context can take on many forms and often involves the school counselor working closely with stakeholders (e.g., parents, teachers, administration, other school counselors) to discuss skills and resources that benefit students (Cholewa et al., 2017). Within this chapter, we focus on the concept of peer consultation as the intentional collaboration *between counseling colleagues* for the explicit purpose of improving and refining counseling practice. Unfortunately, similar to clinical supervision in schools, peer consultation groups may not be readily available, and it is important for school counselors to consider how they might creatively seek out or design peer consultation groups themselves in order to collaborate with other counseling professionals to further support their development.

Advocating for School Counseling Consultation Groups

School counselor consultation groups typically involve a group of school counselors who meet regularly to consult on student issues, service delivery, intervention ideas, and/or new skills. In rare cases, opportunities exist where school counselors receive consultation services from individuals outside of the school system (e.g., a seasoned mental health counselor, a counselor educator from a local training program). School counselors who report working in isolation must be especially mindful of the need to extend their networking and professional development opportunities outside of their respective schools. Consultation and forming consultation groups is a great way to start.

Leading "Outside" Peer Consultation Groups

When school counselors recognize that they are not receiving enough clinical supervision and appropriate professional development within their home schools or districts, it becomes ethically important that they seek further assistance (American School Counselor Association, 2016, Section B.3.h; CACREP, 2016, Section G.3.m). This often necessitates that they use their advocacy skills to form a network of other counselors who are willing to engage in group consultation, especially for school counselors who practice independently in a school district. Meeting regularly with other district school counselors and pupil personnel services staff in groups is an important way to both give and receive much needed clinical support. Additionally, advocating for monthly consultation group meetings with out-of-district colleagues is another way in which school counselors receive ongoing support. Here we offer ideas on how school counselors might conceptualize establishing peer consultation groups.

First, consider rotating schools each month. Each month, the school counselor at the designated school can host the supervision group and even take on the role of group leader for that particular session. Another option that has become popular amid the COVID-19 global pandemic is creating virtual groups where different counselors lead a discussion, present concerns from their schools, and share resources. This offers a great way for school counselors to increase their knowledge and skill sets and bring fresh ideas into their schools. It also allows for facilitators to practice their group leadership skills and receive feedback from colleagues.

Within these peer consultation groups, another suggestion includes facilitators focusing on a topic for each meeting, such as asking members to bring and discuss an example of a current group intervention that they are running with students. This targets specific skills and topics and promotes shared experiences. As suggested by scholars in the field (e.g., Davis, 2003, Sangganjanavanich & Lenz, 2012), experiential learning using roleplays and audio tape recordings may also be especially helpful during these meetings and can be planned to mirror case conferences often used as part of the clinical supervision process.

When creating school counselor/peer-led consultation groups, as with any group formation, school counseling group leaders use their screening skills to ensure that adult members are a good fit for the goals of the group, and that group rules and norms are consistent with the scope and sequence of each session. School counseling leaders use their group facilitation skills to help draw out and connect members, which assists in cultivating a safe space in which to conceptualize difficult cases and share ideas.

Professional Development

As referenced earlier, professional development opportunities offered by local schools and school districts are often teacher or classroom instruction focused. Unless a school system has leadership that is committed to implementing a school counseling program with high fidelity, local professional development offerings for school counselors can be insufficient to promote continued skill development. In cases such as this, it is the job of school counselors to both advocate for appropriate professional development for themselves and to encourage leadership to be involved in professional development that increases their knowledge of the appropriate role of the school counselor.

One option for appropriate professional development that engages the working relationship with school leadership and assists in advancing advocacy efforts for skill development is attending training focused on a variety of school counselor evaluation tools. For example, readers may consider attending training based on the ASCA school counselor performance appraisal template; the New Jersey school counselor evaluation model (New Jersey School Counselor Association, 2017); the Ohio school counselor evaluation model (Ohio Department of Education, 2016); the Iowa school counselor evaluation supplement (Iowa School Counselor Association, 2019); or the Danielson Group's school counselor rubric (Danielson Group, 2015). Each of these documents includes school counselor evaluation around responsive services like group counseling. After attending professional development sessions on models such as these, school counselors can review these evaluation tools with administrators to help advocate for increased feedback and professional development opportunities specific to group counseling and skill development.

Additionally, attending professional development with school leadership on the importance of using data to drive a school counselor program is valuable. The ability to link group counseling interventions with outcome data points (e.g., attendance, behavior, academics) provides a stronger rationale for administrators to support school counselors' continued professional development in the area of group counseling, as these interventions are seen to service a larger number of students at one time. Requesting that non-counseling supervisors attend state school counseling [classes, courses, seminars, symposia], regional counselor education and supervision, or local group-work conferences and workshops presents opportunities to garner support for more group-leader-specific supervision. The bottom line is, when school counselors can show how group interventions make a difference in the academic, social/emotional, and career development of students, administrators are likely to provide more support for continued counselor development in these areas.

Conclusion

Small-group counseling is an important Tier 2 intervention in schools; yet for many reasons, small groups are not initiated as often as needed. This is likely due in part to a lack of focus on small-group leadership skill development post graduate education. This chapter offers ways in which school counselors can collaborate with stakeholders and other professionals to advocate for appropriate supervision, and it provides suggestions for ways in which school counselors can lead and participate in peer consultation groups and professional development to further enhance their clinical skills and increase their group leading confidence.

Personal Reflection Questions

- Now that you have read about the challenges to school-based supervision, peer consultation, and professional development, how do you feel about your ability to advocate for each?
- How can you plan to overcome some of the challenges involved in seeking supervision related to running school-based groups?

Advice From the Expert/Author

It is important to ask about ways of receiving ongoing support during the interview process for prospective jobs as well as after you are hired. Schools that value the school counselor's work will be open to professional development opportunities (e.g., attending conferences or online workshops) and will also want to hear any ideas you might have about school counselor evaluation, peer consultation, and clinical supervision in the counseling department.

Check Out These Resources

- Linton, J. M., & Deuschle, C. J. (n.d.). *Meeting school counselors' supervision needs: Four models of group supervision* (EJ901142). ERIC. https://files.eric.ed.gov/fulltext/EJ901142.pdf
- Ockerman, M. S., Mason, E. C. M., & Chen-Hayes, S. F. (2013). School counseling supervision in challenging times: The CAFE supervisor model. *Journal of Counselor Preparation and Supervision, 5*(2), Article 4. https://doi.org/10.7729/51.0024

References

American School Counselor Association. (2015). *The school counselor and annual performance appraisal* [Position statement]. https://schoolcounselor.org/Standards-Positions/Position-Statements/ASCA-Position-Statements/The-School-Counselor-and-Annual-Performance-Apprai

American School Counselor Association. (2016). *ASCA ethical standards for school counselors*. https://www.schoolcounselor.org/getmedia/f041cbd0-7004-47a5-ba01-3a5d657c6743/Ethical-Standards.pdf

American School Counselor Association. (2019). *ASCA national model: A framework for school counseling programs* (4th ed.).

Bernard, J. M. (1979). Supervisor training: A discrimination model. *Counselor Education and Supervision, 19*(1), 60–68. https://doi.org/10.1002/j.1556-6978.1979.tb00906.x

Bernard, J. M., & Goodyear, R. K. (2014). *Fundamentals of clinical supervision* (5th ed.). Allyn & Bacon.

CACREP. (2016). *2016 CACREP standards*. https://www.cacrep.org/for-programs/2016-cacrep-standards/

Cholewa, B., Goodman-Scott, E., Thomas, A., & Cook, J. (2017). Teachers' perceptions and experiences consulting with school counselors: A qualitative study. *Professional School Counseling, 20*(1), 77–88. https://doi.org/10.5330/1096-2409-20.1.77

Cinotti, D. A., & Springer, S. I. (2016). *Examining the impact of non-counseling supervisors on school counselor self-efficacy*. American Counseling Association. https://www.counseling.org/docs/default-source/vistas/article_71_2016.pdf?sfvrsn=63e5482c_4

Cleveland, R. E., & Hartline, J. (2017). *School counselor evaluation instrument pilot project: A school counselor association, department of education, and university collaboration* (EJ1158291). ERIC. https://eric.ed.gov/?id=EJ1158291

Danielson Group. (2015). *School counselors rubric: Example framework for school counselors*. https://www.k12.wa.us/sites/default/files/public/tpep/frameworks/danielson/schoolcounselorrubric.pdf

Davis, K. M. (2003). Teaching a course in school-based consultation. *Counselor Education and Supervision, 42*(4), 275–285. https://doi.org/10.1002/j.1556-6978.2003.tb01819.x

DeKruyf, L., Auger, R. W., Trice-Black, S. (2013). The role of school counselors in meeting students' mental health needs: Examining issues of professional identity. *Professional School Counseling, 16*(5), 271–282. https://doi.org/10.1177/2156759X0001600502

Iowa School Counselor Association. (2019). *School counselor evaluation supplement.* https://www.iowaschool-counselors.org/resources/Documents/Professional%20Development/ISCA_Supplement_2019.pdf

Krell, M. M., & Donohue, P. (2018). Using supervision mapping to enrich school counseling fieldwork supervision. *Journal of Counselor Preparation and Supervision, 11*(1), Article 9. https://repository.wcsu.edu/jcps/vol11/iss1/9

Ladany, N., & Bradley, L. J. (2011). *Counselor supervision.* Routledge.

Luke, M., & Bernard, J. M. (2006). The school counselor supervision model: An extension of the discrimination model. *Counselor Education and Supervision, 45*(4), 282–295. https://doi.org/10.1002/j.1556-6978.2006.tb00004.x

Luke, M., & Goodrich, K. M. (2019). The discrimination model for school counseling supervision. In C. T. Dollarhide & M. E. Lemberger-Truelove (Eds.), *Theories of school counseling for the 21st century* (pp. 297–317). Oxford University Press.

New Jersey School Counselor Association. (2017). *New Jersey school counselor evaluation model.* https://static1.squarespace.com/static/5a56b9aa017db276cd76b240/t/5a6f82ece4966b5767b68863/1517257454116/Evaluation_Model.pdf

Ohio Department of Education. (2016). *Ohio school counselor evaluation model.* https://education.ohio.gov/getattachment/Topics/Career-Tech/Career-Connections/Resources-for-School-Counselors/School-Counselor-Standards-and-Evaluation/OSCES-Model.pdf.aspx

Sangganjanavanich, V. F., & Lenz, A. S. (2012). The experiential consultation training model. *Counselor Education and Supervision, 51*(4), 296–307. https://doi.org/10.1002/j.1556-6978.2012.00022.x

Splete, H. H., & Grisdale, G. A. (1992). The Oakland Counselor Academy: A professional development program for school counselors. *School Counselor, 39*(3), 176–182. https://www.jstor.org/stable/23899933

Springer, S. I. (2016). Examining predictors of group leader self-efficacy for preservice school counselors. *Journal for Specialists in Group Work, 41*(4), 286–311. https://doi.org/10.1080/01933922.2016.1228723

Thompson, C. L., & Henderson, D. A. (2011). Consultation. In C. L. Thompson & D. A. Henderson (Eds.), *Counseling children* (8th ed). Brooks/Cole.

Yalom, I. D., & Leszcz, M. (2020). *The theory and practice of group psychotherapy* (6th ed.). Basic Books.

Structured Feedback to Enhance Preservice School Counselors' Group Leader Skills

Jonathan H. Ohrt, PhD
University of South Carolina

Shelby Gonzales
University of South Carolina

LEARNING OBJECTIVES

1. Describe how the major aspects of the discrimination model of supervision and the supervision of group work model aid in the development of group leadership skills and improve group leader self-efficacy.
2. Recognize the components of the school counseling supervision model (SCSM) and discuss how the individual and group advisement domain of SCSM is used to enhance school counselor group leadership.
3. Recall effective group leadership skills to promote positive group outcomes at the intrapersonal, interpersonal, and group-as-a-whole levels.
4. Explain how the Group Leader Feedback Form (GLFF) is used to provide group leadership feedback to preservice school counselors.

CONSIDER THIS SCENARIO

Monica is a school counseling practicum student completing her clinical experience under your supervision at your school. Monica has demonstrated strong individual counseling skills during role-plays and practice sessions; however, she has verbalized that she is much more comfortable in one-on-one sessions and is anxious about counseling in the small-group setting. In your first supervision session with Monica, she expresses to you that she is very anxious about receiving feedback on her group skills. She lets you know that "I am not going to be very good at it. I am nervous about receiving feedback on the feedback form you are using."

CONSIDER THESE QUESTIONS FOR DISCUSSION

- What advice or words of encouragement might you offer Monica to help ease her anxiety?
- What are your personal thoughts regarding the benefits of receiving feedback on your group-leading skills?

Introduction

Group leadership requires skills that are beyond the scope of individual counseling. Group leaders, educators, and researchers consistently report that more group leadership training is needed during graduate-level training programs in order to keep up with continued implementation of the group modality (Burlingame et al., 2019; Ohrt et al., 2014a; Springer et al., 2018). In order for preservice school counselors to develop effective group leader skills, adequate training, feedback, and supervision are needed. In this chapter, we discuss group training and supervision strategies for preservice school counselors. Additionally, we review the Group Leader Feedback Form (GLFF), which can be used to provide formal, structured feedback on group leader skills to enhance preservice school counselors' leadership development.

Training in Group Leadership

Although the majority of training models in counselor education are focused on individual counseling skills, several authors have proposed models specific to group work. Stockton et al. (2014) described training models that focus on group process, skill acquisition, or an integration of both. Process models include a focus on trainees gaining a firm understanding of group dynamics and stages. These models often include didactic strategies related to content, but primarily emphasize experiential activities such as observing a group, coleading a group with a more experienced leader, and participating in a group as a member. Yalom and Leszcz (2005) recommended that trainees colead a group with a more experienced counselor and then participate in post-group meetings to receive feedback. By participating in a group as a member, students better identify process-related issues (e.g., stage development, subgrouping, cohesion) so they can more accurately address these aspects when they become a leader (Ohrt et al., 2014ab). The overall goal of process model strategies is to help future group leaders become more aware of how a group works so they are prepared to effectively lead in the future.

Skill-acquisition models emphasize helping trainees learn group-specific techniques and interventions. For example, Jacobs et al. (2016) developed a model in which students first observe a group, either live or through a video, and then practice the skills they observed. In their model, students practice skills during an authentic small-group experience as opposed to a role-play. Smaby et al. (1999) described a similar model termed the skilled group counseling training model (SGCTM). In the SGCTM, students learn increasingly more advanced leadership skills through instructor demonstrations, video observations, leadership practice, and performance feedback. Stockton (2009) described the perceiving, selecting, and risking (PSR) model that integrates learning about process with skill acquisition. Within the PSR model, the instructor first uses didactic strategies to help students learn about group dynamics and therapeutic factors. Next, the instructor focuses on assisting the student in developing basic group techniques (e.g., member-to-member feedback, promoting learning to outside the group), microskills (e.g., linking, drawing out), and more advanced skills (e.g., promoting therapeutic factors). The instructor uses strategies such as training videos, instructor modeling, skill practice, and feedback.

Each counselor educator and supervisor will approach training from a different perspective based on individual style and program structure. Most school counselor training programs include a combination of didactic instruction on content and process-oriented experiential learning, as well as a focus on group skill acquisition. Nevertheless, what appears to be most important is that preservice school counselors receive training in both group process and skill acquisition through experiential learning, observation, practice, and feedback. Springer et al. (2018) found that preservice school counselors desired more opportunities to observe groups, found it helpful to colead a group with a more experienced leader, and valued supervision and feedback. Ohrt et al. (2016) found preservice school counselors valued opportunities for observation and practice when learning about larger group facilitation. Similarly, Ohrt et al. (2014a) found that experiential participation as a member, observation of groups, opportunities for practice, and supervision were helpful aspects of group leader training.

Supervision Models Applied to Group

As preservice school counselors begin to develop their skills in group work, school counseling supervisors must be just as adequately prepared to supervise the work in which their supervisees are engaged (Springer et al., 2018). Dollarhide and Miller (2006) recognized that there is a lack of clinical supervision in school counseling, and there is a critical need for qualified, trained counseling supervisors for the development of preservice school counselors. The implementation of instruction and activities are through large-group, classroom, small-group, and individual settings. However, the American School Counselor Association (ASCA) 2020 School Counselor and Group Counseling Position Statement proclaims that "group counseling ... is an efficient, effective and positive way of providing direct service to students with academic, career and social/emotional developmental issues and situational concerns" (p. 35). Today's K–12 students are likely to need assistance with special issues (e.g., coping skills, emotional regulation, family, social skills). It is imperative that professional school counselors who work with K–12 students have not only a firm foundation on their understanding of developmental counseling but also a thorough understanding of effective group interventions with students. In the following section, we provide a brief overview of a popular supervision model as it pertains to group work in a school counseling setting. Although there are other models of supervision specified for school counseling—solution-focused (Limberg et al., 2012), systems model (Wood & Rayle, 2006), integrated approach (Nelson & Johnson, 1999), and peer supervision (Agnew et al., 2000)—for the purposes of this chapter, we will focus on the use of the discrimination model for supervision of school counselors and, more specifically, supervision of group work.

The Discrimination Model

The discrimination model developed by Bernard (1979, 1997) aids supervisors in organizing their supervision sessions by allowing them to establish focus for supervision (intervention, conceptualization, personalization skills). It also establishes the ways in which the supervisor operates within the supervisor role (teacher, counselor, and consultant). Within each role, supervisors are able to turn their focus upon the supervisee's work with their client. Intervention skills include all observable behaviors displayed by a clinical counselor; this can be as simple as a use of basic counseling skills such as a head nod or as complex as the delivery of a counseling strategy. Conceptualization skills involve the selection of an appropriate intervention for the student(s), identifying and discussing client themes, the examination of outcome goals, and the demonstration of an understanding of what is occurring in the session. Lastly, personalization skills refer to the counselor's ability to integrate their own personal style of counseling while ensuring that personal issues, cultural biases, and countertransference are tempered.

Once supervisors have an understanding concerning their supervisee's abilities within each focus area, they must decide on a role to accept (teacher, counselor, or consultant) that will benefit that individual and, in turn, accomplish their supervision goals. As a teacher, the supervisor provides structure: giving instruction, modeling, and direct feedback. In the role of counselor, the supervisor aims to support the supervisee in examining their thoughts, activities, or internal reality. Finally, if the supervisor opts out of the consultant role, they become a resource for the supervisee, encouraging autonomy and trusting his or her own insights, feelings, and insights about their work.

Application of this model first to group work and secondly to school counseling has yet to come to fruition; however, Rubel and Okech (2006) adapted the discrimination model for the supervision of group leaders. The supervision of group work model (SGW) integrates aspects of the discrimination model, drawing parallels between the roles supervisors adopt in typical supervision but is revised to include roles that emerge within group work supervision. Additionally, the focus of supervision (intervention, conceptualization, and personalization skills) is extended to include the individual, interpersonal, and group-as-a-whole interactions (Donigian & Malnati, 1997; Kline, 2003; Rubel & Okech, 2006).

Utilizing the SGW model, a supervisor in the teaching role works to identify knowledge gaps of the supervisee, brings it to their attention, and then provides the information that is lacking. Acting within the counselor role, supervisors assist in the exploration of the supervisee's ability to conceptualize their group members at the individual, interpersonal, and group-as-a-whole level. Lastly, within the consultant role, supervisors enable supervisees to identify their focus of supervision and issues within their focus and then allow them to find their own solution to the identified issues while providing necessary assistance, information, and perspective (Rubel & Okech, 2006). Supervisors should anticipate overlap in their roles due to the complexity of the live supervision process and ever-present dynamics of group work and the skills entailed. When selecting their role, supervisors should consider the skills of the supervisee; factoring in how well they are able to identify supervision issues and needs, and how the supervisee perceives their own knowledge deficits or emotional needs.

Utilizing the SGW model allows supervisors to draw attention to the supervisee's comprehension of group dynamics; this understanding is imperative for supervisees to understand as group leaders. Supervisors should be prepared to consider how the supervisee is understanding the individual level of group member interactions when focusing on a single individual in the group. This can look like providing individualized intervention, conceptualizing an individual's well-being and their experience of the group, and becoming cognizant of how their reactions to individual group members impact the group as a whole. Therefore, supervisors should be prepared to aid supervisees with interventions, conceptualizations, and personalization skills for the individuals that participate in their groups (Rubel & Okech, 2006). Furthermore, interactions between group members are vital to understand when working with groups. According to Kline (2003) the interpersonal level is the most useful but often the most underutilized skill during group interactions. At the interpersonal (or subsystem) level of interaction, supervisors must be equipped to guide supervisees through intervention skills that enable them to intervene, interact with, understand, and be aware of group member relationships throughout the duration of the group. This can look like facilitating communication, connection, or confrontation between group members or becoming aware of their own reactions to group member dynamics and how that can impact the relationships established within the group (Rubel & Okech, 2006). Finally, the group-as-a-system level is where interactions are assessed as a whole. At this level, supervision occurs related to the supervisee's implementation of whole-group interventions, conceptualization of group dynamics, and identification of their own reactions to group occurrences or instances and how they impact the group (Rubel & Okech, 2006).

The selection of focus (intervention, conceptualization, and personalization) in supervision can seem like a daunting task; however, following Bernard's (1997) suggestion of paying attention to the supervisee's actions in session, live or video recorded, will give the best insight into areas of strength and growth for intervention, conceptualization, and personalization skills. In addition to the challenge of selecting a focus, the selection of a group-level (individual, interpersonal, group-as-a-whole) focus may be just as, if not more, challenging because each level of interaction has its own implications and impact on the remaining levels. It should be noted that the three levels of interactions are not separate but intertwined within one another; therefore, supervisors should encourage supervisees to conceptualize all three levels at once, linking intervention, conceptualization, and personalization skills (Rubel & Okech, 2006).

As the SGW model provides direction for supervision of group work, what group work in the schools looks like along with the supervision of that work needs to be considered as well. Also building on the discrimination model established by Bernard (1979, 1997), Luke and Bernard (2006) added an additional four-part domain to the initial three by three (teacher, counselor, consultant and intervention, conceptualization, personalization) grid. Recognizing that clinical supervisors who work outside of the school system may lack a thorough understanding of the setting, population, needs, contexts, and role of a school counselor, there is a need for professional school counselors to be prepared and comfortable with providing supervision to novice school counselors. The extended domains included in Luke and Bernard's (2006) school counseling supervision model (SCSM) include (a) large group intervention, (b) counseling and consultation, (c) individual and group advisement, and (d) planning, coordination, and evaluation. The domains, originating from common components of a comprehensive school counseling program, provide a point of entry for supervisors to discuss the multifaceted roles and tasks of the school counseling profession (Luke & Bernard, 2006). For the purposes of this chapter, we mainly focus on the individual and group advisement domain. Within this domain, supervisors have the ability to target the development of a supervisee's intervention, conceptualization, and personalization skills in group work and group interactions with students, parents, teachers, and other school-based professionals. Examining how preservice school counselors are facilitating small-group work with students, parent-teacher conferences, and small-group peer mediations, for example, will give supervisors opportunities to evaluate intervention, conceptualization, and personalization skills through live or recorded supervision, leading the supervisor to choose a role (teacher, counselor, consultant) to address the needs of the supervisee. As mentioned earlier in the chapter, although the structure of the SCSM gives a 3×3×4 model in separate parts, each section should not be treated independently. All domains interact with and impact the other; therefore, supervisors must be consistently aware of how each domain, role, and focus interacts, exchanges, and influences the other.

Springer et al. (2018) provided some practical recommendations for preservice school counselor site supervision specific to group work. The authors suggested that site supervisors intentionally plan and organize supervision sessions and allocate time to discuss group-specific concerns during supervision sessions. Springer et al. (2018) and Ohrt et al. (2016) recommended providing preservice school counselors with the opportunity to construct a group from start to finish (i.e., planning, organizing, and facilitating the group). Springer (2016) also suggested that supervisors provide interns with specific feedback about group knowledge and skills in addition to supporting them through processing their emotional responses to group experiences. Furthermore, Ohrt et al. (2014a) found that preservice group leaders desired constructive feedback from their supervisors based on their recorded group sessions.

Effective Group Skills

Burlingame et al. (2019) found that cohesion is a consistent predictor of group counseling outcomes. Experienced group leaders also report that attention to group dynamics such as cohesion and universality among group members is a critical aspect of successful group outcomes (Ohrt et al., 2014a). In order to promote cohesion and ultimately successful outcomes, group leaders must utilize skills that promote personal awareness and member engagement, build rapport, manage member interactions, and facilitate group process in general. Although there is not a consensus list of group skills in the literature and the research is still evolving in this area, Luke (2014) categorized common group skills that are used at the intrapersonal, interpersonal, and group-as-a-whole levels based on group systems theory (Connors & Caple, 2005). Intrapersonal interventions are focused on individual members' experiences, thoughts, and feelings. Interventions at the intrapersonal level include support, drawing out, and blocking. Interpersonal interventions are focused on the dynamics and interactions between members and include modeling, linking, and feedback. Group-level interventions focus on the development of the whole group and include reframing, self-disclosure, and processing. Although this is not an exhaustive list, it is a useful framework to conceptualize important skills.

The timing and effectiveness of specific skills that a group leader implements are inextricably linked with the dynamics at play within a group (Luke, 2014). In other words, group leaders will emphasize different skills based on group stage, group climate, and individual members' characteristics. Throughout the supervision process, supervisors must take into account the various types of groups preservice school counselors are leading. Based on the type of group (task, psychoeducational, counseling, and psychotherapy) (Association for Specialists in Group Work, 2000), school counseling supervisors need to be aware of the leadership skills required by the developing school counselor for each specific group type, the group members, and the group setting. Although psychotherapy groups are not often facilitated in schools, task, psychoeducational, and counseling groups are. Unsurprisingly, different skills are needed to lead different types of groups. For instance, supervisors must be mindful of the interventions that are most appropriate for psychoeducational groups; these are often skills based and typically structured to improve interpersonal relationships or growth of members, and task groups may be more directive, physically productive, and tangibly focused. Developing competency to work with diverse group members should also be noted as a priority for group leaders. Group leaders should be well equipped to respond effectively to diverse group members, understand how diversity impacts group processes and dynamics, and assist members in their own awareness, knowledge, and exploration of working alongside individuals who come from a different background than themselves (Haley-Banez et al., 1999).

Assessment and Feedback for Skill Development

Preservice school counselors who lead groups benefit from receiving constructive feedback about their skill development (Ohrt et al., 2014a; Ohrt et al., 2016). Therefore, providing intentional, structured supervision to preservice school counselors is an essential aspect of developing effective group leader skills. Ohrt et al. (2014a) found that group leaders desired specific feedback based on a supervisor reviewing their session (not just their own conceptualization). Springer (2016) also found that preservice school counselors' group leadership self-efficacy was related to feedback they received from their site supervisors.

In this section, we describe the Group Leader Feedback (GLFF) Form, which is a formal form that can be used by counselor educators and supervisors to provide feedback to students about their group leader skill development. Additionally, we provide a case example of how the form is to be used in practice. We developed the feedback form based on best practice training standards (Association for Specialists in Group Work, 2000), previous literature on essential group skills (Corey & Corey, 2018; Luke, 2014; Ohrt, 2014a), and research on group outcomes (Burlingame et al., 2019). I (Jonathan) use the feedback form when I supervise preservice school counselors who are leading groups (e.g., in a practicum, internship, or group class). The feedback form is divided into four sections of group leader skills and includes performance indicators related to planning, active listening, facilitating, and group climate. Ratings on each indicator range from "0" ("did not meet skills competency; missed all opportunities") to "4" ("leader demonstrates exemplary skill competency; successful in ~85% of opportunities"). There is also space for narrative comments and feedback. An example of the GLFF is included in Appendix A at the end of this chapter.

When I use the form, I present it to my students and discuss that I will use it to provide concrete feedback. I also explain that I use the form to help us have a shared understanding of progress when providing them with feedback on their leadership skills and that it is not meant as a punitive evaluation tool. Processing how the form functions helps alleviate the students' anxiety related to performance evaluation. Prior to students facilitating a group, I meet with them to discuss their plan for the group. If they are facilitating a psychoeducational group, I also discuss lesson plans, content, and any activities they are using. Students then facilitate the session and record it so I can review it. Students submit a copy of the recorded session as well as a reflection of the session, in which they discuss what went well and what they would like to improve. While reviewing the session, I complete the feedback form and provide narrative feedback about relative strengths and growth areas. After students receive their feedback, I meet with them to process the session, brainstorm how they can improve, and reinforce what they are doing well.

Supervision and feedback are key aspects of preservice school counselor group leadership development. For example, using the SGW model, the supervisor can use the GLFF to facilitate discussion around group intervention skills, how the supervisee is conceptualizing the group dynamics and intervening, and the supervisee's reaction to the group. Based on the feedback discussion, the supervisor may work in multiple roles through (a) teaching the supervisee how to implement a specific skill (teacher role), (b) helping the supervisee work through insecurities confronting group members (counselor role), or (c) brainstorming effective interventions to use during termination (consultant role). School counselor educators and supervisors process feedback using their personalized models of education and supervision. However, the GLFF provides educators and supervisors with a way to organize formative feedback to preservice school counselors so there are shared expectations and understanding related to group leader skill development.

Conclusion

Groups are an effective counseling modality that will continue to be widely implemented in school settings. The outcomes of groups are influenced by the leader's ability to effectively use skills and interventions within groups. School counselor educators and supervisors can enhance preservice school counselors' leadership abilities through structured training and supervision activities that include constructive feedback. We conclude this chapter with some concrete recommendations to enhance training and supervision activities of preservice school counselors.

CONNECTING TO CHAPTER CONTENT

Personal Reflection Questions

- What parts of receiving feedback are challenging for you? Are you uncomfortable being praised/hearing about what you are doing well? Do you become anxious or uneasy when you think about ways you could improve your counseling practice?

- Consider aspects of giving feedback that make you uncomfortable. Are you nervous about providing someone with information they may not have thought of? Does it make you feel uneasy to talk with someone about the ways they could improve their counseling practice?

Advice From the Expert /Author

When supervising Monica, you can spend some time processing her feelings of anxiety related to leading groups. Try to get a sense of what specifically she is concerned about so you can support her self-efficacy in those areas. It is also important to be clear that the feedback form is meant to be developmental and not punitive. I like to have students complete the form in addition to receiving feedback from me. I typically find that students rate themselves lower than I do in most areas. This process is helpful in starting the conversation about what areas are going well and providing feedback and support in areas that need improvement. Of course, it is a continuous formative feedback process and not a one-time evaluation.

Consider These Questions for Discussion

- The supervision process in school counseling is different from traditional clinical supervision and therefore the supervision of group work is also different. Think about the experiences you had as a supervisee. What worked well for you? What do you feel was lacking? What can you empower yourself with as you begin supervising group leaders in a school counseling setting?
- There are different types of groups that group leaders run in the school system (counseling, task, and psychoeducational). How do you plan on facilitating the development of novice school counselors in their group skills? What skills do you want your supervisee to display or know before they start working as a group leader? Will you utilize live and/ or recorded sessions, or rely on the supervisee report to provide supervision?
- When conducting small groups in the school setting, it's common to have students with diverse backgrounds, which will require group leaders to be culturally competent but also able to facilitate group interactions, experiences, and growth for individual members of the group. Thinking about the demographics and culture of the school your supervisee is working in, what are key multicultural considerations that you should review before they begin group work?

Training and Supervision Recommendations

- Provide training in group dynamics, group climate, group stages, therapeutic factors, and group process.
- Train students in skills that increase group cohesion.
- Provide opportunities for observation of groups.
- Ensure site supervisors have adequate training and resources for supervision.
- Provide opportunities for coleadership with a more experienced group leader.
- Ensure supervisors are dedicating specific time to discuss group-specific concerns. This includes logistics of how to plan for the group as well as case conceptualization and skill development. Counselor education programs may need to specify this requirement in practicum and internship agreements.
- Provide guidance on how to plan and implement the group, but also allow students autonomy to coordinate the group from start to finish.
- Provide concrete feedback on group leader skill development (i.e., using a feedback form like the one presented in this chapter). Provide feedback based on the supervisor's observation, not just the group leader's recollection of the group.

Check Out These Resources

ASCA Strategies for Site Supervisors

American School Counselor Association, (n.d.). *ASCA strategies for site supervisors* [Video]. https://videos.school-counselor.org/strategies-for-site-supervisors

Discrimination Model for School Counseling

Rubel, D., & Okech, J. E. A. (2006). The supervision of group work model: Adapting the discrimination model for supervision of group workers. *Journal for Specialists in Group Work, 31*(2), 113–134. https://doi.org/10.1080/01933920500493597

Solution-Focused Supervision Model

Limberg, D., Bell, H., & Lambie, G. (2012). Developmental, solution-focused supervision for counselors-in-training. *Wisconsin Counseling Journal, 26*(1), 3–14.

Supervision of Group Work Model

Luke, M., & Bernard, J. (2006). The school counseling supervision model: An extension of the discrimination model. *Counselor Education and Supervision, 45*(4), 282–295. https://doi.org/10.1002/j.1556-6978.2006.tb00004.x

Systems Supervision Model

Wood, C., & Rayle, A. D. (2006), A model of school counseling supervision: The goals, functions, roles, and systems model. *Counselor Education and Supervision, 45*(4), 253–266. https://doi.org/10.1002/j.1556-6978.2006.tb00002.x

References

Agnew, T., Vaught, C. C., Getz, H. G., & Fortune, J. (2000). Peer group clinical supervision program fosters confidence and professionalism. *Professional School Counseling, 4*(1), 6–13.

American School Counselor Association. (2020). *The school counselor and group counseling* [Position statement]. https://www.schoolcounselor.org/Standards-Positions/Position-Statements/ASCA-Position-Statements/The-School-Counselor-and-Group-Counseling

Association for Specialists in Group Work. (2000). Association for Specialists in Group Work: Professional standards for the training of group workers. *Journal for Specialists in Group Work, 25*(4), 327–342. https://doi.org/10.1080/01933920008411677

Bernard, J. M. (1979). Supervisor training: A discrimination model. *Counselor Education and Supervision, 19*(1), 60–68. https://doi.org/10.1002/j.1556-6978.1979.tb00906.x

Bernard, J. M. (1997). The discrimination model. In C. E. Watkins, Jr. (Ed.), *Handbook of psychotherapy supervision* (pp. 310–327). Wiley.

Burlingame, G. M., McClendon, D. T., & Yang, C. (2019). Cohesion in group therapy. In J. C. Norcross & M. J. Lambert (Eds.), *Psychotherapy relationships that work: Evidence-based therapist contributions* (Vol. 1, 3rd ed., pp. 205–244). Oxford University Press.

Connors, J. V., & Caple, R. B. (2005). A review of group systems theory. *Journal for Specialists in Group Work, 30*(2), 93–100. https://doi.org/10.1080/01933920590925940

Corey, M. S., & Corey, G. (2018). *Groups: Process and practice* (10th ed.). Brooks/Cole.

Dollarhide, C., & Miller, G. (2006). Supervision for preparation and practice of school counselors: Pathways to excellence. *Counselor Education and Supervision, 45*(4), 242–252. https://doi.org/10.1002/j.1556-6978.2006.tb00001.x

Donigian, J., & Malnati, R. (1997). *Systemic group therapy: A triadic model*. Brooks/Cole.

Haley-Banez, L., Brown, S., Molina, B., D'Andrea, M., Arrendondo, P., Merchant, M., & Wathen, S. (1999). Association for Specialists in Group Work principles for diversity-competent group workers. *Journal for Specialists in Group Work, 24*(1), 7–14. https://doi.org/10.1080/01933929908411415

Jacobs, E.E., Schimmel, C. J., Masson, R. L., Harvill, R. L. (2016). *Group counseling: Strategies and skills* (8th ed.). Cengage.

Kline, W. (2003). *Interactive group counseling and therapy*. Merrill/Prentice Hall.

Limberg, D., Bell, H., & Lambie, G. (2012). Developmental, solution-focused supervision for counselors-in-training. *Wisconsin Counseling Journal, 26*(1), 3–14.

Luke, M. (2014). Effective group leader skills. In J. L. DeLucia-Waack, C. R. Kalodner, & M. T. Riva (Eds.), *Handbook of group counseling and psychotherapy* (2nd ed., pp. 107–119). Sage.

Luke, M., & Bernard, J. (2006). The school counseling supervision model: An extension of the discrimination model. *Counselor Education and Supervision, 45(4)*, 282–295. https://doi.org/10.1002/j.1556-6978.2006.tb00004.x

Nelson, M. D., & Johnson, P. (1999). School counselors as supervisors: An integrated approach for supervising school counseling interns. *Counselor Education and Supervision, 39(2)*, 80–100. https://doi.org/10.1002/j.1556-6978.1999.tb01220.x

Ohrt, J. H., Blalock, S., & Limberg, D. (2016). Preparing school counselors-in-training to conduct large group developmental guidance: Evaluation of an instructional model. *Journal for Specialists in Group Work, 41(2)*, 96–116. https://doi.org/10.1080/01933922.2016.1146377

Ohrt, J. H., Ener, E., Porter, J., & Young, T. L. (2014). Group leader reflections on their training and experience: Implications for group counselor educators and supervisors. *Journal for Specialists in Group Work, 39(2)*, 95–124. https://doi.org/10.1080/01933922.2014.883004

Rubel, D., & Okech, J. E. A. (2006). The supervision of group work model: Adapting the discrimination model for supervision of group workers. *Journal for Specialists in Group Work, 31(2)*, 113–134. https://doi.org/10.1080/01933920500493597

Smaby, M. H., Maddux, C. D., Torres-Rivera, E., & Zimmick, R. (1999). A study of the effects of a skills-based versus a conventional group counseling training program. *Journal for Specialists in Group Work, 24(2)*, 152–163. https://doi.org/10.1080/01933929908411427

Springer, S. I. (2016). Examining predictors of group leader self-efficacy for preservice school counselors. *Journal for Specialists in Group Work, 41(4)*, 286–311. https://doi.org/10.1080/01933922.2016.1228723

Springer, S. I., Moss, L. J., Cinotti, D., & Land, C. W. (2018). Examining pre-service school counselors' site supervisory experiences specific to group work. *Journal for Specialists in Group Work, 43(3)*, 250–273. https://doi.org/10.1080/01933922.2018.1484537

Stockton, R. (2009). Model for supervision of group leaders. In C. F. Salazar (Ed.), *Group work experts share their multicultural activities: A guide to diversity-competent choosing, conducting and processing.* Association for Specialists in Group Work.

Stockton, R., Morran, K., & Chang, S. (2014). An overview of current research and best practice for training beginning group leaders. In J. L. DeLucia-Waack, C. R. Kalodner, & M. T. Riva (Eds.), *Handbook of group counseling and psychotherapy* (2nd ed., pp. 133–145). Sage.

Wood, C. and Rayle, A. D. (2006), A model of school counseling supervision: The goals, functions, roles, and systems model. *Counselor Education and Supervision, 45(4)*, 253–266. https://doi.org/10.1002/j.1556-6978.2006.tb00002.x

Yalom, I. D., & Leszcz, M. (2005). *The theory and practice of group psychotherapy* (5th ed.). Basic Books.

Appendix A.

Group Leadership Feedback Form (GLFF)

Group leader(s): J and K

Group type/topic: Psychoeducation/Body Image   **Session #** 1

N/A = no opportunity to demonstrate skill

0 = leader did not demonstrate skill competency, missed all opportunities, or is harmful to the group

1 = leader did not meet expectations/ demonstrates minimal skill competency (successful in ~25% of opportunities)

2 = leader is near expectations / developing toward skill competency (successful in ~50% of opportunities)

3 = leader meets expectations / demonstrates adequate skill competency (successful in ~70% of opportunities)

4 = leader exceeds expectations / demonstrates exemplary skill competency (successful in ~85% of opportunities)

Group Leader Skill	Rating	Comments
Planning		
The leader collaborated with the coleader (if applicable) to plan the group and was well prepared to facilitate.	N/A 0 1 2 3 **4**	
The leadership responsibilities were balanced.	N/A 0 1 2 3 **4**	
The session followed a logical order (warm-up, working, closing).	N/A 0 1 2 3 **4**	Good job checking in and checking out.
The leader used appropriate evaluation methods (e.g., pretest/posttest) to assess the effectiveness of the group.	N/A 0 1 2 3 **4**	
Active Listening		
Tracking—the leader demonstrated interest in the sharing member by using eye contact and attending skills.	N/A 0 1 2 3 **4**	
Scanning—the leader monitored the group members and noted their reactions and attentiveness.	N/A 0 1 2 3 **4**	Nice job pointing out member reactions.
Minimal encouragers—the leader encouraged the members to elaborate ("uh huh" and head nods)	N/A 0 1 2 3 **4**	
Facilitating Skills		
Initiating—the leader provided direction or set topics to facilitate group discussion.	N/A 0 1 2 3 **4**	Good initiation activities (concise) and questions.

Skill	Rating	Comments
Drawing out—the leader invited group members to be involved.	N/A 0 1 **2** 3 4	Good job doing this through rounds. Work on doing it more during spontaneous discussion.
Supporting—the leader encouraged and reinforced appropriate participation.	N/A 0 1 2 **3** 4	Work on doing this a little more after disclosures.
Questioning—the leader maintained a good balance of open and closed questions to elicit information from members.	N/A 0 1 2 **3** 4	
Linking—the leader identified themes and connected members' stories.	N/A 0 1 2 **3** 4	Pretty nice job of this in general. Try to do it more with individual members as well.
Modeling—the leader modeled appropriate group interactions for members (e.g., giving feedback, disclosure).	N/A 0 1 2 3 **4**	
Clarifying—the leader checked their own and other members' understanding of what group members shared.	N/A 0 1 2 **3** 4	
Confronting—the leader addressed discrepancies between what a group member said and their behavior.	**N/A** 0 1 2 3 4	
Summarizing—the leader tied together the main content and group interactions for the group.	N/A 0 1 2 **3** 4	
Blocking—the leader "cut off" or redirected members who were inappropriately storytelling, gossiping, or probing.	N/A 0 **1** 2 3 4	Work on doing this a little more when the group gets too light.
Protecting—the leader protected members from attacks from other members or from unnecessary psychological risks (e.g., premature disclosure).	**N/A** 0 1 2 3 4	
Promote interaction among members—the leader cultivated opportunities for members to interact and give each other feedback.	N/A 0 1 **2** 3 4	The interaction was pretty good. Work on promoting more of it. "Can anyone relate to ___?" "Does anyone have feedback for ____?"
Check-ins/check-outs—the leader provided each member the opportunity to express how they were doing presently (i.e., at the beginning and end of group).	N/A 0 1 2 3 **4**	
Rounds—the leader took opportunities to solicit each members' thoughts about a topic (consensus taking).	N/A 0 1 2 3 **4**	
Insight and meaning attribution—the leader helped members process what the group means to them and/or what they learned.	N/A 0 1 2 3 **4**	Really nice job of this at the end of the group.
Group Climate		
Emotional stimulation—the leader fostered a safe environment where members felt safe to express themselves.	N/A 0 1 2 3 **4**	

Here-and-now focus—the leader maintained a present-moment awareness and focused on what was happening in the group.	N/A 0 1 2 3 4	Continue to work on this. "What was it like to share with the group?" "I notice laughing ... what's going on for you all?"
Moderating—the leader ensured that multiple perspectives were heard when topics were discussed; addressed cultural and diversity factors.	N/A 0 1 2 3 4	Very nice job of facilitating discussion about both sides of the issue.
Checking emotional temperature—the leader was aware of the mood of the group (e.g., exhausted, frustrated, hopeful), illuminated it to the group, and shifted the mood when appropriate.	N/A 0 1 2 3 4	Try to do some of this. Your group was a little light at points. Check in about it.

Narrative Feedback

Areas of Strength

Overall, you did a very nice job of preparing for the group. You and your coleader worked well together and appeared to be on the same page. The leadership responsibilities were balanced. Good idea to sit across from the group leader. That helps with scanning the room. Great job involving members through check-ins, check-outs, and rounds. The video was a creative initiation strategy. Good job moderating to ensure all perspectives were heard. Good job noticing members' reactions. Nice job linking general themes.

Areas for Improvement

It might help to do the check-in quickly before jumping into any content or the video. That can help to "warm" the members up. Try to touch on process a little more—"What's it like to share?" Try to promote more interaction during the "working" part of the discussion—"Can anyone relate to (...) ?" Good job encouraging involvement through rounds. Try to do it more during general discussion. Some members were quieter. Do a summary of the session prior to the check-in? Remember to use basic reflecting skills.

General Impressions

Overall, you did a really nice job.

Instructor/Supervisor: _____ **Date:** _____

PART V
Plans

Anxiety Groups

Introduction

Anxiety is a normal reaction to stress and provides beneficial outcomes in many situations. For some people, however, anxiety becomes excessive. At times, children and adolescents may be aware that they are experiencing overwhelming anxiety, yet they may have difficulty controlling it—causing it to negatively affect their day-to-day living at home and/or at school. With signs, symptoms, and diagnoses of anxiety reaching epidemic proportions in the United States, it is increasingly important for school counselors to intervene when manifestations impact the learning environment.

Characterized by sensations of worry, fear, or dread that are disproportionate to the circumstances, anxiety disorders can have a profound impact on many aspects of an individual's life. Children and adolescents who experience anxiety are thereby at risk of facing increased barriers to achieving their academic, career, and social/emotional goals.

Given the increasingly intense and high-stakes academic environment of American culture and schools, in addition to the effects of COVID-19, many children experience increased rates of anxiety. While symptoms of anxiety are typically manageable at first, they may quickly escalate—that is, if coping strategies to mitigate sensations of anxiety are never acquired and applied, symptoms may worsen. Luckily, small-group responsive services provide school counselors with an optimal intervention to help students manage anxiety and its ill effects. The following session plans provide creative and comprehensive ways for school counselors to implement small groups for students experiencing symptoms of anxiety.

Data Discussion

Being able to collect and analyze data effectively is key to developing your comprehensive school counseling program, and is also important for your small-group counseling program (see Chapter 3 for more). Examining data that are accurate and appropriate for the goals of your small group is imperative in garnering support for a more robust small-group counseling program. Here are steps we hope you take as you review the sample sessions on anxiety.

Discuss Data Collection With a Peer/Colleague

Nothing helps school counselors boost their confidence and motivation like consulting and collaborating with other professionals! While working with peers and colleagues helps us feel more efficacious about the interventions we are planning, it also aligns with the ASCA National Model for School Counseling programs. Collaboration and consultation represent school counseling best practice and help us remain data driven and intentional with intervention planning. Based on the sessions you choose when considering your particular school, consult with a peer or colleague about your rationale/selections and your data collection plan.

Take a Walk With Data Related to Anxiety

For each of the sessions focused on anxiety, we ask that you engage in the following steps for thought and discussion either with your colleague(s) or your course instructor(s):

Step 1—General Data Consideration

Read the Learning Objectives for each small group on anxiety and then:

Ask yourself, What kinds of data might be relevant to collect based on the learning objectives stated? Are you most interested in the number of students served (participation) or are you more concerned with how your small group meets the ASCA mindsets and behaviors that are the target of your group (surveys, pretest/posttest)? Are you most concerned with examining the reduction of anxiety and how that might impact improved student academics (outcome)?

Disaggregating your data to determine if certain subgroups of students are disproportionately impacted is essentially important to the small-group planning process. Do you have suspicions that anxiety plays a role in how underserved or marginalized students are treated in your school? Do you suspect that anxiety is impacting an underserved or marginalized group of students more than another (e.g., undocumented students report higher levels of generalized anxiety than other subgroups of students)?

Step 2—Thoughts on Participation Data

After reading the general outline for the session:

What is a plan that would help you collect participation data? What would the collection of participation data look like in your anxiety group? To answer these questions, consider who the group will serve. In other words, how will you screen group members? Will the group consist of students from a particular grade? Or maybe all group members have missed a certain amount of class due to the anxiety they experience. There are many factors you can consider. Take some time to outline as specifically as possible who the group will serve. Once you are clear about who will qualify as a group member, consider how you will record and track participation data. Whether it be in written form or electronically recorded in a computer program (i.e., Excel, Google Forms), it is important that you document who participates in your group; this is true for groups that meet once and for those that meet over the course of several sessions. Tracking exactly what you did and who participated is key to understanding your post-group data.

Step 3—Thoughts on Mindsets and Behaviors Data

After reading the Closing Discussion Questions/Activities section for each session, ask:

When considering collecting mindsets and behaviors data, how might a pretest/posttest survey of group members look? What questions would you want to ask to determine if the mindsets and behaviors you targeted were achieved? Once you determine who your group will serve (as outlined in the Participation Data section above), you will need to clarify what you want them to know or be able to do as a result of participating in the group. The mindset and behavior standards provide a framework of developmentally appropriate skills and abilities to help you plan. For example, for a group designed to meet the needs of students struggling with anxiety at school, you might be most interested in addressing Mindset Standard M 2., "Self-confidence in ability to succeed," and/or M 6., "Positive attitude toward work and learning." Additionally, you might find that behavior standards such as B-LS 7., "Identify long- and short-term academic, career, and social/emotional goals," and/or B-SMS 7., "Demonstrate effective coping skills when faced with a problem," are aligned with the group intervention you are planning. The *ASCA Mindsets and Behaviors* database (https://scale-research.org/mandb/public_html/) provides a quick reference and additional resources for school counselors developing interventions such as groups designed to support students who want to reduce/manage their anxiety.

Step 4—Thoughts on Outcome Data

Upon reading the entire group plan, consider this:

If we think of "outcome data" as most often relating to attendance, behavior, and academics, what is a metric you could examine to determine if this group helps improve academics? Are you most concerned with examining regularly scheduled diagnostic classroom assessments to monitor academic improvement (e.g., DRA, spelling test), or is it more important to consider how your group impacted state or district standardized assessment data, school report card data, or the overall academic mission of the school? Are you most concerned with examining group members' abilities to attend class despite the anxiety they experience (attendance)? Finally, consider examining any metrics related to student behavior that is tied to anxiety (e.g., group member discipline referrals to administration, classroom behavior issues). One final note about outcome data: pick one! It is not always necessary to evaluate all three areas—attendance, behavior, and academics—for your small group. Target one area and let that guide your evaluation of the group's impact!

ANXIETY SESSION **PLAN 1**

LEVEL	SESSION TITLE	TOPIC
Elementary, Middle & High	Sometimes There Aren't Enough Rocks	Anxiety

STAGE ☒ Orientation ☐ Working ☐ Closing

ASCA Mindsets Standards

Belief in development of whole self, including a healthy balance of mental, social/emotional, and physical well-being.

ASCA Behavior Standards

Learning Strategies

Apply self-motivation and self-direction to learning.

Self-Management Skills

Demonstrate ability to overcome barriers in learning.
Demonstrate effective coping skills when faced with a problem.

Social Skills

Use effective oral and written communication skills and listening skills.
Create positive and supportive relationships with other students.
Demonstrate empathy.

Learning Objectives

1. Students will reflect on the ways anxiety impacts their bodies, minds, and relationships.
2. Students will experience and process a strategy for releasing anxiety.

Materials

1. One sheet of paper per student
2. Pencils/pens
3. Recycling bin

Session Procedure

1. The school counselor will introduce this activity by asking students if they have ever thrown rocks into a creek or lake.
2. The school counselor will ask students to write down one worry that has frequently been on their minds. The school counselor will indicate that students do not have to share what they have written if they do not feel comfortable.
3. The school counselor will instruct students to make "rocks" out of their papers by crumpling them into paper balls.
4. The school counselor will ask students to close their eyes and silently imagine their rock as representing the identified worries.
5. The school counselor will ask the students to feel the weight of the paper in their hands, consider where in their bodies they feel that worry, and how that worry has weighed down their lives.

6. The school counselor will ask students to stand up and walk over to the recycling bin.
7. The school counselor will ask them to breathe in and out, feel their feet touching the floor, and feel the rock in their hands.
8. The school counselor will then ask students to throw their rocks into the recycling bin and walk back to their seats.
9. The school counselor will ask students to share how it felt to throw away their rocks and how they feel differently now than when the session began.

Closing Discussion Questions/Activities
1. What situations or people make you feel anxious? How do you know when you are feeling anxious? What are ways you can let go of your "rocks" in those situations?
2. How do you feel and act when you are experiencing anxiety as opposed to when you are feeling calm?
3. What part of letting go of your worries is particularly difficult?
4. Does letting go mean that we should forget about what made us anxious? How is letting go different than just "not worrying about it?"

About the Group Worker
Phillip Waalkes is an Assistant Professor in Counselor Education at the University of South Dakota.

Appendix A
Pretest/Posttest

1. What are three ways that anxiety impacts your life?

_____

_____

_____

_____

2. How does your body feel when you are anxious?

_____

_____

_____

3. How does your body feel when you are calm?

   _____

   _____

   _____

4. What are some strategies for letting go of your anxiety?

   _____

   _____

   _____

ASCA Mindsets Standards

Belief in development of whole self, including a healthy balance of mental, social/emotional, and physical well-being.

Self-confidence in ability to succeed.

ASCA Behavior Standards

Learning Strategies

Apply self-motivation and self-direction to learning.

Self-Management Skills

Demonstrate effective coping skills when faced with a problem.

Social Skills

Demonstrate social maturity and behaviors appropriate to the situation and environment.

Learning Objectives

1. Students will identify the sensations, thoughts, and feelings that accompany their experiences of nervousness or anxiety during tests.
2. Students will learn how to categorize sensations, thoughts, and feelings nonjudgmentally.
3. Students will use thought diffusion to cope with anxiety in the classroom.

> Now that you have read the LOs for this lesson, ask yourself, What kinds of data might be relevant to collect based on the LOs stated?

Materials

1. Train of Thought handouts (see Appendix A)
2. Mindfulness Script (see Appendix C)
3. One large image drawn on the chalkboard or whiteboard with anxiety sensations, thoughts, and feelings listed on sticky notes (see Appendix B)
4. Pencils/pens

Session Procedure

Activity One: Train of Thought

1. The school counselor will explain that some anxiety or nervousness during tests or exams can be normal and can help ensure that students prepare adequately; however, sometimes the anxiety can become too intense, making it hard for students to think clearly and concentrate on a task and it can get so bad that sometimes one can feel sick.
2. The school counselor will introduce either the "Train of Thought" handouts to each student (for older students) or reference the whiteboard drawing (for younger students). The school counselor will list each of the train cars: sensations, thoughts, and feelings.

3. The school counselor will state that symptoms of test anxiety will be different for each person: one student might notice uncomfortable physical sensations, whereas another might notice thoughts that make it hard to concentrate.

4. The school counselor will list and describe several experiences from each category and explain how these experiences might influence test taking. For example, the school counselor might say, "Some students taking a test may think, 'I don't know any of the answers and I'm going to flunk this exam,' while another student might look around the room and see students working and feel discouraged because other students are moving onto the second page while they are still working on the first page."

5. The school counselor will ask students to think about their own experiences of taking tests and describe any related sensations, thoughts, or feelings common for them. Using the chalkboard or whiteboard, the school counselor can have students take turns placing symptom sticky notes on the board in the category where they fit best. For younger children, it might be easier to go category by category (e.g., sensations, then thoughts, then feelings). To reduce confusion for students using handouts, students can write in their own symptoms.

6. Once the thoughts are listed on the board or handout, the school counselor can have students share their unique experiences and make links between group members to normalize the experience. The school counselor should mention that identifying one's own anxiety symptoms makes it easier to recognize them if or when they occur during a classroom task.

Activity Two: Mindful Attention

1. The school counselor will explain that sensations, thoughts, and feelings caused by anxiety can make it very difficult to take tests or engage in other school tasks because they can intensify anxiety and discomfort and possibly discourage the test taker from continuing in the task.

2. The school counselor will also discuss how distracting it can be to focus on these sensations, thoughts, and feelings while taking a test.

3. The school counselor should discuss several symptoms and ask students how they may have tried to avoid or get rid of each anxiety symptom. At the end of this brief discussion, the school counselor can discuss which responses, if any, have been helpful and reinforce adaptive coping strategies (e.g., taking slow and deep breaths, repeating a positive affirmation).

4. The school counselor will introduce the idea of stepping back and observing our experiences nonjudgmentally. The counselor will start by identifying different parts of the body and by asking the students to pay attention to each part, reminding students to attend to how it feels instead of focusing on whether it feels good or bad. The school counselor will then mention that this mindful attention can be used with thoughts and our senses.

5. When the first minute has passed, the school counselor will ask students to describe the sensations they felt (e.g., carpet under feet, ticking of the clock, hardness of the chair), the thoughts they had (e.g., this is weird, when's lunch), and the emotions they felt (e.g., happy, confused). The counselor will normalize and validate each student's experience and reinforce that these are normal experiences, not necessarily good or bad.

6. The school counselor will now connect this observation exercise with the image of the train.

7. The school counselor will ask the students to close their eyes again or direct vision downward and imagine their "Thought Train" and use or adapt the following mindfulness script.

8. The school counselor will read the mindfulness script to the students.

9. Once students transition back into the group, the school counselor will ask students what they observed, followed by normalizing and linking responses.

10. The school counselor will ask students to name a specific class setting in which they might like to practice this new skill. The school counselor should remind students that this skill can be used at any time when needing to focus attention while sensations, thoughts, and feelings could distract them from completing their tasks.

Closing Discussion Questions/Activities

1. What did you notice when you closed your eyes and observed your surroundings?
2. If you found your mind wandering or getting distracted, what was it like to identify with what was going on?
3. Why might it be helpful to know what symptoms are common for you?
4. What was it like grouping the symptoms into sensations, thoughts, and feelings?
5. How do you think this exercise might help you during a test or a stressful task or event in school?

> When considering collecting mindsets and behaviors data, what might a pretest/posttest survey of group members in this group look like? What questions would you want to ask to see if the mindsets and behaviors you were targeting were achieved?

About the Group Worker

Susannah Coaston, PhD, is an assistant professor at Northern Kentucky University and teaches group counseling courses for undergraduate and graduate students. She is also a counselor and supervisor at Greater Cincinnati Behavioral Health Services. In both positions, Dr. Coaston encourages creative approaches to engage students and clients in both individual and group counseling.

Additional Resources

Anxiety and Depression Association of America. (2016). *Test anxiety.* https://www.adaa.org/living-with-anxiety/children/test-anxiety

Hayes, S. C., Strosahl, K. D., & Wilson, K. G. (2012). *Acceptance and commitment theory: The process and practice of mindful change* (2nd ed.). Guilford Press.

Zeidner, M. (1998). *Test anxiety: The state of the art.* Plenum Press.

Appendix A
Train of Thought

Train of Thought

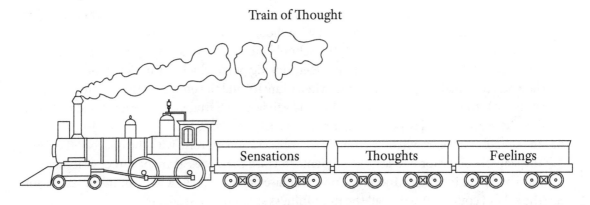

Appendix B
Sensations, Thoughts, and Feelings of Anxiety

Sensations	Thoughts	Feelings	You can create your own sensations, thoughts, or feelings below
Headache	I'm going to fail this test.	Withdrawn	
Stomachache or cramps	I'm totally stuck.	Irritable	
Sleeping too much/Eating too little	I don't remember anything.	Confused	
Tight muscles	The time is running out.	Frustrated	
Eating too much/ Eating too little	I'm never going to finish this.	Overwhelmed	
Breathing changes or difficulties	What if I get held back?	Disappointed	
Sweating	My parent(s) will be mad if I fail.	Helpless	
Heart beating fast	This wasn't covered in class.	Ashamed	
Needing to go to the bathroom	My mind is totally blank.	Inadequate	
Mouth feels dry	I just can't do this.	Embarrassed	
Fidgety	I don't understand anything.	Afraid	
Biting nails	My teacher will think I'm stupid.	Hopeless	
Chest feels tight	I can't even focus.	Miserable	
Sleepy	I'm so stupid.	Angry	
Dizzy	I will never understand this.	Bummed	
Too hot/ Too cold	This is hopeless.	Distressed	
Panicky	I should just give up.	Intimidated	
Nauseated	My thoughts are racing.	Numb	
Weak	What is wrong with me?	Panic	

Appendix C
Mindfulness Script

Take several deep breaths and get comfortable in your chair.

[Pause]

I want you to imagine that you are looking at a small train on a track. This train has many cars and is moving slowly in front of you.

[Pause]

As you watch the train, you will notice that there is writing on each of the cars.

On one car, it says "sensations"; the next says "thoughts"; the next one says "feelings"; the next car says "sensations" again.

The train continues moving slowly in front of you.

I am going to list some of the symptoms of anxiety we discussed earlier. While you watch the train, take each of the symptoms you hear and place them in the train car where it best fits.

[The school counselor will list the shared symptoms identified by the group in a random order.]

Notice how you can observe each sensation, thought, or feeling and place it on the train without judging it as good or bad, holding onto it as a fact, or judging yourself.

Now I want you to continue to watch the train and pay attention to the room around you.

You might hear the clock ticking or feel the arm of the chair under your elbow, while thinking about what you will do after school or feel happy because it is almost the weekend.

With each of these sensations, thoughts, and feelings, you will place each of them into the corresponding train car.

Now sit quietly and pay attention to the sensations, thoughts, and feelings around you.

[Pause for fifteen seconds]

If you find yourself getting distracted by a sensation, thought, or feeling, identify it and place it in the train car.

Remember, it is normal for your mind to wander.

[Pause for 30–45 more seconds]

Okay, now take three deep, slow breaths and when you are done, slowly open your eyes.

ANXIETY SESSION **PLAN 3**

LEVEL	SESSION TITLE	TOPIC
Elementary	Worry-Eaters: A Coping Skill for Fear	Anxiety

STAGE   ■ Orientation   ☒ Working   ■ Closing

ASCA Mindsets Standards

Belief in development of whole self, including a healthy balance of mental, social/emotional, and physical well-being.

ASCA Behavior Standards

Learning Strategies

Demonstrate creativity.

Gather evidence and consider multiple perspectives to make informed decisions.

Self-Management Skills

Demonstrate self-discipline and self-control.

Demonstrate effective coping skills when faced with a problem.

Social Skills

Demonstrate social maturity and behaviors appropriate to the situation and environment.

Demonstrate advocacy skills and ability to assert self, when necessary.

Learning Objectives

1. Students will demonstrate awareness of bodily sensations, thoughts, and feelings that are associated with fear.
2. Students will incorporate coping skills in the classroom setting.
3. Students will understand why fear and anxiety are important to their well-being.

Materials

1. Markers/colored pencils/crayons
2. Mini Worry Eating boxes (or find a cube template and cut it out to make a box)
3. Blank body template for each student
4. Construction paper
5. Glue
6. Googly eyes
7. *Inside Out Box of Mixed Emotions* (*Fear* book) by Brittany Candau (2015)

Session Procedure

Activity One: Fear

1. The school counselor will read the *Fear* book from the *Inside Out Box of Mixed Emotions*.
2. The school counselor will ask students what it looks like when someone is fearful, scared, or anxious.
3. The school counselor will ask students where in their bodies they feel fear or anxiety.
4. The school counselor will distribute blank body templates to each student.

Discussion Questions: What do scared, fearful, or anxious people look like? Show me your best scared face. What do people act like when they are scared? Show me your scariest move (encourage students to get up and move their bodies). What makes you scared or anxious?

5. Using the body template and a purple crayon, the school counselor will instruct students to color the places on their bodies where they feel scared.

Activity Two: Worry-Eating Monster

1. The school counselor should show the premade Worry-Eating Monster to the students, which can be made out of a small box or cube template. The box should have an opening.
2. The school counselor will instruct students to decorate their monsters in any ways that they desire.
3. The school counselor will tell students, "We are going to make Worry-Eating Monsters. You can decorate the box or cube by drawing on it or cutting out paper to glue on the box. You can put googly eyes on the monster or make whatever kind of monster you choose. These are friendly Worry-Eating Monsters because you can write your worries down or whisper them in their ears, and they will gobble up any worries or fears that you have. But the trick is that before you write down or whisper your worry to the monster, you have to take three deep breaths, write down your worry, and give it away to the monster to eat, never to be thought of again!"
4. The school counselor will wrap up the activity by asking a few students to volunteer to talk about their Worry-Eating Monster.

Closing Discussion Questions/Activities

1. What have you learned about fear and anxiety? How is fear and anxiety helpful to us?
2. How are you going to use your Worry-Eating Monster?

About the Group Worker

Megan Numbers, LPC, is a military family life counselor specializing in working with children in North Carolina. In her previous position, she worked as a school-based behavioral health specialist with K–12 students, in which she conducted a variety of different group counseling activities. Ms. Numbers is passionate about working with children and is working on obtaining her Registered Play Therapist credentials.

References

Candau, B. (2015). *Inside out box of mixed emotions*. Disney Press.

ASCA Mindsets Standards

Belief in development of whole self, including a healthy balance of mental, social/emotional, and physical well-being.

Self-confidence in ability to succeed.

Positive attitude toward work and learning.

ASCA Behavior Standards

Learning Strategies

Gather evidence and consider multiple perspectives to make informed decisions.

Self-Management Skills

Demonstrate self-discipline and self-control.

Demonstrate ability to overcome barriers to learning.

Demonstrate effective coping skills when faced with a problem.

Social Skills

Demonstrate social maturity and behaviors appropriate to the situation and environment.

Learning Objectives

1. Students will understand the concepts of negative thoughts and self-talk.
2. Students will identify negative thoughts that lead to anxious feelings and behaviors, and challenge themselves with positive self-talk and affirmations.
3. Students will apply what they have learned about changing unhelpful thoughts into helpful thoughts in the classroom setting.

Materials

1. Situation, Unhelpful Thoughts and Helpful Thoughts worksheets (see Appendix A)
2. Positive Affirmation worksheets (see Appendix B)
3. Whiteboard/chalkboard
4. Preprinted pictures of objects for discussion on thoughts (e.g., snake, rollercoaster, math test, big waves in the ocean)

Session Procedure

Activity One: Understanding Thoughts and Feelings

1. The school counselor will start by discussing the difference between thoughts and feelings.
2. The school counselor will explain to the students that "thoughts normally occur in our heads, so only we can hear them. In order for other people to know what we are thinking, we must tell them. What we say to ourselves is called 'self-talk,' which can be either helpful or unhelpful. Feelings are typically associated with our thoughts and self-talk. Some feelings are positive and some are negative."

Discussion Questions: What types of feelings do you think are associated with negative self-talk? What about helpful and positive self-talk?

3. The school counselor will help students identify thoughts that lead to feelings through a brief exercise by stating, "It is important to realize that people can have different thoughts and feelings about the same thing. As a group, let's look at the following pictures, and share what we feel" (e.g., snake, rollercoaster, math test, big waves in the ocean).

Discussion Questions: What is making you feel this way? What are your thoughts when you see this picture? The objective is to make sure that the students can backtrack to a thought and understand the impact that this thought has on how they feel.

Note: Responses will vary and the school counselor should point out the differences that students may have. For example, the counselor should explain, "Some children feel excited and think that snakes are cool, while others will feel frightened and think they are scary and may bite; some students feel brave and think that roller coasters are fun and go fast, while others will feel nervous and think they are too high and may get stuck; certain students feel proud and think a math test is super easy and they will finish right away, whereas other students will feel anxious, think math tests are very hard, and that they are not smart enough; or some students feel that big waves are so much fun to jump and boogie board on while some students may think they will get pulled under or see a huge shark.

4. The school counselor will link negative self-talk to the topic of anxiety. In doing so, the counselor will guide students to think of their own examples using the "Situation, Unhelpful Thoughts and Helpful Thoughts" worksheet.

5. The school counselor will explain that, for example, "When we think or expect something bad is going to happen, we tend to feel anxious and worried. Our unhelpful self-talk is what leads us to feel badly. The good news is that we can change the way we think! By thinking positively and using positive self-talk, we can completely change what we expect to happen and in turn, how we will feel about a situation."

6. The school counselor will have the students complete their "Situation, Unhelpful Thoughts and Helpful Thoughts" worksheet while thinking about what was just discussed in group.

Discussion Questions: Can you think of a situation when you felt worried or nervous? What did you think to yourself? What is a helpful thought that you could have had that would have made you feel better?

Activity Two: Challenging Negative Thoughts by Using Positive Affirmations

1. The school counselor will define positive affirmations by telling students "When we are feeling anxious and having unhelpful thoughts, positive affirmations are statements we can say to ourselves in order to make ourselves feel happy, confident, and brave. Positive affirmations help us challenge the negative self-talk we may have and can serve as the statements to help us think positively."

2. The school counselor will provide examples for the group to review together and lead the group in a discussion about the importance of positive affirmations and how students can recite these statements to themselves while practicing deep breathing in stressful or anxious moments (e.g., before a big test, prior to presenting or speaking in front of the class).

Discussion Questions: Can anyone think of any other statements we may want to include on our list?

3. The school counselor will conclude the session by directing students to choose one positive affirmation they like the most.

4. The school counselor will guide the students through a very brief deep belly breathing exercise by having students silently recite the affirmation in their heads in order to practice what they would do in an actual stressful situation.

5. The school counselor will instruct students by telling them, "Let's finish what we have learned today by practicing doing a brief deep belly breathing exercise. Once you have chosen the positive affirmation you want to use, close your eyes and sit up in a comfortable position. As you take a deep breath in through your nose, say the positive statement to yourself silently and then breathe out through your mouth."

6. The school counselor will have students repeat the deep breathing positive affirmation exercise three to five times, until students are familiar with the exercise.

7. The school counselor should explain that this is a great way to calm ourselves down and increase our confidence in our ability to get through a stressful situation or accomplish a difficult task.

8. The school counselor should emphasize that whenever we catch ourselves reciting negative self-talk, we can challenge those thoughts by doing exactly what we just practiced.

Closing Discussion Questions/Activities

1. Think of a situation that may occur this week when you will use what we have learned about challenging negative self-talk that leads to anxiety.

2. Choose one positive affirmation statement that you liked the most, and use it this week. Share with the group.

About the Group Worker

Stephanie Probert is an elementary school counselor in northern New Jersey. She is very passionate about group work as it is an efficient and effective method to reach students of all ages and address trends occurring in the academic, career, and social/emotional domains. Ms. Probert believes that group counseling is a very powerful tool because it allows students to work through similar situations in an empathetic and peer-supported environment.

Additional Resources

Anxiety Canada. (2014). *Healthy thinking for younger children.* https://www.anxietycanada.com/sites/default/files/Healthy_Thinking_for_Younger_Children.pdf

Pursuit of Happiness. (2016). *Mindfulness and positive thinking.* http://www.pursuit-of-happiness.org/science-of-happiness/positive-thinking/

Yu, C., & Keddis, V. (2014, March 20). *Helping your anxious child: What it looks like and what parents can do* [Video]. Anxiety Canada. https://www.anxietycanada.com/articles/helping-your-anxious-child-what-it-looks-like-and-what-parents-can-do/

Appendix A
Situations, Unhelpful Thoughts, and Helpful Thoughts

Situation	Unhelpful Thought	Helpful Thought

Appendix B
Positive Affirmations

I am kind.

I am strong.

I am brave.

I am smart.

I can do this.

I believe in myself.

I am perfect just the way I am.

I always try my hardest.

I will do my best and that is always enough.

I love myself.

I will learn from my mistakes.

Appendix C
Pretest/Posttest

1. I can change how I feel by changing my thoughts:
   a. Yes
   b. No
   c. Sometimes

2. I can tell when I am having an unhelpful thought that makes me feel anxious:
   a. Yes
   b. No
   c. Sometimes

3. I use positive affirmations to help calm me down in class during stressful situations:
   a. Yes
   b. No
   c. Sometimes

4. I think positively while using deep breathing techniques to help calm me down when I feel anxious in class:
   a. Yes
   b. No
   c. Sometimes

ASCA Mindsets Standards

Belief in development of whole self, including a healthy balance of mental, social/emotional, and physical well-being.

ASCA Behavior Standards

Learning Strategies

Demonstrate creativity.

Self-Management Skills

Demonstrate self-discipline and self-control.

Demonstrate effective coping skills when faced with a problem.

Social Skills

Create positive and supportive relationships with other students.

Demonstrate social maturity and behaviors appropriate to the situation and environment.

Learning Objectives

1. Students will create a peace jar as a coping strategy to help regulate their emotions.
2. Students will choose a name for their jar that correlates with the emotion they feel that impacts them the most.
3. Students will determine and explain when they might use their jars in practice.

Materials

1. 8-ounce Mason jars
2. Sticky labels
3. Water
4. Glitter
5. Colored glitter glue
6. Clear glitter glue
7. Food coloring
8. Krazy Glue©
9. Fork/whisk
10. Microwave or stovetop
11. Bubble wrap (optional)

Session Procedure

1. The school counselor will present the emotions/mind jar to the students, which can represent any emotion students think they can use to help them outside of the group or school setting. The jar is filled with glitter that, when shaken, represents the racing thoughts and feelings

an individual has in mind when emotions are heightened. As the glitter slowly settles, it represents emotions settling.

2. The school counselor should instruct students to think about what to do next after the glitter has settled rather than reacting when their minds are spinning. Further, students should be instructed that staring at the jar while the glitter is spinning can cause a distraction that will help them regulate their emotions in order for them to think rationally.

3. The school counselor will distribute one Mason jar and one sticky label to each student and ask students to fill it with warm water.

4. The school counselor should have students decorate their labels with a title for their jars, which represent their respective emotions.

5. The school counselor will instruct students to apply the sticky label to their jars.

6. The school counselor should instruct students to leave some space at the top of their jars.

7. The school counselor will have students choose one color of glitter glue and have students add a decent amount of the glitter glue to their jars, which will look like spaghetti as it drops to the bottom of the jar.

8. Using a fork or whisk, the school counselor should have students stir the water and glitter glue until all of the glitter is floating freely in the jar and no longer looks like spaghetti.

9. If the glue does not completely dissolve, the school counselor can microwave the jar without the lid.

10. Once the solution has been completely dissolved, the school counselor should have students add some additional glue to help thicken the mixture.

11. If students would like, the school counselor can suggest that students add a few drops of food coloring and dry glitter to help emphasize the glitter glue solution.

12. The school counselor will instruct students to screw the lid onto the jar tightly and shake the jar to see if it produces the desired effect. Students can be reminded that they can always add more glue to the jar so that the glitter suspends longer in the water.

13. Once students are satisfied with their mixture of glue and water, the school counselor should have each student unscrew the lid from the Mason jar and apply some Krazy Glue© to the lid, and screw the lid on tightly once again, which will prevent the jar from opening.

14. The school counselor should have each student share a real-life example of when they can use the jar with the other members of the group and can model how they would use it outside of school.

Optional: The school counselor should have students wrap their jar with bubble wrap to transport it home safely.

Closing Discussion Questions/Activities

1. Can you describe how this jar represents your mind?
2. What are some situations where this jar would be useful?
3. Which emotions do you think this jar will help?
4. How does the jar help you calm down?
5. How might this jar remind you of your personal goals?

About the Group Worker

Cindy Weiner, LPC, works in private practice serving children and adolescents and is a school counselor working with fourth- and fifth-grade students who experience high levels of academic and social anxiety.

Additional Resources

Mindful Schools. (2015, January 26). *"Just breathe" by Julie Bayer Salzman & Josh Salzman (Wavecrest Films)* [Video]. YouTube. https://www.youtube.com/watch?v=RVA2N6tX2cg

Willard, C. (2019, May 30). *How to create a glitter jar for kids.* Mindful. http://www.mindful.org/how-to-create-a-glitter-jar-for-kids/

ANXIETY SESSION PLAN 6

LEVEL	SESSION TITLE	TOPIC
Middle & High	Embrace Your Imperfections	Anxiety

STAGE ☐ Orientation   ☒ Working   ☐ Closing

ASCA Mindsets Standards

Belief in development of whole self, including a healthy balance of mental, social/emotional, and physical well-being.

Self-confidence in ability to succeed.

ASCA Behavior Standards

Learning Strategies

Participate in enrichment and extracurricular activities.

Self-Management Skills

Demonstrate effective coping skills when faced with a problem.

Social Skills

Demonstrate empathy.

Demonstrate social maturity and behaviors appropriate to the situation and environment.

Learning Objectives

1. Students will understand the concept of self-compassion and how to practice it in everyday situations.
2. Students will demonstrate how to use yoga to manage emotions and improve self-confidence.
3. Students will use self-compassion techniques in the classroom setting in order to manage anxiety and improve self-confidence.

Materials

1. Yoga script (see Appendix A)
2. Letter sent home to inform parents/guardians that students will need to wear loose clothing and bring in a yoga mat or towel (see Appendix B)
3. Yoga mat or towel for each student—school counselor should provide one to students who are unable to bring one
4. Device to play music
5. Four colored circles of paper taped at eye level on all four walls of the room
6. Note cards
7. Envelopes
8. Pencils/pens
9. Floor space

Session Procedure

Activity One: Self-Compassion Yoga Sequence

1. The school counselor will ask the students to place their yoga mats or towel in a circle and sit in an upright, cross-legged position.
2. The school counselor will ask students to think of and share a situation where they feel nervous or frustrated with themselves or others.

Discussion Questions: How does your body feel when you are in this difficult situation? What thoughts are you having? How would you treat a friend who is feeling the way you just described?

3. The school counselor will introduce the concept of self-compassion by explaining that people are always told to be kind and compassionate to others who are in need but we are not often told to treat ourselves with the same amount of respect and acceptance. Self-compassion is the practice of talking to ourselves and treating our bodies with kindness and acceptance, particularly during difficult situations.

4. The school counselor will explain that if students make a habit of practicing self-compassion, it can reduce their physical and emotional stress and increase their self-confidence.
   Discussion Questions: What do you think it means to treat yourself with acceptance? What activities do you like to do to relax and get into a more positive frame of mind?

5. The school counselor will explain the practice of yoga and how it serves as a way to practice self-compassion as "Yoga is an ancient practice that trains our breath, bodies, and our minds to reduce physical and emotional stress, in addition to bringing us back to our natural state of happiness and peace. Yoga not only helps us manage negative emotions but it helps us to perform better in school and in other activities and, in this way, yoga gives us a way to practice self-compassion."

6. The school counselor will instruct the students to sit up straight in a cross-legged position on their mats, while placing one hand on their stomachs and the other hand on their chests with their eyes closed. The school counselor will then ask students to notice their breathing without judgment and ask mindful questions related to the students' breathing patterns. For example, "Is your breathing short? Is it slow? Where in your body is your breath coming from?"

7. The school counselor will lead a breathing exercise by instructing students to "breathe in deeply, expand your ribcage like a balloon and exhale out through your mouth." The school counselor will tell students to continue breathing deeply on their own for one minute.

8. While the students are breathing, the school counselor will provide behavioral guidelines for the yoga exercise.
   Example: "In a moment, we will begin to do some stretches to relieve any tension or frustration that we are holding in our bodies. Try to be aware of your body without judging yourself. Only do what you are capable of doing; challenge yourself when you need to and take it easy when you need to. Remember that this is a time to keep our voices quiet and to listen to our bodies. Now let us begin."

9. The school counselor will turn on the music to a low volume.

10. The school counselor will ask students to open their eyes and will give instructions for the yoga sequence. The school counselor can choose to do the exercises with the class or walk around the room. No prior training is required; however, the school counselor should practice the script so it flows naturally. The yoga sequence will last ten minutes and is designed for students of any size or athletic ability. Modifications are necessary to accommodate physical disabilities.

11. The school counselor will begin reading the yoga script to the students.

12. Once the yoga script has been fully read, the school counselor will turn the music off.

13. The school counselor will ask students to open their eyes and reflect on the experience.
    Discussion Questions: How did you feel about doing the yoga before we started? How do you feel now having completed the yoga sequence?

14. The school counselor will remind students that the theme today was "self-compassion."
    Discussion Questions: How did you practice self-compassion today during our yoga activity? If you felt a pose was challenging or difficult, what did you do or say to yourself to get through it?

Activity Two: Thank You, Body

1. The school counselor will pass out a note card, envelope, and writing utensil to each student, asking them to write a thank you letter to their body.
   Discussion Questions: What are some of the reasons that you are grateful for your body? What do you think your body needs to hear from you? You can reflect on today's yoga activity or other experiences; you will be keeping this letter, so write about what is most meaningful to you.
2. Once everyone has finished, the school counselor will ask if any students would like to share what they wrote or thought about with fellow members.

Closing Discussion Questions/Activities

1. What are some areas of your life in which you could increase your self-compassion?
2. Share one goal you have for practicing self-compassion this week.
3. When might you be able to use yoga practices as a way to demonstrate self-compassion?

About the Group Worker

Carey Gilchrist is working toward her Science in Clinical Mental Health Counseling master's degree at Loyola University New Orleans. She is also a certified youth yoga instructor and aims to incorporate this training into her group counseling work.

Additional Resources

Raes, F., Pommier, E., Neff, K. D., & Van Gucht, D. (2011). Constructions and factorial validation of a short form of the self-compassion scale. *Clinical Psychology and Psychotherapy, 18*(3), 250–255. https://doi.org/10.1002/cpp.702

Butzer, B. (2016). *Research repository: Yoga, meditation and mindfulness for children, adolescents and in schools.* YogaKids. https://yogakids.com/wp-content/uploads/2016/05/Yoga-and-Meditation-for-Children-Adolescents-Schools-Research-Repository-11-22-16.pdf

Appendix A
Yoga Script

Neck Rolls

Take a deep breath in. As you exhale, slowly roll your neck around to the right. When you are finished, inhale and exhale as you slowly roll your neck to the left. Do this twice.

Torso Rolls

Place your hands on your knees, inhale and sit up tall as you exhale, then circle your torso to the right. Circle to the right one more time. Now inhale, sit up tall and exhale while you circle from the waist to the left. Circle to the left one more time. Do this twice.

Seated Twists

Place your left hand behind you and your right hand on your left knee. Inhale, sit up taller, and as you exhale, twist your waist so that you are looking over your left shoulder. Inhale, relax and exhale. Twist a little deeper. Inhale, exhale and come back to the center. Place your right hand behind you and your left hand on your right knee. Inhale, sit tall, and as you exhale, twist your waist and look over your right shoulder. Inhale, relax and exhale. Deepen into the twist. Inhale, exhale, and then come back to the center.

Mountain Pose

Stand and place your palms on the floor. Tuck your head, inhale and slowly exhale while you roll your spine to stand up. Your head should be the last part of your spine to come up. Stand up tall with your arms at your sides and focus on the colored piece of paper on the wall in front of you.

Balance on One Foot

While keeping your eyes glued to a spot on the wall, shift your weight onto your right foot and start to bend your left knee. Grab hold of your left ankle with your left hand. If you wobble, that's okay—just come back to the position. Now gently put your left foot down and plant your left foot into the ground and begin to bend your right knee. Grab your right ankle with your right hand. This side might be easier or harder, either way is fine—just focus on breathing and keeping your feet glued to the ground. And release your left ankle.

Tree Pose

If you would like to try to balance in the pose we just did again, that is fine. If you want to try something different, then let's try the tree pose. Place both palms together in front of your chest. Looking straight ahead at one spot, begin to shift your weight onto your right foot. Lift your left heel and slide your foot up your ankle with your knee bent to the side like the number "4." If you want a bit more of a challenge, you can slide your foot further up your right leg, being careful not to place it against your knee. Remember to breathe and if you wobble, remember that trees sway too! Let's put our left foot down and shake our arms and legs. Now shift your weight onto your left foot. Lift up your right heel and slowly slide your foot up onto your left ankle. Keep breathing. Try sliding your right foot further up if you want. Remember to smile—this is just for fun! And bring your right foot back down. Shake everything out and give yourself a pat on the back!

Appendix B
Letter for Parent/Guardian

[Today's Date]

Dear Parent/Guardian,

I am writing to inform you about a special activity that we will be doing during our counseling session next week on [insert date].

As part of the school counseling department's mission to maximize the emotional well-being of each student, we teach strategies that help students manage anxiety and stress and promote relaxation. Students will be learning about self-compassion and self-care. We will put these concepts into action by practicing yoga next week. There is a growing body of research regarding the use of yoga in schools, which indicates that it increases emotional and physical health and improves self-esteem. Given these significant findings, I believe that your child will benefit from learning how to use yoga as a strategy to implement self-care and self-compassion.

Below I have provided a list of supplies and reminders that will ensure each student's comfort and safety during this yoga activity.

Please make sure your child:

- Wears comfortable, loose clothing.
- Does not wear long, dangly jewelry or is prepared to remove it.
- Brings a yoga mat or towel.
- Ties hair back if it is long.

If you have any questions or concerns, please do not hesitate to reach me by email or phone. Thank you for your cooperation and assistance in ensuring the success of this activity for our students.

Sincerely,
[Name/Title]
[Contact Information]

ASCA Mindsets Standards

Belief in development of whole self, including a healthy balance of mental, social/emotional, and physical well-being.

ASCA Behavior Standards

Learning Strategies

Apply self-motivation and self-direction to learning.

Self-Management Skills

Demonstrate self-discipline and self-control.
Demonstrate effective coping skills when faced with a problem.

Social Skills

Use effective collaboration and cooperation skills.
Demonstrate advocacy skills and ability to assert self, when necessary.

Learning Objectives

1. Students will understand the definition of anxiety.
2. Students will demonstrate ways in which self-confidence can be used as a coping mechanism in order to self-soothe and manage emotions.
3. Students will set a goal related to their personal experience with anxiety.

Materials

1. 10- to 40-pound weighted kettle bells
2. 15 plastic cones
3. 5 hula hoops
4. 3 soft kickballs
5. 2 footballs
6. A set of badminton rackets with birdies

Session Procedure

1. The school counselor will ask students to identify some personal experiences of fear or worry associated with anxiety with school transition, career planning, and peer pressure (e.g., test taking, socializing with peers, conflict with peers).
2. The school counselor will discuss the definition of anxiety with the students.
   Discussion Questions: Can you think of any times when you felt certain emotions (e.g., fatigue, irritability, difficulty focusing, sleep problems, feeling tense or on the edge)? What did your body feel like when you experienced certain emotions?

3. The school counselor will discuss the idea that an obstacle course can be used as a tool that can help students increase their awareness and acceptance of emotions in the present moment.

4. The school counselor will utilize each section of the course as an analogy (as described below) to introduce a negative emotion related to anxiety.

5. The school counselor will explain that anxiety and anxious behaviors can be inherited, learned, or both. For example, anxiety is connected with panic attacks and phobias.

6. The school counselor will describe an event related to a parent or role model displaying similar tendencies during childhood. Therefore, the student can react to certain experiences correlated with their behaviors.

7. The school counselor will explain that when completing each obstacle, it will allow students to develop certain techniques to address their feelings of anxiety in the moment.

8. Following this introduction, students will complete the five-stage obstacle course described below, and the school counselor will attach each emotion to each obstacle after the students process these emotions:
   Stage 1: Carry weighted kettle bell thirty yards (irritability).
   Stage 2: Run through ten cones that are placed in a difficult design (feeling fatigue).
   Stage 3: Throw two footballs in a hula hoop that is laying on the ground ten yards away (difficulty focusing).
   Stage 4: Roll three kickballs into a hula hoop twenty yards away (muscle tension).
   Stage 5: Hit a birdie with a badminton racket over a line that is created by cones eight yards away (feeling tense).

9. After students have attempted the obstacle course, the school counselor will ask them to self-reflect on their experiences. As each student is processing, the counselor will ask a series of open-ended questions to promote coping skills in order to manage their symptoms (e.g., taking deep breaths, imagining a safe place, taking a time-out, slowly counting to ten). If a student is unable to complete the course, the school counselor will model the obstacle side by side with the student in order to motivate his or her engagement.
   Discussion Questions: What is your body currently feeling in this very moment? What are some techniques that you can use when in a stressful environment?

10. The school counselor will have each student go through the obstacle course one more time, paying particular attention to their emotional reactions, which will allow each student to regain self-control in order to reduce or eliminate the symptoms associated with anxiety.

11. The school counselor will ask each student to regroup and collaborate with their classmates in order to share their second experience on each obstacle and how they handled their emotions differently during the second attempt.

12. The school counselor will have the students identify their negative and positive feelings regarding this activity.
    Discussion Questions: How did your feelings of anxiety change from the start to the end of this activity when you were completing each obstacle stage? How did your body feel as you completed it the second time?

Closing Discussion Questions/Activities

1. What did you notice about yourself regarding how you manage emotions and challenges after participating in this activity?

2. What are some instances in which you think you could use either of these activities?

3. What is one goal for using these techniques in the classroom or at home this coming week?

About the Group Worker

Keith LaBadie is working toward his Education in School Counseling master's degree at Caldwell University. He currently works full time at Bridgewater-Raritan High School in New Jersey as a one-on-one special education assistant. Mr. LaBadie implemented an after-school program at his internship site called #GetSocial, which promotes self-awareness, social skills, team leadership, emotional intelligence and coping mechanisms to handle stressful situations. #GetSocial was held once a week after school for developmentally disabled students and was supervised by Dr. Diana Wildermuth, NCC, LPC, during the pilot of this group.

Additional Resources

American School Counselor Association. (2014). *ASCA mindsets & behaviors for student success: K–12 college-and career-readiness standards for every student.* https://www.schoolcounselor.org/getmedia/7428a787-a452-4abb-afec-d78ec77870cd/Mindsets-Behaviors.pdf

Kagan, J., & Snidman, N. (1999). Early childhood predictors of adult anxiety disorders. *Biological Psychiatry, 46*(11), 1536–1541. https://doi.org/10.1016/S0006-3223(99)00137-7

Potter, C. M., Wong, J., Heimber, R. G., Blanck, C., Liu, S., Wang, S., & Schneier, F. R. (2014). Situational panic attacks in social anxiety disorder. *Journal of Affective Disorder, 167*, 1–7. https://doi.org/10.1016/j.jad.2014.05.044

ANXIETY SESSION PLAN 8

LEVEL	SESSION TITLE	TOPIC
Middle & High	Presently & Patiently	Anxiety

STAGE   ☐ Orientation   ☒ Working   ☐ Closing

ASCA Mindsets Standards

Belief in development of whole self, including a healthy balance of mental, social/emotional, and physical well-being.

ASCA Behavior Standards

Learning Strategies

Demonstrate critical-thinking skills to make informed decisions.

Identify long and short academic, career, and social/emotional goals.

Self-Management Skills

Demonstrate self-discipline and self-control.

Demonstrate effective coping skills when faced with a problem.

Demonstrate ability to balance school, home, and community activities.

Social Skills

Demonstrate advocacy skills and ability to assert self, when necessary.

Demonstrate social maturity and behaviors appropriate to the situation and environment.

Learning Objectives

1. Students will recognize personal anxiety triggers.
2. Students will utilize breathing techniques to mitigate anxiety
3. Students will articulate healthy self-talk.

Materials

1. Boxes of LEGO© each of which creates a specific model for each student
2. Pencils/pens
3. Paper
4. Timer

Session Procedure

Activity One: LEGO©, Round 1

1. The school counselor will distribute LEGO© sets, pens/pencils, and two blank sheets of paper to each student.
2. The school counselor will ask students to carefully empty the content of the box of LEGO© out onto their personal space and instruct the students to refrain from playing with them.
3. The school counselor will inform the students that a timer will be set for 3 minutes in which time they must attempt to build the designed image pictured on the box of LEGO©.
4. Once the students understand the instructions, the school counselor will ready the students and start the timer.

5. After 3 minutes have passed, the school counselor will ask the students to stop assembling the LEGO©.

   Discussion Questions: How did you feel trying to complete the task in 3 minutes? When else have you experienced a similar feeling? How do you calm yourself down when you have these kinds of feelings? Can you calm yourself down when you are in the middle of feeling such strong emotions?

Activity Two: LEGO©, Round 2

1. The school counselor will instruct the students to take apart whatever they have assembled and to lay out all pieces of the LEGO©.
2. The school counselor will introduce a breathing technique, instructing the students to count each breath inhaled and exhaled up to 10 (one in, two out, three in, four out, and so on).
3. The school counselor will have students practice this exercise. Afterward, the school counselor will ask the students to try this technique if they feel stressed or rushed on the next attempt to build with the LEGO©.
4. The school counselor will inform the students that the timer will be set again for 3 minutes; however, the students can take the 3 minutes to build whatever they want. The students should be instructed to be creative and told that there is no correct way to construct the LEGO©.
5. If the students appear to feel rushed, the school counselor should remind them to use the breathing technique previously practiced.
6. The school counselor will start the timer. At the end of the 3 minutes, the school counselor will ask the students to record their feelings. Afterwards, the counselor will ask the students to share what they created.

   Discussion Questions: What did you notice that was different between the first and second attempt? Although the time for each attempt was the same, which attempt did you like more? Why? Did you use the breathing technique during the second attempt? If so, did you find it helpful or not?

7. The school counselor will explain the following to students: "In attempting to achieve our goals in life, we sometimes have this 'perfect' picture in our minds of what outcomes will look like. This can lead to putting unnecessary pressure on ourselves. By doing so, this may keep us from being fully present, and we may thus look past how individual achievements are unique to us. Our lives don't have to be the 'perfect' image we have or that someone else has for us. Your best effort is all you can ask of yourself."

Activity Three: Positive Mantras

1. The school counselor will explain what a personal mantra is and give the students an example of one. The school counselor will explain how a personal mantra can be a reminder to the students to breathe and center themselves when life gets chaotic or feels rushed.
2. After the introduction and example of mantras, the school counselor will ask students to come up with their own personal positive mantras that they can repeat to themselves anytime they feel the rush of anxiety.

Closing Discussion Questions/Activities

1. What did you learn about yourself through the LEGO© activities today?
2. Which attempt was your favorite and why?

About the Group Worker

William A. McAleenan is working toward his School Counseling master's degree at Northern Kentucky University. He is currently working as an AmeriCorps VISTA leader in the state of Kentucky and is also president of Northern Kentucky University's Chi Sigma Iota–Nu Kappa Counseling Honors Society.

Appendix A
Pretest/Posttest

1. Do you know any breathing techniques to calm yourself down when you start to feel anxious, nervous, or rushed?
   a. Yes
   b. No

2. What are some things that make you feel anxious or nervous?

   _____

   _____

   _____

3. Do you have an understanding of how to apply mindfulness to your life?
   a. Yes
   b. No

4. What are some coping skills, strategies, or techniques that you can use to calm yourself down?

   _____

   _____

   _____

ASCA Mindsets Standards

Belief in development of whole self, including a healthy balance of mental, social/emotional, and physical well-being.

Self-confidence in ability to succeed.

ASCA Behavior Standards

Learning Strategies

Use time-management, organizational, and study skills.

Self-Management Skills

Demonstrate ability to overcome barriers to learning.

Demonstrate effective coping skills when faced with a problem.

Social Skills

None

Learning Objectives

1. Students will evaluate their current feelings attached to standardized testing situations.
2. Students will demonstrate coping strategies for anxiety related to standardized testing.
3. Students will use coping strategies during a frustrating standardized testing situation.

Materials

1. ACT Math Practice Questions 1 worksheets (see Appendix A)
2. ACT Math Practice Questions 2 worksheets (see Appendix B)
3. Two pieces of paper per student
4. Pencils/markers/colored pencils/crayons
5. Whiteboard/chalkboard
6. Clock/stopwatch
7. Small prizes for students (e.g., candy, t-shirts, school supplies)

Session Procedure

1. The school counselor will start the group with a brief check-in to find out when each student has their next standardized test.
2. The school counselor will hand out the ACT Math Practice Questions 1 worksheet to the students.
3. The school counselor will inform the students that they have 5 minutes to complete the five questions and that there is no talking allowed, including any questions.

4. The school counselor can either have students discuss how they felt while taking the practice questions, or the counselor may use the pieces of paper to collect the students' answers and process them together while writing on the whiteboard or a piece of paper on the wall.
   Discussion Questions: How did you feel while taking this test?

5. The school counselor will focus on the answers that address anxiety or stress by asking students to describe the feelings in further detail.
   Discussion Questions: Can you explain what your body feels like when you feel
   [insert feeling]?

6. The school counselor will go through all of the feelings expressed by the students and discuss where in their bodies they feel the physical effects of anxiety.

7. The school counselor will hand out another piece of paper to each of the students and instruct them to write a sentence they can tell themselves when they begin to feel stressed during testing.
   Examples: "I know this information"; "No one knows all of these answers"; "I can do this"; "I am more than just a number"; "Relaxing helps me do my best"; "Staying calm helps me think clearly."

8. The school counselor will have students read their sentences aloud with their eyes closed.

9. The school counselor will demonstrate what a relaxing belly breath looks like by explaining to the students that "It is important for the shoulders to stay down and the stomach to expand. For example, five counts in and five counts out at least twice."

10. The school counselor will have the students practice the relaxing belly breaths at least five times.

11. The school counselor will go through the answers of the questions from ACT Math Practice Questions 1 [Answers: 1 = a; 2 = b; 3 = b; 4 = d; 5 = c].

12. The school counselor will hand out the ACT Math Practice Questions 2 worksheet to the students. Note: this worksheet does not have the correct answers as an option.

13. The school counselor will inform the students that they have 5 minutes to complete the five questions and that there is no talking allowed, including questions; however, the students who get more questions correct will receive prizes.
    Discussion Questions: How did you feel completing the second worksheet? Did anyone feel anxious or stressed? What was going through your head to cause anxiety?

14. The school counselor will process through the responses of the students.
    Discussion Questions: Did anyone say their sentence to themselves during the second practice worksheet? Did anyone try the relaxing belly breath?

15. The school counselor will process students' reactions.

16. The school counselor will inform the students that the correct answers were not listed on the paper in order to cause heightened stress and anxiety.

Closing Discussion Questions/Activities

When can you use your sentence or relaxing belly breaths to relax yourself during your testing?

About the Group Workers

Rebecca L. H. Meidinger, Christina N. Jurekovic, and Johnsa B. Phares are professional school counselors; two are currently practicing at public urban high schools and one practices at a private international secondary school. All three are also doctoral students in Counselor Education and Supervision at Adams State University. Their love of group counseling emerged during their Advanced Group Counseling course.

References

American College Testing. (2005). *Preparing for the ACT (2005–2006)*.

Appendix A

ACT Math Practice Questions 1

Directions: You have 5 minutes to complete this quiz. Calculators are not permitted.

1. The perimeter of a parallelogram is 72 inches and one side measures 12 inches. What are the lengths, in inches, of the other three sides?
   a. 12, 12, 36
   b. 12, 18, 18
   c. 12, 24, 24
   d. 12, 30, 30

2. If $2x^2 + 6x = 36$, what are the possible values of x?
   a. -12 and 3
   b. -6 and 3
   c. -3 and 6
   d. -3 and 12

3. Television screen sizes are the diagonal length of the rectangular screen. Hector recently changed from watching a television with a 13-inch screen to a television with a similar 19-inch screen. If a boxcar appeared 8 inches long on the 13-inch screen, how many inches long, to the nearest inch, will it appear on the 19-inch screen?
   a. 10
   b. 12
   c. 14
   d. 16

4. When graphed in the standard (x, y) coordinated plane, the lines $x = -3$ and $y = x - 3$ intersect at what point?
   a. $(0, -3)$
   b. $(-3, 0)$
   c. $(-3, -3)$
   d. $(-3, -6)$

5. What does the absolute value of $7(-3) + 2(4)$ equal?
   a. -28
   b. -13
   c. 13
   d. 28

Appendix B

ACT Math Practice Questions 2

Directions: You have 5 minutes to complete this quiz. Calculators are not permitted.

1. If $7 + 3x = 22$, then $2x = ?$
   a. 5
   b. 12
   c. 14
   d. 20

2. The total cost of renting a car is $30.00 for each day the car is rented plus 28.5¢ for each mile the car is driven. What is the total cost of renting the car for 5 days and driving 350 miles? (Note: No sales tax is involved.)
   a. $104.75
   b. $159.98
   c. $300.00
   d. $1,147.50

3. The product $(2x^4y)(3x^5y^8)$ is equivalent to:
   a. $5x^9y^9$
   b. $6x^9y^8$
   c. $5x^{20}y^8$
   d. $6x^{20}y^8$

4. In a bag of 400 jelly beans, 25% of the jelly beans are red in color. If you randomly pick a jelly bean from the bag, what is the probability that the jelly bean picked is NOT one of the red jelly beans?
   a. 1/2
   b. 1/4
   c. 1/16
   d. 15/16

5. Meg pounded a stake into the ground. When she attached a leash to both the stake and her dog's collar, the dog could reach 9 feet from the stake in any direction. Using 3.14 for pi (π), what is the approximate area of the lawn, in square feet, the dog could reach from the stake?
   a. 28
   b. 57
   c. 113
   d. 283

Appendix C
Pretest/Posttest

1. What are your feelings about standardized testing (check all that apply)?
   □ Stressed   □ Anxious   □ Calm
   □ Relaxed   □ Frustrated   □ Angry
   □ Annoyed   □ Excited   □ Confident

2. I feel prepared for standardized tests (e.g., ACT, SAT, AP, PSAT, state/district testing).
   □ Strongly disagree   □ Slightly disagree
   □ Slightly agree   □ Strongly agree

3. I use the following coping strategies during standardized testing (check all that apply).
   □ Deep breathing
   □ Self-talk/positive thinking
   □ Mindfulness
   □ Other: _____
   □ None

ASCA Mindsets Standards

Belief in development of whole self, including a healthy balance of mental, social/emotional, and physical well-being.

ASCA Behavior Standards

Learning Strategies

Gather evidence and consider multiple perspectives to make informed decisions.

Self-Management Skills

Demonstrate effective coping skills when faced with a problem.

Demonstrate ability to manage transitions and ability to adapt to changing situations and responsibilities.

Social Skills

Demonstrate social maturity and behaviors appropriate to the situation and environment.

Learning Objectives

1. Students will be able to discuss the main function of the amygdala.
2. Students will understand the 90-second amygdala response and be able to apply the 90-second principle when feeling anxious.
3. Students will understand how to use the Name It to Tame It strategy when feeling anxious.

Materials

1. Amygdala Response handouts (see Appendix A)
2. *The Neuroanatomical Transformation of the Teenage Brain* by Jill Bolte Taylor
3. Stopwatch

Session Procedure

1. The school counselor will open the discussion by asking students how they think their brains are connected to experiencing anxiety and by explaining that the group will be talking about the brain by stating, "Today's discussion will focus on the part of the brain that is in the limbic system: the amygdala. The amygdala is about the size of an almond and serves as the fear response. The amygdala scans our surroundings and helps keep us safe—like a watchdog on the lookout. However, when it is in overdrive, it leads to a heightened sense of emotions, especially anxiety."
2. The school counselor will distribute the Amygdala Response handout to each student.
3. The school counselor will instruct the students that "On this handout you will see a green zone indicating that when you feel calm, your amygdala hasn't been triggered. You will also see the red zone, which indicates that the amygdala is in high fear response mode. For example, you may be afraid of dogs. When you are walking in the park and see a dog, your

amygdala is fired, igniting your fear response. This takes you into the red zone. Your prefrontal cortex (or the thinking part of the brain) then reminds the amygdala that the dog is on a leash and that you are safe. You should then take a deep breath and return to the green zone area. This response helps you to notice how you are feeling and checks in with the thinking location of your brain to tell you that you are safe from danger. When we do not engage the thinking area of our brain, our emotional response stays activated, causing us to stay in that fear response or red zone."

4. The school counselor should emphasize to the students that the amygdala is always asking, Am I safe?
   Discussion Questions: What are you thinking about your watchdog response? When are some instances when your watchdog has been set off? Where in the red zone were you during that instance? Did you stay in the red, or were you able to get back to the green zone?

5. The school counselor will briefly explain to the students how feelings, behaviors, and bodily responses are affected when individuals are in the green and red zones.
   Discussion Questions: What behaviors would a student in the green zone exhibit? What about a student's behaviors when he or she is in the red zone? What feelings may be experienced in the green and red zones? How does your body feel when you are in the red zone?

6. The school counselor will provide students with a few examples of behaviors that are experienced in both zones by stating, "For example, some behaviors that are experienced in the green zone include active listening, maintaining eye contact, and being engaged in the conversation. Some examples that are experienced in the red zone include being distracted or looking around the room, lack of eye contact, and pacing nervously."

7. The school counselor will provide students with a few examples of feelings that occur in both zones by stating, "For example, some feelings that occur in the green zone include feeling calm, relaxed, and satisfied. Some examples that occur in the red zone include feeling worried, frustrated, angry, and agitated."

8. The school counselor will provide students with a few examples of bodily responses that happen in both zones by stating, "For example, some bodily responses that happen in the green zone include deep breathing, feeling completely relaxed, and lack of muscle tension. Some examples that happen in the red zone include rapid breathing, rapid heartbeat, sweaty palms, nausea, muscle tension, and dry mouth."

9. The school counselor will now introduce two brief strategies to help students return to the green zone when feeling anxious.

10. The school counselor will explain the first strategy, the 90-second rule, by telling the students that "Dr. Jill Bolte Taylor explains that emotions last for less than 90 seconds. When our emotional response lasts longer, then that means we have not engaged our thinking parts of our brain and have added our own fear story to the initial trigger. Basically, think of it as 'We have decided to hold on to that emotion.'"

11. The school counselor will now have students participate in the 90-second rule strategy.

12. The school counselor will take out their stopwatch and instruct the students to close their eyes.

13. After 90 seconds has passed, the school counselor should have students open their eyes.
    Discussion Questions: What was it like trying to gauge ninety seconds? Did it feel like it took a long time? When you think about times you have felt anxious, how long did those feelings last?

14. The school counselor will now explain the second strategy, Name It to Tame It, which was developed by Dr. Dan Siegel, by telling the students, "When we pause after we notice our amygdala has been triggered by asking ourselves, 'What am I feeling?' we have engaged our thinking areas of the brain. This strategy will help keep us from staying emotionally triggered and help us work to find out how to think about whether we are safe and how to return to the green zone more quickly. For example, thinking back to seeing the dog in the park, I notice my anxiety or amygdala is triggered because I am fearful of dogs. I can name my feeling: being scared. Taking a moment to think about what we are feeling helps to both acknowledge the 90-second rule and makes us use the thinking parts of our brain so we can begin to work to get back to the green zone."

Discussion Questions: What are some feelings you can name when you think about events that cause you anxiety? When you name that feeling, how can you stay in your thinking brain in order to come up with the ways to reduce your anxious feelings?

15. The school counselor should invite students to respond to the empty box on the Amygdala Response handout.

Discussion Questions: How will you engage your amygdala in order to return to the green zone more quickly?

Closing Discussion Questions/Activities

Can you share one word or phrase that you learned today about your brain and anxiety?

About the Group Worker

Brandie Oliver, PhD, is an assistant professor in the School Counseling Department at Butler University. Previously, she worked as a middle school counselor. She has taught the group counseling course and has experience facilitating numerous groups over the last 8 years. Dr. Oliver strongly believes in the power of group counseling and its benefit to students learning in this format of counseling. She is dedicated to the training, development, and supervision of school counselors who strive to be change agents in P–12 education.

References

Bolte Taylor, J. (2016, May 12). *B is for Jill Bolte Taylor: Her stroke of insight* [Video]. The Positive Encourager. http://www.thepositiveencourager.global/jill-bolte-taylors-stroke-of-insight-video-2/

Siegel, D. (2014, December 8). *Dan Siegel: Name it to tame it* [Video]. YouTube. https://www.youtube.com/watch?v=ZcDLzppD4Jc

Appendix A
Amygdala Response Handout

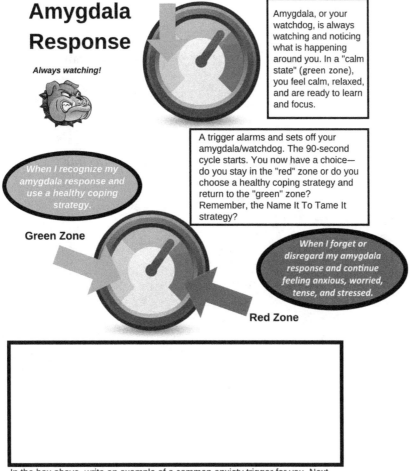

In the box above, write an example of a common anxiety trigger for you. Next, write how you will respond when your amygdala/watchdog is triggered and a healthy coping strategy you will use to return to the "green" zone.

© 2018, Dr. Brandie Oliver

Appendix B
Pretest/Posttest

1. I know what the role of the amygdala is:
   a. Strongly disagree
   b. Disagree
   c. Agree
   d. Strongly agree

2. After my amygdala has been set off, my emotional responses last approximately:
   a. 30 seconds
   b. 1 minute
   c. 90 seconds
   d. 3 minutes

3. When I am feeling anxious, I know how to use the Name It to Tame It strategy:
   a. Strongly disagree
   b. Disagree
   c. Agree
   d. Strongly agree

4. The amygdala functions as the _____ response in my brain:
   a. Anger
   b. Fear
   c. Joy
   d. Sleep

5. I have strategies that I can use when I feel my amygdala is going into the red zone of fear and anxiety:
   a. Strongly disagree
   b. Disagree
   c. Agree
   d. Strongly agree

Answer Key: 1. n/a, 2. c, 3. n/a, 4. b, 5. n/a

ANXIETY SESSION **PLAN 11**

| LEVEL | SESSION TITLE | TOPIC |
| Elementary, Middle & High | The Ties That Bind | Anxiety |

STAGE   ☐ Orientation   ☐ Working   ☒ Closing

ASCA Mindsets Standards

Belief in development of whole self, including a healthy balance of mental, social/emotional, and physical well-being.

ASCA Behavior Standards

Learning Strategies

Gather evidence and consider multiple perspectives to make informed decisions.

Self-Management Skills

Demonstrate effective coping skills when faced with a problem.

Demonstrate the ability to manage transitions and the ability to adapt to changing situations and responsibilities.

Social Skills

Create positive and supportive relationships with other students.

Demonstrate empathy.

Learning Objectives

1. Students will be able to verbalize at least one accomplishment achieved throughout the group.
2. Students will be able to identify how they can be a source of support to other students.
3. Students will be able to demonstrate empathy toward their peers.

Materials

1. A bolt (or spool) of ribbon or string
2. An assortment of multicolored children's jewelry beads

Session Procedure

1. The school counselor will take the students to an open space and ask them to sit in a circle.
2. The school counselor will pass around the box of assorted jewelry beads and ask each student to pick two beads.
3. The school counselor will remind the students of all the tasks they have worked on accomplishing over the entire group (increasing self-esteem, decreasing anxiety, and preparing for transition out of this group, class, or school).
4. The school counselor will state the following verbal directions for the activity: "I will be asking the group two questions. When it is your turn, please thread the ribbon or string through the hole in your bead and hold your bead firmly in your hand as you answer the question. When you are finished answering the question, give the end of the ribbon to another student in the group. While holding onto your bead in front of you, allow the ribbon or string to move freely through the bead. The end of the ribbon or string does not have to be given to the person sitting directly next to you—any order is acceptable."

5. Holding the bolt (or spool) of ribbon or string in his or her hand, the school counselor will take the end of the ribbon and hand it to a student in the group.
   Discussion Questions: Think back to where you were at the beginning of our time together. What was something that you accomplished over our time together that surprised you? What is something you were able to do that you did not think was possible?

6. The school counselor should have each student thread the ribbon or string through their bead and give the students the opportunity to answer these questions.
   Discussion Questions: What is something that makes you anxious about leaving this group or going on without this group? Does anyone have any suggestions for how to deal with this particular anxiety?

7. The school counselor should instruct the students that as they answer the question, they should slide the ribbon or string through the hole in the bead. Once that student is finished answering the question and receives advice from a peer, they will hold onto their bead firmly and hand the end of the ribbon or string to another peer.
   Discussion Questions: Looking at what you have made [the spider web of ribbon or string]—what do you see and what does this say about the group?

8. The school counselor will close the group by commenting, "What I see is that, yes, you are all similar and many of you faced the same obstacles, fears, and anxieties, but you also leaned on each other. You have come to support each other and become a resource for one another. As you go forward, I encourage you to remember the time you had together and continue to act as a source of support for each other."

Closing Discussion Questions/Activities

1. What are some challenges you imagine that you may encounter in the future?
2. What have you learned from this group that would help you deal with those challenges?
3. How might you be a resource or source of support for a peer?

About the Group Worker

Christine Ebrahim, PhD, is currently an associate professor at Loyola University New Orleans, where she teaches courses in school counseling. Dr. Ebrahim also has a private practice in which she works with adolescents and is a former high school counselor.

CREDITS

Social Skills Groups

Introduction

Formal education has a clear impact on students' social skills development. Prior to enrolling in school, many young children experience limited social interactions, which often occur at the behest of their parents. As children enter school, the hub of academic learning, they also enter a forum where their social education begins. Often referred to as the hidden curriculum of the PreK–12 learning environment, school-aged children are expected to learn to function appropriately with peers, teachers, and other adults with whom their daily paths cross.

The school setting becomes a place where individuals make and maintain friends and experience daily social interactions. For many, learning appropriate social skills and interdependence requires minimal effort. For others, making friends and understanding appropriate interpersonal behaviors does not come as easily. Symptoms of negative or poor social skills sometimes do not emerge until prompted by changes associated with adolescence. Moreover, mental health issues may further complicate interpersonal functioning.

Regardless of the causes or symptoms, lacking appropriate social skills undoubtedly affects an individual's academic, career, and social/emotional development. Therefore, school counselors should consider appropriate direct services to meet the needs of students who experience related challenges. Small-group responsive services offer an ideal, Tier 2 intervention to support students in developing essential social skills through role-plays and modeling. The session plans included in the following section provide small-group counseling sessions that address various aspects of students' social skills development.

Data Discussion

Being able to collect and analyze data effectively is key to developing your comprehensive school counseling program, and is also important for your small-group counseling program (see Chapter 3 for more). Examining data that are accurate and appropriate for the goals of your small group is imperative in garnering support for a more robust small-group counseling program. Here are steps we hope you undertake as you review the sample sessions on social skills.

Discuss Data Collection With a Peer/Colleague

Consultation and collaboration are inherent in the role of school counseling. By working with others in the field, we build our professional skills and confidence and increase alignment of our work with the ASCA National Model for School Counseling programs. Collaboration and consultation also represent school counseling best practice and help us remain data driven and intentional with intervention planning. Based on the sessions you choose when considering your particular school, consult with a peer or colleague about your rationale/selections and your data collection plan.

Take a Walk with Data Related to Social Skills

For each of the lessons focused here on social skills, we ask that you engage in the following steps either with your colleague(s) or your course instructor(s):

Step 1—General Data Consideration

Read the Learning Objectives for each small group on social skills and then:

Ask yourself, What kinds of data might be relevant to collect based on the learning objectives stated? Are you most interested in the number of students served (participation), or are you more focused on how your small group meets the mindsets and behaviors that are the target of your group (surveys, pretest/posttest)? Are you concerned about examining how students' social skills development might improve student academics (outcome)?

Disaggregating your data to determine if certain subgroups of students are disproportionately impacted is also essential in small-group planning. As such, do you have any suspicions that poor social skills and awareness play a role in how underserved or marginalized students are treated in the school (e.g., students with IEPs self-reporting greater conflict with peers; Black and Brown students receiving more behavior referrals than other segments of your student body)?

Step 2—Thoughts on Participation Data

After reading the general outline for the session:

What plan would help you collect participation data for your social skills group? For example, when taking attendance for your group, which identifiers are you most concerned about? In reality, social skills development is beneficial across all grade levels, and many students need to build on their skills in this area. As such, indicators such as grade level or class room assignment are common participation data points to consider when deciding what data are most important for you to track related to your small group. Also, think about how you will organize this information. Will you keep a notebook with an attendance roster to indicate which students participate in each session, or do you prefer electronic means for organizing your participation data (e.g., Microsoft Excel; Google Sheets)? It is important for school counselors to select organization tools that are both efficient and functional so that data are tracked consistently.

Step 3—Thoughts on Mindsets and Behaviors Data

After reading the Closing Discussion Questions/Activities section for each session, ask:

When considering collecting mindsets and behaviors data, how might a pretest/posttest survey of group members in this group look? What questions would you want to ask to determine if the mindsets and behaviors related to the social skills targeted were achieved? Consider what particular social skills and knowledge you want students to walk away with once they have participated in the group. For example, developing a "sense of belonging in the school environment" (Standard M.3) might be the mindset you choose for a small group. Consider which behavior standards you will select to accompany this mindset. For instance, you may decide to focus on Standard B-SS 6., "Use effective collaboration and cooperation skills," and/or Standard B-SS 9., "Demonstrate social maturity and behaviors appropriate to the situation and environment." Consider accessing the *ASCA Mindsets and Behaviors* database (https://scale-research.org/mandb/public_html/) for help to quickly identify and assess content based on the developmental needs of students as they relate to appropriate student competencies and standards.

Step 4—Thoughts on Outcome Data

Upon reading the entire group plan, consider this:

The term outcome data refers to the "big picture" data and are therefore typically connected to attendance, behavior, and academics metrics. Consider what data you might examine to see if the session(s) you decide to implement improve academics. Undoubtedly, examining any change in behaviors around discipline referrals, suspensions, or expulsions related to social interactions with others is valid. For example, will you focus on students' improvements related to reported bullying or conflicts with others? Are you focused on a measurable behavior related to participants' social skills (e.g., amount of time they are able to interact appropriately with peers or number of times they appropriately take turns in a group)? Think about what you want as your big picture take-aways for students who participate in your groups. One final note about outcome data: pick one! It is not always necessary to evaluate all three areas—attendance, behavior, and academics—for your small group. Target one area and let that guide your evaluation of the group's impact!

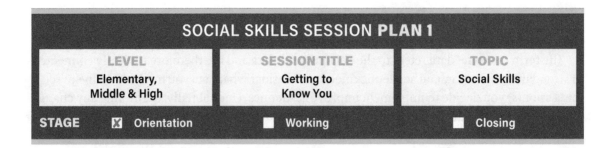

ASCA Mindsets Standards

Belief in development of whole self, including a healthy balance of mental, social/emotional, and physical well-being.

Sense of belonging in the school environment.

ASCA Behavior Standards

Learning Strategies

Participate in enrichment and extracurricular activities.

Self-Management Skills

Demonstrate ability to manage transitions and ability to adapt to changing situations and responsibilities.

Social Skills

Create positive and supportive relationships with other students.

Create relationships with adults that support success.

Learning Objectives

1. Students will share their experiences of being new to the school.
2. Students will gain knowledge of school culture.
3. Students will gain a sense of citizenship within the school by meeting strategic faculty and staff and becoming familiar with surroundings.

Materials

1. Icebreaker Questions (see Appendix A)
2. New Student Coupon Books (see Appendix B)
3. Slips of paper
4. School map (if available)

Session Procedure

Activity One: Icebreaker

1. The school counselor will discuss the purpose of building universality.
2. The school counselor will begin the icebreaker activity with the students. All questions may be used or the school counselor can select specific questions to ask.
   Discussion Questions: Can you identify with any of the answers another person shared? How did you feel when you heard other people talk about their experiences as a new student? How did you feel before talking with one another?

3. The school counselor will place slips of paper in the middle of the group with each student's name on one slip of paper.
4. The school counselor will instruct students to choose one slip of paper, identify the person whose name is on the slip, and recall the information shared by that student from the questions previously asked.
5. After the icebreaker activity, the school counselor will discuss group expectations: confidentiality, respect, working together, listening to each other, and taking turns.

Activity Two: Getting to Know You

1. The school counselor will pass out the pretest to students.
2. After taking the pretest, the school counselor will ask the students if they knew all the answers. After the students respond, the counselor will state that it is fine for not to know all of the answers and that the purpose of the group is to learn about the school and make friends at the same time.
3. The school counselor will give students time to reflect and discuss their experiences taking the pretest.
   Discussion Questions: What are some similarities you noticed about your responses to the pretest? What are some differences that you noticed? How do you feel after hearing each other talk about answers and about being a new student?
4. The school counselor will ask students to name strategic people in the school (e.g., media specialist, nurse) and explain where those people are located in the building as students may not know this information.
5. The school counselor will give each student a New Student Coupon Book, which contains the names of the strategic people within the school.
6. The school counselor will pair preselected new students with a classmate or classroom ambassador (outside of the group) to meet the staff in the coupon book and learn where they are located in the building. The coupon book will be a keepsake for the new student. The school counselor may also provide a school map.
7. The school counselor will instruct students to write their names on the lines labeled "Student's Name," so that the respective school staff will know who they are. The school counselor will ask that students have the school staff sign their name after that student has been introduced by the classmate or ambassador.
8. After reviewing the New Student Coupon Book, students will share one thing they learned from the group meeting and how they feel after meeting other new students.
   Discussion Questions: What is one thing you learned from being in group today? How are you feeling after meeting other new students?

Closing Discussion Questions/Activities

1. Who are some people you could sit next to at lunch or hang out with at recess this week?
2. How are you feeling after meeting other new students?
3. Between now and next week, try to meet every adult in your coupon book. We will discuss who you met and where they are located when we meet again.

About the Group Worker

Malti Tuttle is an assistant professor in the Department of Counseling at Auburn University. Prior to becoming a professor, she was a practicing school counselor for 13 years. She enjoys facilitating small groups because of its powerful impact on student change.

Appendix A
Icebreaker Questions
Where are you from?

How do you feel about coming to this school?

What do you like about this school?

How is this school different from your old school?

What would you like to know more about this school?

What is your favorite thing to do?

What is something cool about yourself?

What is your favorite _____?

Appendix B
New Student Coupon Book Template

Welcome to:

_____ School

[Place Picture of Staff Member Here]

Coupon for _____

_____   _____

Student's Name   Nurse

Appendix C
Pretest/Posttest

1. I have made more than two friends at this school:
   a. Yes
   b. No
   c. Not sure

2. I know how to get around the school by myself:
   a. Yes
   b. No
   c. Not sure

3. I believe I am the only person who knows what it is like to be a new student:
   a. Yes
   b. No
   c. Not sure

4. I know two or more people whom I can ask for help if I need help:
   a. Yes
   b. No
   c. Not sure

5. My school counselor is available to help me if I need help with school, home and friends:
   a. Yes
   b. No
   c. Not sure

6. I know the name of the nurse:
   a. Yes
   b. No
   c. Not sure

7. I feel like I fit in at this school:
   a. Yes
   b. No
   c. Not sure

8. I know the media specialist's name:
   a. Yes
   b. No
   c. Not sure

9. I feel safe at this school:
   a. Yes
   b. No
   c. Not sure

ASCA Mindsets Standards

Belief in development of whole self, including a healthy balance of mental, social/emotional, and physical well-being.

ASCA Behavior Standards

Learning Strategies

Identify long- and short-term academic, career, and social/emotional goals.

Self-Management Skills

Demonstrate self-discipline and self-control.
Demonstrate effective coping skills when faced with a problem.
Demonstrate personal safety skills.

Social Skills

Demonstrate social maturity and behaviors appropriate to the situation and environment.

Learning Objectives

1. Students will recognize the emotions that may occur prior to becoming angry.
2. Students will recognize that anger is an acceptable emotion.
3. Students will learn how to appropriately express anger and practice management strategies.

Materials

1. Sample Scenarios (see Appendix A)
2. Cup
3. Paper
4. Pencils/pens

Session Procedure

Activity One: Introduction

1. The school counselor should begin by talking about anger, its consequences, and how to manage it.
   Discussion Questions: Can everyone remember a time when you were angry—what feelings did you experience? What did you do? What were your thoughts?
2. The school counselor should have students brainstorm answers to the following questions regarding anger expression.
   Discussion Questions: What are the physical signs of anger? What are some inappropriate ways to express anger? What are examples of strategies to handle anger appropriately?

Activity Two: Anger Scenarios

Note: The school counselor will use Appendix A scenarios for the following activity.

1. The school counselor will place students into groups of two.
2. The school counselor will have students draw one sample scenario from the cup.
3. The school counselor will instruct each member to brainstorm times when they would use at least two anger management strategies that were talked about in the previous activity.
4. The school counselor will instruct students to respond to their scenarios by writing them on sheets of paper. Students will be given 10 minutes to complete the activity. Students may offer other dyads support if needed.
5. After 10 minutes have passed, the school counselor will have all dyads share their scenarios and responses to the other groups.

Closing Discussion Questions/Activities

1. Describe your thoughts about the scenario responses shared by all dyads.
2. What are some appropriate and inappropriate ways to handle anger?
3. When do you need to ask for help if you are angry with another person?
4. What is an appropriate way that you can control your anger outbursts this week?

About the Group Workers

Teddi Cunningham, PhD, is an associate professor at Valdosta State University. Dr. Cunningham has taught the group work class at Valdosta State University for over 10 years.

Heather Kelley, PhD, is an assistant professor at Valdosta State University. Dr. Kelley is an educational psychologist who uses group strategies when instructing her classes.

Appendix A
Sample Scenarios

Scenario #1:

The group must create a story about a child who is angry because someone would not share with them. Include two ways the child could manage their anger.

Scenario #2:

The group must create a story about a child who is angry because they weren't chosen to participate in the school play and include two ways that the child could manage their anger.

Scenario #3:

The group must create a story about a child who is angry with their teacher because they did not pass their test.

Scenario #4:

The group must create a story about a girl who is angry at her friend because someone told her that the friend was talking about her.

Appendix B
Pretest/Posttest

Please answer true or false about yourself to the following statements:

1. ____ When I am angry, I can identify where I feel the anger in my body.
2. ____ I know how to identify what makes me mad.

3. ___ It is normal to be angry sometimes.
4. ___ Anger can make me say hurtful things to others.
5. ___ I have a strategy to handle my anger.
6. ___ When I am angry, I know how to ask for help.

Please choose the best answer to the following questions:

1. Which of the following feelings might indicate when someone is angry?
   a. Face turns red
   b. Screaming
   c. Frowning
   d. All of the above

2. Jack is feeling angry because he did not get to go to recess. Which of the following is the best way for him to calm down?
   a. Hold his feelings inside
   b. Yell at his teacher
   c. Take a few deep breaths
   d. Kick a desk

3. Mary forgot to bring her colored pencils to school and she is feeling angry. Which of the following is the best way for her to calm down?
   a. Refuse to participate in class
   b. Take colored pencils from a classmate without permission
   c. Kick the table
   d. Ask the teacher for help on how to manage her anger

4. Lucy notices that someone is sitting in her favorite seat and she knows this is a trigger that makes her angry. Which of the following is the best way for Lucy to avoid this trigger?
   a. Lucy should yell at the person in her seat
   b. Lucy should take a deep breath, count to 10, and sit in another seat
   c. Lucy should kick the chair
   d. Lucy should hold her feelings inside and yell at the student later at recess

SOCIAL SKILLS SESSION **PLAN 3**

LEVEL	SESSION TITLE	TOPIC
Elementary	Talk to the Chair	Social Skills

STAGE   ☐ Orientation   ☒ Working   ☐ Closing

ASCA Mindsets Standards

Belief in development of whole self, including a healthy balance of mental, social/emotional, and physical well-being.

ASCA Behavior Standards

Learning Strategies

Gather evidence and consider multiple perspectives to make informed decisions.

Self-Management Skills

Demonstrate effective coping skills when faced with a problem.

Social Skills

Demonstrate effective oral and written communication skills and listening skills.
Create positive and supportive relationships with other students.
Demonstrate ethical decision-making and social responsibility.
Demonstrate advocacy skills and ability to assert self, when necessary.
Demonstrate social maturity and behaviors appropriate to the situation and environment.

Learning Objectives

1. Students will understand the importance of communicating their needs and wants in a respectful manner.
2. Students will demonstrate assertiveness through self-expression.
3. Students will use "I" messages to practice communicating their feelings, needs, and wants.

Materials

1. Feelings Chart handouts (see Appendix A)
2. "I" statements template individually typed onto strips of paper (Appendix B)
3. Two chairs

Session Procedure

Activity One: Expressing Yourself

1. The school counselor will begin the session by welcoming students and asking them to describe their current emotional state based on a feeling that is written in the chart (see Appendix A).
2. The school counselor will ask students to reflect upon previous group sessions.
   Discussion Questions: Can you think about a time when someone said or did something to you that you did not like? How did you and your body feel in that moment? What made it difficult for you to speak up in that moment?
3. The school counselor will use basic counseling skills (e.g., reflecting feelings, paraphrasing, summarizing, linking) to process these experiences with the group members.

4. The school counselor will then describe the concept behind making "I" statements and invite students to share a time when making "I" statements could have helped them communicate more effectively.

   Example Statement: You can use "I" statements with your classmates and friends. "I" statements are statements that you can use to explain how you feel about something that has happened, that was said, or that you need. This is important because sometimes when we communicate how we feel or what we need from other people, we feel better inside. "I" statements allow us to communicate our feelings in a respectful manner. Remember that all feelings are okay—it's how we express our feelings that is important.

5. The school counselor will use the "I" statements template to demonstrate a variety of ways that students can make "I" statements based on situations shared in Step 4. As an extension to this, the school counselor can create situations for the students to role-play.

Activity Two: Talk to the Chair

1. The school counselor will sit in one of the two chairs and pretend to speak with another person sitting in the empty chair, demonstrating a variety of ways to express "I" statements.

2. The school counselor will give students the opportunity to practice making "I" statements with others using the empty chair. The school counselor will ask the other students to observe their peer sitting in the chair and provide them with encouraging feedback on their use of "I" statements.

Closing Discussion Questions/Activities

1. The school counselor will ask for volunteers to summarize this session.

2. The school counselor will ask students to identify a peer with whom they are currently struggling or a situation in which they could possibly use "I" statements to appropriately express their feelings, needs, and wants.

3. The school counselor will encourage students to use "I" statements outside of the group and ask them to be prepared to share their experiences with the group during the next session.

About the Group Worker

Glenda S. Johnson is an assistant professor in the Professional School Counseling Program at Appalachian State University. Ms. Johnson worked as a special education counselor for 3 years and a general education counselor for 14 years at the elementary, middle, and high school levels. She has found group work to be an enjoyable way to provide counseling services to a variety of students who have shared similar experiences.

Appendix A
Feelings Chart

Happy	Embarrassed	Angry
Scared	**How do you feel?**	Lonely
Disgusted	Surprised	Sad

Appendix B
"I" Statements Template

I feel _____ (feeling word) when you _____ (action). I would like for you to _____ (replacement behavior).

I like being your friend. When you _____ (action), I feel _____ (feeling word). Next time, can you _____ (action)?

Hey, let's go play _____ (action). But before we go, can I share something with you? I feel _____ (feeling word) when you _____ (action). Will you _____ (replacement behavior)?

_____ (student's name), can I talk to you? I want to let you know that I feel _____ (feeling word) when you _____ (action). Will you _____ (action) instead? I like being your friend but I'm not sure if we can continue being friends if you continue _____ (action).

ASCA Mindsets Standards

Belief in development of whole self, including a healthy balance of mental, social/emotional, and physical well-being.

ASCA Behavior Standards

Learning Strategies

Demonstrate critical thinking to make informed decisions.
Demonstrate creativity.

Self-Management Skills

Demonstrate ability to assume responsibility.
Demonstrate effective coping skills when faced with a problem.

Social Skills

Demonstrate empathy.
Demonstrate advocacy skills and ability to assert self, when necessary.
Demonstrate social maturity and behaviors appropriate to the situation and environment.

Learning Objectives

1. Students will learn about bullying and the different forms it can take.
2. Students will learn about the effects of bullying.
3. Students will learn to advocate for themselves and others when faced with bullying situations.

Materials

1. Paper
2. Sheets of colored paper precut into the shape of a bumper sticker
3. Stick Together to Drive Out Bullying poster with the large image of the back of a car on it
4. Markers
5. Glue

Session Procedure

Activity One: The Crumple Paper Activity

1. The school counselor will explain the definition of bullying and discuss its different forms (e.g., name calling, physical abuse, exclusion, and gossiping) (Olweus, 1993).
   Discussion Questions: Can you think of some other examples of bullying? How did it make you or others feel?
2. The school counselor will pass out blank sheets of paper to the students.
3. The school counselor will give the students 30 seconds to crumple up their papers as much as they can.

4. Upon completion of the exercise, the school counselor will instruct the students to uncrumple their paper as much as possible.
   Discussion Questions: What do your sheets of paper look like now? Are they still wrinkled?

5. The school counselor will explain how the effects of bullying are like the paper: once the damage has been done, the paper will never look the same.

6. The school counselor will go over different consequences associated with bullying behaviors.

Activity Two: Stick Together to Drive Out Bullying

1. The school counselor will go over some examples of how students can deal with bullying.
   Discussion Questions: What are some things you can do if you are getting bullied or see someone else getting bullied?

2. The school counselor will emphasize that students can take action to do something about bullying while emphasizing the importance of students only doing what feels safe for them.

3. The school counselor will show the students the poster with the car and explain that they will be coming up with their own ideas of how to "stick together to drive out bullying" and attach them to the poster.

4. The school counselor will pass out the pieces of colored paper and markers and explain to the students that they should come up with their own ideas about how to deal with bullying.

5. The school counselor will instruct students that they will need to write their ideas on the colored paper, which will be their bumper stickers; students can make multiple bumper stickers if they would like.

6. The school counselor will have the students bring their bumper stickers to the school counselor to glue onto the poster wherever the student would like.

7. Upon completion of the activity, the school counselor will go over each of the bumper stickers aloud and provide positive reinforcement for the ideas the students provided.

Closing Discussion Questions/Activities

1. What have you learned about the different forms of bullying and how bullying makes the victim feel?

2. What situations can you think of which you can use these ideas to deal with bullies?

About the Group Worker

Ashley Lopez is working toward her in Clinical Mental Health Counseling master's degree at Loyola University New Orleans. She also volunteers at Raphael Academy during the school year by assisting teachers in working with students with special needs.

References

Olweus, D. (1993). *Bullying at school: What we know and what we can do.* Blackwell.

Additional Resources

PBS Newshour Extra. (n.d.). *Crumpled paper-lesson plan.* https://d43fweuh3sg51.cloudfront.net/media/media_files/Crumpled_Paper.pdf

Privette, M. (2012, February 16). *Stick it to bullies.* The Creative Counselor. http://thecreativecounselor.blogspot.com/2012/02/stick-it-to-bullies.html?m=1

SOCIAL SKILLS SESSION **PLAN 5**

LEVEL	SESSION TITLE	TOPIC
Elementary	Flexible Friends Have More Fun!	Social Skills

STAGE   ☐ Orientation   ☒ Working   ☐ Closing

ASCA Mindsets Standards

Belief in development of whole self, including a healthy balance of mental, social/emotional, and physical well-being.

Sense of belonging in the school environment.

ASCA Behavior Standards

Learning Strategies

Participate in enrichment and extracurricular activities.

Self-Management Skills

Demonstrate self-discipline and self-control.

Demonstrate effective coping skills when faced with a problem.

Social Skills

Create positive and supportive relationships with other students.

Use effective collaboration and cooperation skills.

Demonstrate social maturity and behaviors appropriate to the situation and environment.

Learning Objectives

1. Students will play cooperatively with peers in less structured activities, such as pretend play or playground games.
2. Students will understand ways to select which person goes first and/or determine the sequence of turn-taking for an activity.

Materials

1. Selection of materials for open-ended creative and expressive play (e.g., sand, clay, blocks, dolls and doll house, play kitchen, puppets, art materials)
2. A variety of tools or strategies to determine which child goes first
3. One flexible item (e.g., pipe cleaner)
4. One rigid item (e.g., ruler)

Session Procedure

Preparation

1. The school counselor will select nondirective play materials that allow for a variety of types of self-expression in less structured group play interactions. Materials such as sand, clay, blocks, construction toys, plastic animals (domestic and wild animals, including dinosaurs) dolls and doll house, play kitchen, puppets, and art materials allow for this type of play. *Note:* Board games are not recommended for this group because they typically provide for more structured play with clear rules.

2. The school counselor will gather materials that can be used to determine which student will be the "leader" of the group for the session, such as spinners, dice, playing cards, drawing straws, and hand rhymes (e.g., "one potato, two potato").

Activity: Flexible Friends Have More Fun!

1. The school counselor will introduce the group to the students by stating, "This is a special group for the four of you which will allow each of you to be in charge of what we play during our time together but here is the challenge: You will have to be 'flexible' because you might not get to be in charge of what we play together today! Flexible means that you can handle it when you do not get to be leader or you do not like what the leader chooses."

2. The school counselor will demonstrate how the pipe cleaner/flexible item can change its shape and won't break when it has to change but the ruler/rigid item, on the other hand, remains firm and might break if it has to change shape. The school counselor will discuss how people can be flexible by changing their thinking and behavior when faced with a challenge or a change of plans.
   Discussion Questions: When was a time you had to change your mind or had to be flexible with a change of plans?

3. The school counselor will explain the group limits by telling students, "Even if you do not want to play what the leader chooses, you will still stay with us. We will help each other be 'flexible' so we all have fun."
   Discussion Questions: What do you do when you don't like to play what your friends want to play? What helps you have fun even if you don't want to play the same game as them?

4. The school counselor will explain, "Everyone will get to be the group leader at some point but only one person will be the leader right now." The school counselor will demonstrate how a given leader selection method works (e.g., dice, spinner).
   Discussion Questions: What ways do you know to pick the leader for a game?
   The school counselor will coach students in positive self-talk in case they are not chosen as the leader. For example, the school counselor will tell students, "Be ready in case you do not get chosen to be the leader today. Let's practice saying to ourselves, 'I'm disappointed I did not get to be leader today but I will play and have fun anyway!'"
   Discussion Questions: What are some other things you could say to yourself if you are not chosen today?

5. The school counselor will lead the group in determining the session leader.

6. The school counselor will coach the students who were not selected as the leader with positive self-talk by saying, "It is okay to be sad if you were not chosen today. You will get another chance to be the leader."

7. The school counselor will show the leader the materials they may choose from for the group activity and tell the student, "You may choose one toy for all of us to play with today."

8. The school counselor will coach students using positive self-talk with the remaining group members in case they do not like the activity selected by the leader. For example, the school counselor can tell students, "I would like to play with my favorite toy but if [leader's name] does not choose it, I will have fun anyway! When it is my turn, I can choose the toy I like."
   Discussion Questions: What are some other things you could say to yourself if you don't like the toy or activity that the leader chooses?

9. Once the leader has made their choice of activity/toy, the school counselor will facilitate a group play session using the least amount of structure necessary to allow students to gain practice in cooperative play with minimal adult intervention. If a child opts out of the activity, the school counselor can coach that student to remain with the group. For example, the

school counselor can tell students, "You may still have fun by staying with your friends during the group time. Please come sit and talk with us. You could say, 'I do not want to play [toy/activity] but I will stay and talk with you'."

Discussion Questions: What was a time you didn't want to play with the same toys your friends were using but you had fun with them anyway?

10. At the end of the group session, the school counselor will facilitate cleanup and give specific positive feedback to each group participant about flexibility and participation.

    Note: The school counselor may wish to have future group sessions follow the same format until each child has had a chance to be leader.

Closing Discussion Questions/Activities

How did it feel today when you were not chosen to be the leader but went along with the activity anyway?

About the Group Worker

Laura Tejada, PhD, LMFT, LPC, Registered Play Therapist-Supervisor, is a former elementary classroom teacher and school counselor who earned the Registered Play Therapist credential during her years as a school counselor. Dr. Tejada is an assistant professor in the Department of Counselor Education at Northeastern Illinois University.

Additional Resources

Kestly, T. A. (2014). *The interpersonal neurobiology of play: Brain-building interventions for emotional well-being.* Norton.

Landreth, G. (1991). *Play therapy: The art of the relationship.* Accelerated Development.

Landreth, G., Homeyer, L. E., Glover, G., & Sweeney, D. S. (1998). *Play therapy interventions with children's problems.* Jason Aronson.

Peoples, C. (1983). Fair play therapy. In C. E. Schaefer & K. O'Connor (Eds.), *Handbook of play therapy* (pp. 76–88). Wiley.

Pfaff-Henk, J. (2009, September). Using play in group therapy with young children. *Play Therapy Magazine, 4*(3), 10–12.

Schaefer, C. E., Jacobsen, H. E., & Ghahramanlou, M. (2000). Play group therapy for social skills deficits in children. In H. E. Kadusen C. E., & Schaefer (Eds.), *Short-term play therapy for children* (pp. 296–344). Guilford Press.

Slavson, S. R. (2000). Play group therapy. In H. E. Kadusen & C. E. Schaefer (Eds.), *Short-term play therapy for children* (pp. 242–252). Guilford Press.

Appendix A

Pretest/Posttest

Note: This is for the adult to read to students and is not intended as an assessment that students complete independently.

1. When I play with my friends on the playground, I can handle it when they don't play what I want to.

I can do it!   I need help.   I have trouble with this.

2. When I play with my friends, I know how to share and take turns.

I can do it!   I need help.   I have trouble with this.

3. When I play with my friends on the playground, I can handle it when I don't get to go first.

I can do it!   I need help.   I have trouble with this.

ASCA Mindsets Standards

Belief in development of whole self, including a healthy balance of mental, social/emotional, and physical well-being.

Sense of belonging in the school environment.

ASCA Behavior Standards

Learning Strategies

Demonstrate creativity.

Self-Management Skills

None

Social Skills

Create positive and supportive relationships with other students.

Demonstrate empathy.

Use effective collaboration and cooperation skills.

Learning Objectives

1. Students will identify the qualities and characteristics of growth-fostering friendships.
2. Students will identify the qualities and characteristics that influence negative friendships.
3. Students will work toward improving patterns of interpersonal communication with peers.

Materials

1. Positive & Negative Friends handout (see Appendix A)
2. Whiteboard/chalkboard
3. Colored construction paper
4. Pencils/markers/colored pencils/crayons
5. Scissors
6. Clear adhesive tape

Session Procedure

Activity One: Positive vs. Negative Influences

1. The school counselor will distribute the Positive & Negative Friends handout to each student.
2. The school counselor will ask students to list the influences of productive and unproductive relationships.
3. The school counselor will give students five minutes to come up with five characteristics for each type of relationship.
4. One at a time, the school counselor will ask students to write one of each characteristic on the chalkboard.

Discussion Questions: What do you think was more difficult, coming up with characteristics of a productive friend or an unproductive friend? Which do you see more often among your friends?

Activity Two: Friends Across the Wall

1. The school counselor will ask students to form a circle with their desks and will distribute a different colored piece of construction paper to each student.
2. The school counselor will instruct students to trace their hand onto their sheet of construction paper, ask that they write their name onto the cuff of their hand, and uniquely design it to their preference.
3. The school counselor will then ask each student to pass the tracing of their hand to the person sitting on their right. Each student will write something positive or something that they like about the person whose hand it belongs to. Students will continue passing each hand to the right so that everyone has a chance to write on each other's sheets.
4. Once each hand has returned to the student who drew it, the school counselor will have each ask everyone to cut their paper hand out and to tape them all together.
5. After the cutouts of all the hands have been taped together, the school counselor will hang the sequence of hands on the wall for discussion.

Closing Discussion Questions/Activities

1. In general, how did reading your peers' comments make you feel?
2. What surprised you about these comments?
3. Are there any characteristics written on your hand that you did not think others noticed about you?

About the Group Worker

Nader D. Manavizadeh is one of the editors of this text. He has his master's degree in Forensic Psychology from Tiffin University, is working toward his master's degree in School Counseling at Kutztown University, and is currently completing the requirements of his internship in secondary school counseling in southeastern Pennsylvania.

Additional Resources

Teacher Vision. (2015). *Friends across the wall.* https://www.teachervision.com/activity/friends-across-wall

Positive & Negative Friends

Positive Friends	Negative Friends

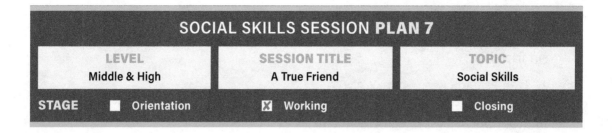

ASCA Mindsets Standards

Belief in development of whole self, including a healthy balance of mental, social/emotional, and physical well-being.

Sense of belonging in the school environment.

ASCA Behavior Standards

Learning Strategies

None

Self-Management Skills

Demonstrate self-discipline and self-control.

Demonstrate personal safety skills.

Social Skills

Create positive and supportive relationships with other students.

Demonstrate ethical decision-making and social responsibility.

Learning Objectives

1. Students will identify when the behaviors of others violate their own sense of trust and belonging.
2. Students will gain a deeper understanding of the qualities they value in a true friendship.
3. Students will identify appropriate choices when determining how to handle troubling situations that may arise within their peer group.

Materials

1. The Friendship Deed of Trust handouts (see Appendix A)
2. Situations printouts (see Appendix B)
3. Paper
4. Pencils/pens
5. Whiteboard/chalkboard

Session Procedure

1. The school counselor should hand each student a writing utensil and piece of scrap paper.
2. The school counselor should write the Ralph Waldo Emerson quote "The only way to have a friend is to be one" on the easel or whiteboard.
3. The school counselor should ask the students to silently process the quote for a few minutes and have them write down what they think the quote means.
4. The school counselor should invite the students to share what they wrote and invite one student to record the responses on the easel pad or whiteboard.

5. The school counselor should distribute The Friendship Deed of Trust handouts to students and have them list the character traits they expect and seek in a "real" friend on the front page.

6. The school counselor should have the students discuss these individual qualities and what they mean to the group, while identifying shared group values and overall thoughts.

7. The school counselor will invite students to turn to the back page and list the qualities and values of people who are not "real" friends.

8. The school counselor will read the sample situations and follow the proceeding discussion questions for each situation.

   Discussion Questions: What would be an appropriate way to handle the situation? Has something similar ever happened to anyone that you know? Does this person have the qualities you seek in a friendship? Let's say the situation only happened once and the two students were really good friends; how could you handle it? What, if any, physical sensations do you feel when you know your friend really isn't your friend? What is the best course of action for breaking up a friendship?

Closing Discussion Questions/Activities

1. How do you know if someone is a true friend?
2. How do you know if someone is not a true friend?
3. How will you handle a situation when you know someone is not being a good friend to you?

About the Group Worker

Julia V. Taylor is an assistant professor of Counselor Education at the University of Virginia. Prior to academia, she spent 10 years as a school counselor at the middle and high school levels.

Additional Resources

Taylor, J. V., & Trice-Black, S. (2007). *Girls in real life situations: Group counseling activities for enhancing social and emotional development.* Research Press.

Appendix A
The Friendship Deed of Trust
Directions:

1. Write down the qualities that you give to and expect from a true friendship. For example, real friends help each other with their problems, real friends are there for each other, and real friends can disagree and still be friends.

2. List what real friends don't do. For example, real friends don't tell secrets about each other unless they think their friends are in danger, real friends don't talk behind each other's back, and real friends don't isolate their friends.

Real Friends Do:

_____

_____

_____

_____

_____

_____

_____

_____

Real Friends Don't:

_____

_____

_____

_____

_____

_____

_____

_____

Appendix B
Situations

Situation 1:
Your friend asks you to hang out after school and cancels at the last minute. A few hours later this friend posts a photo of themselves on Instagram hanging out with other people.

Situation 2:
Your friend asks to copy your homework. You worked really hard on it and don't want to get caught but are also afraid of what might happen if you say no.

Situation 3:
Your friend always puts you down and follows it up with, "Just kidding"; however, you know they are not kidding.

Situation 4:
You feel smothered by one of your friends—they are always where you are, show up at your house uninvited, constantly text you, and won't give you space. When you try to tell them you need some breathing room, they become super emotional, leaving you feeling guilty.

Situation 5:
You have a friend who is really nice to you when you both are alone but ignores you when other people are around.

ASCA Mindsets Standards

Belief in development of whole self, including a healthy balance of mental, social/emotional, and physical well-being.

ASCA Behavior Standards

Learning Strategies

None

Self-Management Skills

None

Social Skills

Use effective oral and written communication skills.

Demonstrate empathy.

Use effective collaboration and cooperation skills.

Demonstrate advocacy skills and ability to assert self, when necessary.

Learning Objectives

1. Students will develop and display effective listening skills, such as paraphrasing, eye contact, and body language.
2. Students will develop assertive communication skills.

Materials

1. Strips of paper containing instructions for Student A (see Appendix A)
2. Strips of paper containing instructions for Student B (see Appendix A)
3. Whiteboard/chalkboard

Session Procedure

1. The school counselor will group students into pairs and ask each pair of students to determine who will be "Student A" and "Student B."
2. The school counselor will provide students with the strip of paper containing the instructions for each respective student.
3. The school counselor will ask that students do not share their instructions with one another.
4. The school counselor will ask that students carry out their instructions for 3 minutes.
5. After 3 minutes have passed, the school counselor will ask students who served as Student A to describe what it was like to interact with Student B.
6. The school counselor will explain that instructions for Student B were to engage in and respond with poor listening skills.

   Discussion Questions: Students who served as Student A, how could you tell that your partner, Student B, was not listening? What were some of the characteristics of poor listening skills that they exhibited?

7. The school counselor will write examples of poor listening skills on the chalkboard as students identify some examples of these.

8. The school counselor will demonstrate examples of effective listening skills as they role-play these skills with a student.

9. The school counselor will demonstrate the three types of communication (aggressive "you" messages, passive communication and assertive "I" messages) as the school counselor role-plays these with a student. For example, the school counselor will discuss examples by stating, "An example of aggressive communication is, 'I cannot believe you said that to him. What is wrong with you?' An example of passive communication is, 'Hey ... umm ... I was wondering if you said anything about what I told you earlier?' Lastly, an example of assertive communication is, 'I am really annoyed. We talked about how I did not want you to tell anyone. Now I am not sure what people know about what I said'."
Discussion Questions: Can you identify which demonstration was an example of aggressive communication? Can you identify which demonstration was an example of passive communication? Can you identify which demonstration was an example of assertive communication?

10. The school counselor will instruct students who served as Student B to identify a time when they were angry with a friend, and students who served as Student A are to pretend that they are the friend with whom Student B is angry or upset.

11. During the role-playing between the pairs of students, the school counselor will instruct those acting as Student B to assertively communicate their anger, using "I" messages. Students acting as Student B's friend are to demonstrate effective listening skills.
Discussion Questions: Students who served as Student B, what was at least one effective communication skill used by your partner? Students who served as Student A, how did it feel to have someone angry or upset with you while you were still trying to understand your partner? Students who served as Student A, what was at least one thing that your partner did to communicate anger to you in a way that you could understand their problem?

Closing Discussion Questions/Activities

1. What were some times when you did not demonstrate effective listening skills?
2. What are some of the consequences of using poor listening skills?
3. How do you know when someone is really listening to you?
4. How do you show someone that you are really listening to them?
5. What is one effective listening skill that you plan to use more frequently during this week?

About the Group Worker

Jered Kolbert, PhD, is the School Counseling Program Coordinator for Duquesne University and has worked as a secondary school counselor in Hanover County, Virginia. Dr. Kolbert co-authored *Introduction to Professional School Counseling* (2016).

Appendix A
Listening Skills Instructions

Instructions for Student A:

Talk to Student B about anything that interests you. Some ideas to talk about include your hobbies, vacation, or the craziest thing that has ever happened to you. Do not ask Student B any questions.

Instructions for Student B:

Do not look at Student A—instead, look around the room, look at your shoes, draw a picture, et cetera.

SOCIAL SKILLS SESSION **PLAN 9**

LEVEL	SESSION TITLE	TOPIC
Middle & High	Friendship—It's Complicated!	Social Skills

STAGE   ☐ Orientation   ☒ Working   ☐ Closing

ASCA Mindsets Standards

Belief in development of whole self, including a healthy balance of mental, social/emotional, and physical well-being.

ASCA Behavior Standards

Learning Strategies

Demonstrate critical-thinking skills to make informed decisions.
Gather evidence and consider multiple perspectives to make informed decisions.

Self-Management Skills

Demonstrate ability to manage transitions and ability to adapt to changing situations and responsibilities.

Social Skills

Create positive and supportive relationships with others.
Demonstrate social maturity and behaviors appropriate to the situation and environment.

Learning Objectives

1. Students will work together to define changing friendships and the feelings associated with these transitions.
2. Students will create and share a self-reflective collage based on their experiences with changing friendships.

Materials

1. Chart paper
2. Markers
3. Poster board
4. Magazines
5. Art supplies (e.g., crayons, scissors, glue, ribbons, pipe cleaners, stickers)

Session Procedure

1. The school counselor will introduce the topic of friendship and highlight how friendships can change during middle school.
   Discussion Questions: How might you define a good friend? What might indicate that your friendships are changing?
2. The school counselor will invite students to share any changing friendship experiences they have had during their time in middle school. While students are sharing, the school counselor will write down key words/phrases that summarize their experiences (e.g., different teams, drama, rumors, changing schools).

Discussion Questions: What are some positive aspects of changing friendships? What are some negative aspects of changing friendships?

3. The school counselor will ask the group to brainstorm a list of feelings associated with their changing friendships and list these next to the key words/phrases about their experiences. *Discussion Questions:* How is it for you to share your feelings? Does anyone feel like they shouldn't feel angry, sad, happy, embarrassed, et cetera.? How are the feelings listed expressed to others?

4. The school counselor will ask students to reflect on this list and create a collage from magazines, representing their personal experiences with changing friendships. The school counselor will encourage creativity and self-expression.

5. The school counselor will invite the students to share their collages with the group.

Closing Discussion Questions/Activities

1. How does it feel to share your experiences with the group?
2. How does it feel to hear their experiences?
3. How can you communicate what you are feeling to your friends?
4. Do you think it is important to clarify your feelings to your friends? Why or why not?

About the Group Worker

Hennessey Lustica, LMHC, has 13 years of experience as a middle school counselor in both suburban and urban settings. She currently works as a mental health counselor in private practice serving children, adolescents, and families and as a clinical supervisor for the Society for the Protection and Care of Children in Rochester, New York. Additionally, Ms. Lustica has served as an adjunct instructor for school counseling graduate students at Alfred University and the University of Rochester, where she is completing her doctorate in Counseling and Counselor Education.

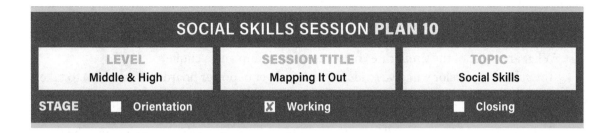

ASCA Mindsets Standards

Belief in development of whole self, including a healthy balance of mental, social/emotional, and physical well-being.

Self-confidence in ability to succeed.

ASCA Behavior Standards

Learning Strategies

Demonstrate critical-thinking skills to make informed decisions.

Gather evidence and consider multiple perspectives to make informed decisions.

Self-Management Skills

Demonstrate ability to manage transitions and ability to adapt to changing situations and responsibilities.

Social Skills

Create positive and supportive relationships with other students.

Demonstrate social maturity and behaviors appropriate to the situation and environment.

Learning Objectives

1. Students will define the difference between a friendship and a clique.
2. Students will create a map of the cafeteria that illustrates the different groups of students in their class.
3. Students will explore their own experiences of belonging to a clique or being influenced by a clique in school.

Materials

1. Chart paper
2. Poster board
3. Art supplies (e.g., crayons, markers, scissors, glue, ribbons, pipe cleaners, stickers)

Session Procedure

1. The school counselor will introduce the topic of friendships versus cliques. For example, the school counselor should explain to the students that "Friendships may be characterized by similar interests, shared experiences, and supportive relationships. Cliques may be characterized by bullying, unequal balances of power, and ostracizing others."
   Discussion Questions: How might you know when someone is your friend? What do you think defines a friendship? What do you think defines a clique?
2. The school counselor will invite students to create two lists on the board: friendships and cliques.

3. The school counselor will have students list the characteristics of each group on the board.
   Discussion Questions: What are some of the differences between a friendship and a clique? What are some of the similarities between a friendship and a clique?
4. The school counselor will give students a large sheet of poster board and ask them to take a moment to close their eyes and picture the cafeteria.
5. The school counselor will then have students work together to map out the cafeteria during their lunch period, which will include the different groups of which students may be a part (e.g., different peer groupings, gender groupings, cultural groupings).
6. The school counselor will remind students to indicate where they sit in their cafeteria map and ask them to think about why they sit there.
   Discussion Questions: How do groups of students typically form? How did you know where to sit on the first day of school? Has your seat changed since the first day of school? Why has your seat changed or not changed since then?
7. The school counselor will ask students to look at their map and share the following information with each other: How do you define each table of students in the cafeteria? Does this map represent friendships or cliques? How do you know the difference between friendships and cliques? If you could sit anywhere, where would it be? Do you think that you belong to a clique? If yes, how do you feel about it? If no, has a clique ever affected your friendships at school?

Closing Discussion Questions/Activities

1. Can you identify two strategies to deal with cliques?
2. The school counselor will post these strategies on the bulletin board outside the cafeteria.

About the Group Worker

Hennessey Lustica, LMHC, has 13 years of experience as a middle school counselor in both suburban and urban settings. She currently works as a mental health counselor in private practice serving children, adolescents, and families and as a clinical supervisor for the Society for the Protection and Care of Children in Rochester, New York. Additionally, Ms. Lustica has served as an adjunct instructor for school counseling graduate students at Alfred University and the University of Rochester, where she is completing her doctorate in Counseling and Counselor Education.

Additional Resources

Gordon, S. (2016). *How to tell the difference between a clique and friends.* Very Well. https://www.verywell.com/a-clique-or-friends-how-to-tell-the-difference-460637

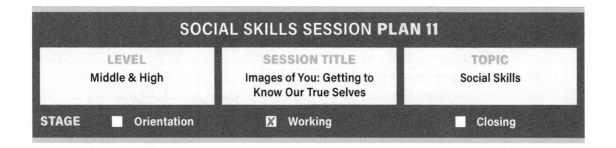

SOCIAL SKILLS SESSION **PLAN 11**

LEVEL	SESSION TITLE	TOPIC
Middle & High	Images of You: Getting to Know Our True Selves	Social Skills

STAGE ☐ Orientation ☒ Working ☐ Closing

ASCA Mindsets Standards

Belief in development of whole self, including a healthy balance of mental, social/emotional, and physical well-being.

ASCA Behavior Standards

Learning Strategies

Gather evidence and consider multiple perspectives to make informed decisions.

Self-Management Skills

Demonstrate ability to assume responsibility.

Social Skills

Create positive and supportive relationships with other students.
Demonstrate empathy.
Demonstrate social maturity and behaviors appropriate to the situation and environment.

Learning Objectives

1. Students will share at least one new thing they learned about another group member.
2. Students will begin to understand the influence of societal messages and articulate at least one gender stereotype that has impacted how they view themselves or make decisions.
3. Students will identify and write down a positive, empowering message for themselves and share the message with at least one other person outside of the group.
   Note: In its current form, this group is intended for girls but could be adapted for a multigender or male group.

Materials

1. Chairs arranged in a circle
2. One full-length mirror
3. Handheld mirror for each member of the group
4. Dry erase marker
5. An empowering song (e.g., *"Brave"* by Sarah Bareilles, 2011; *"Fight Song"* by Rachell Platten, 2014)
6. Printed or electronic image that each student brings to share with the group. (Note: This should not be a photograph of themselves but rather an image that is symbolic of their lives. For example, a student might bring an image of a butterfly emerging from a cocoon or show a GIF of a fireworks display and explain how it uniquely represents this stage of her life. Students should be instructed during the previous group to bring this with them to the next session.)

Session Procedure

Activity One: Sharing Your Image

1. The school counselor will discuss how sometimes we can see "reflections of ourselves" represented in nature, art, or through other images.
2. The school counselor will instruct students to show their images to the group one at a time and explain how they reflect an aspect of their identities.
3. After all students have shared their images, the school counselor will facilitate a discussion and give each student the opportunity to participate.
   Discussion Questions: What is something new you learned about someone else in the group during this activity?

Activity Two: Reflections

1. The school counselor will pull out the full-length mirror and explain that sometimes other people have their own "image" of who we should be based solely on an aspect of our identity, such as gender.
   Discussion Questions: What are messages you have received about how girls should act or what they are "allowed" to be? What does it mean to be "ladylike" or a "good girl"? What things have you heard said about girls or women that bother you?
2. As students share, the school counselor will ask them to come up and write their messages on the mirror with a dry erase marker.
3. Once all of the students have shared and the mirror is filled with messages, the school counselor will ask each student to stand in front of the mirror.
   Discussion Questions: What do you notice when you look in the mirror? Is it harder to see yourself with all of these messages clouding your reflection?
4. The school counselor will explain that sometimes stereotypes and societal messages can be harmful, making it difficult for us to see our "true selves" or be empowered to express our authentic identity to others.
5. Then the school counselor will lead a discussion about students' reactions to the activity.
   Discussion Questions: What is a message that you would like to "erase?" What message would you like to give to yourself and others in the group instead?
6. The school counselor will invite students to erase the harmful messages they identified from the large mirror.
7. The school counselor will give each student a handheld mirror on which to write her new, positive message.
8. The school counselor will ask students to walk around the room and hold up the mirror to another student who will read the message on the mirror aloud. Each student will be instructed to do this with as many group members as possible, while an empowering song is played.
9. At the completion of the song and activity, the school counselor will invite students to take the mirrors home and look in them whenever they need a reminder of who they truly are.
10. To end the session, the school counselor will share the quote, "Strength comes from being in touch with our true selves and being able to make choices from that place." The school counselor can explain how teenage girls often face a lot of pressures and unfair stereotypes; however, being aware of these messages and reflecting on who they truly are can help them to make healthy decisions from a place of authenticity.

Closing Discussion Questions/Activities

1. Think of someone who might benefit from hearing what you learned in the group today. How and when could you share this message with them?
2. Think about a decision you might have to make this week or even further in the future. How could you use what you learned today to make the healthiest decision for your true self?

About the Group Worker

Jill Schwarz, PhD, is a core faculty member in the Department of Counselor Education at the College of New Jersey, where she also serves as the co-coordinator of an International School Counseling Program offered in Portugal. As a former middle school counselor, Dr. Schwarz developed and led empowerment and leadership groups for adolescent girls and was inspired by their growth and support of one another. She regularly presents on gender issues and school counseling and is the sole editor of the textbook *Counseling Women and Girls: Empowerment, Advocacy, and Intervention.*

References

Bareilles, S., & Antonoff, J. (2013). Brave [Recorded by Sara Bareilles]. On *Blessed Unrest* [MP3 file]. Epic Records. (2011).

Platten, R., & Bassett, D. (2015). Fight Song [Recorded by Rachel Platten]. On *Wildfire* [MPS file]. Columbia Records. (2014).

ASCA Mindsets Standards

Belief in development of whole self, including a healthy balance of mental, social/emotional, and physical well-being.

Sense of belonging in the school environment.

ASCA Behavior Standards

Learning Strategies

Demonstrate critical-thinking skills to make informed decisions.

Actively engage in challenging coursework.

Self-Management Skills

Demonstrate ability to overcome barriers to learning.

Social Skills

Use effective oral and written communication skills and listening skills.

Create positive and supportive relationships with other students.

Use effective collaboration and cooperation skills.

Learning Objectives

1. Students will increase effective communication skills.
2. Students will increase trust with other group members during challenging tasks.

Materials

1. Upwards of 100 various items (e.g., tennis balls, wads of paper, football)
2. One full-length mirror
3. Blindfolds (e.g., scarves, handkerchiefs, sleeping masks)
4. Large room with floor space

Session Procedure

1. The school counselor will scatter and evenly distribute the ball-like objects across the entire defined "mine field" space on the floor, leaving enough space to walk through. These ball-like objects will act as "mines."
2. The school counselor will have each student pair up with another group member.
3. Within each pair, the school counselor will ask one student to blindfold the other.
4. The school counselor will have each group member stand on opposite sides of the "mine field" from one another.
5. The school counselor will inform students that the objective of this activity is for the blindfolded student to make it safely across the "mine field" without stepping on any of the ball-like items.

6. The school counselor will instruct the students that the only student allowed to speak or give directions during this activity is the blindfolded student's partner.
7. Once the blindfolded student is ready, their partner will give directions, which should typically include which way to step across the "mine field" and how long the step should be.
8. The school counselor will explain that the challenge will be successfully completed when all students have safely made their way across the "mine field."
9. After each blindfolded participant has completed the course, the school counselor will ask each pair to switch places so that the guiding student becomes the blindfolded student.

Closing Discussion Questions/Activities

1. How does this activity relate to our experiences of being in this group?
2. Which role—blindfolded or guide—was easier?
3. What made communicating during this activity difficult?
4. Why is it so important that we take others' perspectives into account when we are communicating with them?

About the Group Workers

J. Scott Glass, PhD, NCC, LPC, is a professor of Counselor Education at East Carolina University and has worked as a program director for an outdoor adventure-based program that offers a variety of challenging courses and wilderness experiences. In this role, Dr. Glass has worked with thousands of school-aged children in both one-day and overnight experiences. These groups have typically focused on group cohesion, leadership skills and effective communication.

Allison Crow, PhD, NCC, LPC, is an assistant professor of Counselor Education at East Carolina University. Dr. Crow has taught courses in group procedures, creative counseling, and other master's level courses. She enjoys creative and experiential approaches in her clinical work, teaching, and scholarship.

Kylie P. Dotson-Blake, PhD, NCC, LPC, is an associate professor in Counselor Education at East Carolina University. As a school counselor and through grant-funded prevention programming, she has conducted groups with elementary and middle school students. As a counselor educator, Dr. Dotson-Blake focuses on the utilization of experiential activities in the implementation of group counseling in school settings.

Additional Resources

Rohnke, K. (1984). *Silver bullets: A guide to initiative problems, adventure games, and trust activities.* Kendall Hunt.

SOCIAL SKILLS SESSION **PLAN 13**

LEVEL	SESSION TITLE	TOPIC
Elementary, Middle & High	Paper Tattoos	Social Skills

STAGE   ☐ Orientation   ☐ Working   ☒ Closing

ASCA Mindsets Standards

Belief in development of whole self, including a healthy balance of mental, social/emotional, and physical well-being.

ASCA Behavior Standards

Learning Strategies

Demonstrate creativity.

Self-Management Skills

None

Social Skills

Use effective oral and written communication skills and listening skills.
Use effective collaboration and cooperation skills.

Learning Objectives

1. Students will identify a positive interpersonal impact that others have made on them.
2. Students will identify a central theme that has represented the overall interactions described to them by group members.

Materials

1. Paper
2. Pencils/markers/colored pencils/crayons

Session Procedure

1. The school counselor will give students a blank piece of paper and colored drawing utensils.
2. The school counselor will ask students to select a color and that will represent their contributions throughout the activity.
3. The school counselor will describe to the students that "As we complete this group experience, it may be helpful for you to learn the impact that you made on others by sharing something with each group member about the impact that they had on you. We will do this on paper so that you can take it home with you as a reminder of your time in the group and the interpersonal relationships that you built."
4. The school counselor will ask group members to write their names at the top of their papers. The school counselor will indicate that papers will be passed around the circle to each group member so they can add something to them. Then, when returned to the original group member, the paper will have a series of small symbols or shapes on them which reflect what "others learned from you, admired about you, or hoped for your future; ideally, it will make up a larger image as well so that you might see an overall theme emerge."

5. The school counselor will instruct students, "Let's begin. Everyone pass your paper to the person to your right. Now you have another student's paper. Draw a symbol or shape on their paper that symbolizes what you learned from them, what you admire about them, or what you hope for them in the future. At the side of the paper, you can also add a word or two that describes your image and place your initials next to it. When you have finished, pass the paper to the right and continue the process until your paper has come back to you. If you decide to add onto others' images, attempt to make your individual contribution part of a larger image."

6. After the images are complete and each student has contributed, the school counselor will have each student hold their image up one at a time so that other group members can individually discuss their contribution to that image.

   Discussion Questions: Now that you have seen and heard how others view you, can you describe why your peers added these symbols to your paper? Can you identify an overall theme that emerged from all the symbols combined? What might be a meaningful title for your image?

7. After each student has discussed their image, the school counselor can identify additional themes or connections that they noticed collectively from the group. For example, if several students contributed similar images and/or words to a specific drawing, the school counselor may process themes related to a particular interaction that was memorable. The school counselor can also bridge themes across individuals to connect specific students who have similar images or words.

8. If all students are willing, scan or photograph each image and share them with the group.

Closing Discussion Questions/Activities

1. How did you feel about contributing symbols or words to the other group members' papers?
2. How did you feel about seeing the symbols or words on your paper?
3. Did you learn more about the way others view you through this exercise?
4. Has the overall theme that you identified resonated with you?
5. What will you take away from this activity? How will it affect your life beyond the group?

About the Group Worker

Cheryl Pence Wolf, PhD, is an associate professor at Western Kentucky University. Dr. Wolf teaches group supervision for practicum and internship, group counseling, and school counseling. She has also served as the co-director for her program's on-site counseling clinic where she supervised and led groups within the community.

CREDITS

Decision-Making Groups

Introduction

Decision-making is at the very core of students' academic, career, and social/emotional development. Throughout their schooling, students acquire knowledge and skills and are assessed on the application of this information in various capacities. As students move through the educational environment, they are expected to become critical consumers of all sorts of information in order to make sound decisions associated with academics, career choices, peers, social media, et cetera. Within a comprehensive school counseling program, school counselors collaborate with others to support knowledge and skills associated with critical thinking. In doing so, they help students apply this information to their current lives by encouraging them to derive personal meaning from these learning experiences. For instance, elementary school counselors may run study skills groups to help support students who are struggling with executive functioning skills (e.g., organization, test taking). While the academic piece associated with learning study and test-taking skills may not appeal to all students, the process through which they learn these skills in a group setting with peers helps provide accountability and emotional support. Helping students set meaningful and realistic short- and long-term goals likewise helps them to feel more intrinsically motivated to practice these skills, further informing their future decision-making.

As students move through middle school into high school, they use critical thinking and executive functioning skills throughout their course selection and academic processes, while learning to generalize these skills into various community contexts. Providing knowledge, tools, and support, school counselors play an integral role in helping students embrace related challenges. The session plans in this section include decision-making as it applies to career choices, study and academic work skills, goal setting, healthy choices, and social interaction.

Data Discussion

Being able to collect and analyze data effectively is key to developing your comprehensive school counseling program, and is also important for your small-group counseling program (see Chapter 3 for more). Examining data that are accurate and appropriate for the goals of your small group is imperative in garnering support for a more robust small-group counseling program. Here are steps we hope you undertake as you review the sample sessions on decision-making.

Discuss Data Collection With a Peer/Colleague

School counselors are known for their ability to consult and collaborate with stakeholders—practices which help school counselors share best practices, generate new ideas, and align with the ASCA National Model for School Counseling programs. Consider your school's current needs and examine the following session plans related to decision-making. Then identify session plans that could be used to support your students. Next, consult with a peer or colleague about your rationale for the sessions you have selected and the data collection plan you have chosen to ensure you have thought through the issues you intend to address. Be sure to share with your colleague how you will measure progress. Finally, use the following steps to guide your process.

Take a Walk With Data Related to Decision-Making

For each of the sessions focused on decision-making, we ask that you engage in the following steps with either your colleague(s) or your course instructor(s):

Step 1 — General Data Consideration

Read the Learning Objectives for each small group on decision-making and then:

Ask yourself, What kinds of data might be relevant to collect based on the learning objectives stated? Are you most interested in the number of students served (participation) or are you more concerned with how your small group meets the mindsets and behaviors that are the target of your group (surveys, pretest/posttest)? Are you concerned about examining how improving students' decision-making skills might improve their academics (outcome)?

Disaggregating your data to determine if certain subgroups of students are disproportionately impacted is also essential in small-group planning. Do you have any suspicions that the issue of decision-making, or rather poor decision-making, is impacting any underserved or marginalized groups of students more than another (e.g., Black and Brown students are reporting feeling unsupported in their course selection process, or economically disadvantaged students are less often deciding to enroll in advanced curriculum/AP courses)?

Step 2 — Thoughts on Participation Data

After reading the general outline for the session:

What is a plan that would help you collect participation data? What would the collection of participation data look like in your decision-making group? How will you identify participants? What are participants' qualifying characteristics? How many times will participants meet? Will you take attendance at the start of each group? How will you record who attends? Think through these questions and become clear on who is participating in your group, why their participation is meaningful, and how you will document the number of sessions and member attendance so that after the group has ended you can accurately and confidently report participation data to stakeholders.

Step 3 — Thoughts on Mindsets and Behaviors Data

After reading the Closing Discussion Questions/Activities section for each session, ask:

When considering collecting mindsets and behaviors data, how might a pretest/posttest survey of group members in this group look? What questions would you want to ask to determine if the mindsets and behaviors you were targeting were achieved? Be sure to link pretest/posttest questions to the mindsets and behavior standards you intend to address through the group interventions you plan. For example, for a decision-making group, you might focus on Mindset Standard M 5., "Belief in using abilities to their fullest to achieve high-quality results and outcomes," and/or behavior standards B-SMS 1., "Demonstrate ability to assume responsibility," and/or B-SMS 9., "Demonstrate effective coping skills when faced with a problem." The specific mindset and behavior standards you select depends on the presenting problem(s) of your group participants and, relatedly, the purpose of the group.

Remember, you can access the *ASCA Mindsets and Behaviors Database* (https://scale-research.org/mandb/public_html/) for a quick reference and additional resources as you develop group interventions to support students who are working to improve decision-making skills.

Step 4 — Thoughts on Outcome Data

Upon reading the entire group plan, consider this:

The term outcome data refers to attendance, behavior, and academic outcomes. Accordingly, what is a metric you could examine to determine if this lesson helps broadly improve outcome data? Are you most concerned with examining decisions students are making related to their classroom behavior (e.g., office referrals or behavior chart data) or is it more important to consider how your group impacted students' attendance at school (e.g., truancy statistics, absentee rates)? Maybe you want to evaluate students' decision-making skills as they relate to making better choices around homework completion or test preparation (academics). One final note about outcome data: pick one! It is not always necessary to evaluate all three areas—attendance, behavior, and academics—for your small group. Target one area and let that guide your evaluation of the group's impact!

ASCA Mindsets Standards

Belief in development of whole self, including a healthy balance of mental, social/emotional, and physical well-being.

ASCA Behavior Standards

Learning Strategies

Demonstrate critical-thinking skills to make informed decisions.

Gather evidence and consider multiple perspectives to make informed decisions.

Demonstrate creativity.

Self-Management Skills

Demonstrate self-discipline and self-control.

Demonstrate effective coping skills when faced with a problem.

Social Skills

Demonstrate social maturity and behaviors appropriate to the situation and environment.

Learning Objectives

1. Students will be able to identify at least two environmental triggers that have caused them to lose self-control.
2. Students will be able to distinguish at least one inappropriate behavior that they have engaged in and indicate a mature, appropriate replacement behavior.

Materials

1. Paper
2. Pencils/markers/colored pencils/crayons
3. Makeshift stage or space for acting

Session Procedure

1. The school counselor will begin the group session with an opening activity. For this group, a weather report should be used to indicate how students are feeling for the day (e.g., 80 degrees and sunny for a good day).
   Discussion Questions: Who would like to start group today by describing your day using a weather report?
2. The school counselor will ask students about premonitions and have them identify movie scenes where they wish they could have warned the actor or character about what was going to occur. The school counselor will encourage students to make suggestions about what the actor or character could have done instead to avoid the undesired outcome.

3. The school counselor will show students the connection between movie characters and events they could have changed in their own lives. The school counselor will have a student volunteer an event in which they wished to have demonstrated better control of emotions.

4. The school counselor will stop the frame in action and have the student identify negative consequences and "replay" the scene with a better ending.
   Discussion Questions: Identify what was occurring before/during/after the event. Be sure to identify contributing factors (e.g., tired, hungry, location). Freeze frame (or stop) right before undesired behavior and describe any bodily sensations, identifying what you were trying to express and what might have been a better way to express that need. Now can you replay your scene but this time with the desired ending?

5. The school counselor will allow students to write and share their stories, focusing on the aforementioned aspects of their story (e.g., vulnerability, body awareness, alternative way to express need). The school counselor should encourage students to be aware of contributing factors, highlighting that this awareness can help them to pause before they act—this pause can lead to more control over emotional expressions and prevent negative outcomes.

6. In the closing activity, the school counselor will have each student "replay" their movie through acting, writing, or drawing.

7. The school counselor will review the idea of contributing factors, body awareness, and emotional triggers.

Closing Discussion Questions/Activities

1. How did you feel while replaying your movie?
2. How did you feel while watching others' movies?
3. What contributing factors impacted you the most?
4. How can you prevent mistakes you have previously made?
5. When do you see yourself utilizing your emotional control strategies?

About the Group Workers

Diana L. Wildermuth, PhD, NCC, LPC, is an assistant professor in the Department of Counseling Psychology at Temple University. Prior to joining Temple University, she was an assistant professor and the school counseling clinical coordinator at Caldwell University. She previously served as a school counselor and department chairperson for 15 years in southeastern Pennsylvania. Dr. Wildermuth has an extensive background in mental health, stress management, college and career counseling, and research methods, as well as with ESL learners. She has taught courses in counseling theory, group counseling, multicultural counseling, school counseling, and research methods. Her research has focused on factors such as academic resilience and acculturation, the role of the school counselor with ESL learners, and stress management for high anxiety students.

Cassandra Allen, NCC, is a high school counselor at Kennett High School in Kennett Square, Pennsylvania. She has been a counselor for 4 years serving a diverse student population and has experience coordinating social skills, stress management (test anxiety and preparation), and career development groups in high school.

Additional Resources

American School Counselor Association. (2014). *ASCA mindsets & behaviors for student success: K–12 college-and career-readiness standards for every student.* https://www.schoolcounselor.org/getmedia/7428a787-a452-4abb-afec-d78ec77870cd/Mindsets-Behaviors.pdf

Bonner, C. (2002). *Emotional regulation, interpersonal effectiveness, and distress tolerance skills for adolescents: A treatment manual.* Star Center.

ASCA Mindsets Standards

Belief in development of whole self, including a healthy balance of mental, social/emotional, and physical well-being.

Sense of belonging in the school environment.

Understanding that postsecondary education and life-long learning are necessary for long-term career success.

ASCA Behavior Standards

Learning Strategies

Demonstrate creativity.

Apply self-motivation and self-direction to learning.

Identity long- and short-term academic, career, and social/emotional goals.

Gather evidence and consider multiple perspectives to make informed decisions.

Self-Management Skills

Demonstrate ability to overcome barriers to learning.

Social Skills

Use effective oral and written communication skills and listening skills.

Create positive and supportive relationships with other students.

Learning Objectives

1. Students will be able to recognize their differences in a positive way.
2. Students will identify various personal identities.
3. Students will consider how their identities influence career selection/development.

Materials

1. Paper
2. Pencils/markers/colored pencils/crayons

Session Procedure

Activity One: What Is Your Identity?

1. The school counselor will introduce the topic of identity. Depending on the age of the students, the school counselor may ask the group what they think "identity" means.
2. The school counselor will tell students that identity answers the question "Who am I?"
3. The school counselor will provide an example answer, such as "I am kind, a girl, Hispanic, smart, a younger sister, and I love math."
4. The school counselor will give students their first sheet of paper, and tell the students, "Take a few minutes to write down your answer to the question 'Who am I?'"

5. If students are having trouble answering the question, the school counselor should ask them "What are some positive and kind things you know about your peers?"
Discussion Questions: What did you learn about yourself today? What did you learn about your peers today?

Activity Two: Identity Animals

1. The school counselor will give students another sheet of paper and ask the question "What is your favorite animal?"
2. The school counselor will go around the room and let each student answer.
3. The school counselor will instruct students to draw a picture of themselves as their favorite animal doing something that they love and enjoy. For example, students can draw a dog playing soccer or an elephant teaching students.
Discussion Questions: What are some of the attributes of the animal that you drew? How might these attributes help you to be successful in your future? What types of careers would be well-matched with these characteristics?

Closing Discussion Questions/Activities

1. What is one thing that you learned about someone else in group today?
2. What is one thing that you learned about yourself today?

About the Group Workers

Amanda R. Friday, M.Ed, is a third-year doctoral student in the Department of Counseling at George Washington University's Graduate School of Education and Human Development. She has her master's degree in Education from Virginia Commonwealth University and a master's degree in School Counseling from GWU. She is also the senior career counselor for the Graduate School of Education and Human Development at GWU. Ms. Friday's research interests include career transition and development, social justice, intersectionality, teambuilding and group work, and athletic career retirement.

Christian D. Chan (he, him, his), PhD, NCC is an assistant professor in the Department of Counseling and Educational Development at the University of North Carolina at Greensboro and a proud Queer Person of Color. As a scholar-activist, his interests revolve around intersectionality; multiculturalism in counseling practice, supervision, and counselor education; social justice and activism; career development; critical research methodologies; and couple, family, and group modalities with socialization/communication of cultural factors. Dedicated to mentorship for leaders and scholars, he has actively contributed to over 49 peer-reviewed publications in journals, books, and edited volumes and has conducted over 120 refereed presentations at the national, regional, and state levels.

ASCA Mindsets Standards

Belief in development of whole self, including a healthy balance of mental, social/emotional, and physical well-being.

Self-confidence in the ability to succeed.

ASCA Behavior Standards

Learning Strategies

Identify long- and short-term academic, career, and social/emotional goals.

Self-Management Skills

Demonstrate perseverance to achieve long- and short-term goals.

Social Skills

Create positive and supportive relationships with other students.

Demonstrate empathy.

Learning Objectives

1. Students will understand the definition and application of "grit."
2. Students will identify a long- and short-term academic or career goal.
3. Students will share the plans that they have to achieve long- and short-term goals.

Materials

1. Grit Scale (from http://angeladuckworth.com/grit-scale/)
2. Computers
3. Three tennis balls per every 2–3 group members
4. Printed juggling instructions
5. *Grit: The Power Passion and Perseverance* video by Dr. Angela Lee Duckworth
6. *The Power of Believing That You Can Improve* video by Dr. Carol Dweck

Session Procedure

Activity One: Taking the Grit Scale

1. The school counselor will have students begin the session by taking the Grit Scale.
2. The school counselor will explain to the students that these results do not define the individual and that they can change depending on a variety of factors (e.g., taking the scale when healthy vs. taking it when sick).
3. The school counselor will discuss grit, which is defined as having passion and perseverance for very long-term goals.
4. The school counselor will discuss the scale item by item by talking about what the results may mean for academic and career development.

Discussion Questions: What is one long-term goal that you have for your academic career? What is one long-term goal that you have for your career in general?

5. The school counselor will have students highlight similarities in each student's goals.

Activity Two: Developing Grit

1. The school counselor will distribute sets of tennis balls to each student.
2. The school counselor will explain how to juggle by reading the instructions to the students.
3. The school counselor will instruct students to pair up with one another by forming groups of two or three students and having them practice juggling.
4. After 5 minutes have passed, the school counselor will process this exercise with students.
   Discussion Questions: Who has experienced juggling before? What was the process like for those who have never juggled before? What was it like for those who have juggled before? How can you become a "good" juggler or a "better" juggler?
5. The school counselor will discuss how juggling relates to grit by explaining that it takes passion and perseverance to become a really good juggler and that the best jugglers can manage juggling numerous tennis balls.
   Discussion Questions: Have there been times when you've tried something new and ended up giving up? Was there a reason for giving up? Has there ever been something new that you tried that you didn't like at first but then you grew to like it more and more over time?

Activity Three: Grit and How It Relates to Mindset

1. The school counselor will show the students the video *Grit: The Power & Passion of Perseverance* by Dr. Angela Duckworth.
   Discussion Questions: What did you think about what Dr. Duckworth had to say about grit?
2. The school counselor will show the students the video *Fixed Growth vs. Growth Mindset* by Dr. Carol Dweck.
   Discussion Questions: What do you think about what Dr. Dweck had to say about grit and growth mindset? Do you see a relationship between grit and growth mindset? Has there been a time when you felt like you changed your mindset about a particular situation? How did that change in your mindset happen?

Activity Four: Identifying Short- and Long-Term Goals

1. The school counselor will discuss how grit is acquired by students through small steps each day—for example, by comparing grit to playing a musical instrument: "At first, the music may not sound pretty, but with practice, it can be made to sound much better over time. Passion and persistence are key."
2. The school counselor will talk with students about a current or previous long-term goal and discuss the steps needed to meet that goal.
   Discussion Questions: What is one long-term goal that you would like to accomplish? When would you like to achieve this goal? What personal strengths do you have to reach this goal? What can you do on a regular basis to reach that goal? How long would it take to carry out this behavior each week? Is there a way that we as a group can support each other in successfully completing these goals?

Closing Discussion Questions/Activities

1. How confident do you feel in your ability to develop grit?
2. Can you share one academic or career-focused long-term goal that you have and one activity that you can do on a regular basis to meet your goal?

About the Group Workers

Rebekah Reysen, PhD, is the assistant director of Academic Support Programs at the Center for Student Success and First-Year Experience at the University of Mississippi. Dr. Reysen coordinates over 100 sections of academically at-risk students in college each year, including overseeing 64 personal growth groups. She is passionate about helping students discover their calling and career path and utilizes career resources frequently in her practice.

Patrick Perry, EdD, received his bachelor's degree from the University of Memphis and his master's degree and doctorate in Leadership from the University of Memphis. He has worked as director of the Luckyday Scholarship Programs at the University of Mississippi since 2008. Dr. Perry enjoys working with students to identify the best resources needed to reach their goals.

Additional Resources

Duckworth, A. L. (2013, April). *Grit: The power of passion and perseverance* [Video]. TED Conferences. https://www.ted.com/talks/angela_lee_duckworth_grit_the_power_of_passion_and_perseverance?language=en

Duckworth, A. L., Peterson, C., Matthews, M. D., & Kelly, D. R. (2007). Grit: Perseverance and passion for long-term goals. *Journal of Personality and Social Psychology, 92*(6), 1087–1101.

Dweck, C. (2014, November). *The power of believing that you can improve* [Video]. TED Conferences. https://www.ted.com/talks/carol_dweck_the_power_of_believing_that_you_can_improve?language=en

Perry, P., & Reysen, R. (2016). Not so soft skills: Emotional intelligence and grit. In L. Banahan (Ed.), *The Ole Miss first-year experience text* (pp. 113–122). Nautilus.

Reysen, R., Reysen, M., Perry, P., & Knight, R. D. (in press). *Not so soft skills: The importance of grit to college student success*. 12th Annual National Symposium on Student Retention Conference Proceedings.

WikiHow. (n.d.). *How to Juggle*. http://www.wikihow.com/Juggle

DECISION-MAKING SESSION PLAN 4

LEVEL	SESSION TITLE	TOPIC
Elementary	Organizing Our Whatchamacallits	Decision-Making

STAGE   ☐ Orientation   ☒ Working   ☐ Closing

ASCA Mindsets Standards

Belief in development of whole self, including a healthy balance of mental, social/emotional, and physical well-being.

Self-confidence in ability to succeed.

Positive attitude toward work and learning.

ASCA Behavior Standards

Learning Strategies

Demonstrate creativity.

Use time-management, organizational, and study skills.

Set high standards of quality.

Self-Management Skills

Demonstrate ability to assume responsibility.

Demonstrate self-discipline and self-control.

Demonstrate ability to work independently.

Social Skills

Demonstrate advocacy skills and ability to assert self, when necessary.

Learning Objectives

1. Students will identify ways in which organization can positively impact their academic and personal lives.
2. Students will identify and apply specific, creative techniques to organizing their desks at school or their bedrooms at home.

Materials

1. *I Can't Find My Whatchamacallit!!* by Julia Cook
2. Classroom desks filled with various items (e.g., papers, pencils, pieces of trash, books)
3. Three large containers or bins/baskets
4. Paper
5. Markers
6. Tape

Session Procedure

1. Prior to the lesson, the school counselor will write the following phrases on separate pieces of paper and will then attach one sign to each container for a total of one sign per container: "Keep Me," "Toss Me," and "Give Me Away."

2. The school counselor will ask students if they have ever heard of the word *whatchamacallit* and have them make predictions for what it might mean based on previous knowledge or the illustration on the book cover.

3. The school counselor can use the following comprehension/discussion questions while reading the students the book *Whatchamacallit!!*:

   Page 6: When it comes to the organization of your belongings, would you say that you are more like Cletus or his cousin, Bocephus? Why? What does Cletus do with his belongings that makes him disorganized? Do you do these same things, too? What does Bocephus do with his belongings that makes him organized? Do you do these same things, too?

   Page 9: Have you ever had a difficult time finding a particular belonging either in your desk at school or room at home? What were some emotions that you felt while looking for this belonging? What consequences did you experience when you couldn't locate your belonging?

   Page 13: Why do you think it is important to be aware of three things: your brain, your body, and your stuff?

   Pages 18–19: How can we change these questions to help us decide if we need to keep, toss, or give away items located in our desks or backpacks at school?

4. The school counselor will draw the students' attention to the classroom desk located in the room.

5. The school counselor will explain to the students that they are going to engage in the organization of the desk belongings using the "Keep Me, Toss Me, Give Me Away" process used together by Cletus and Bocephus.

6. The school counselor will instruct the students to take turns removing one item at a time from their desks until all items are gone. As they do this, the school counselor will ask that students share each item with one another.

7. If a student needs help deciding, the school counselor will indicate that they may use the "phone a friend" option to elicit assistance from their peers or the school counselor.

   Discussion Questions: What did it feel like when you were trying to decide whether to keep, toss, or give away an item in the desk? What items were harder to decide upon?

8. The school counselor will then challenge students to engage in the "Keep Me, Toss Me, Give Me Away" technique in order to organize their classroom desks within the next few days so that all students can report to the group about their independent organization experience during the next group session.

Closing Discussion Questions/Activities

1. How could you use the "Keep Me, Toss Me, Give Me Away" technique to organize your own desk within the classroom? How about items from your bedroom at home?

2. How do you think that your grade and your relationships with your parents or guardians and classroom teacher might change if you apply the "Keep Me, Toss Me, Give Me Away" technique on your own to organize your personal belongings?

3. In addition to the "Keep Me, Toss Me, Give Me Away" technique, brainstorm one additional way that you can organize your belongings either in school or at home.

About the Group Workers

Julia Cook has her master's degree in Elementary School Counseling. While serving as a school counselor, she often used children's books to enhance her classroom lessons and is now well-recognized as an internationally award-winning children's book author and parenting expert.

With over one million books in print, Ms. Cook has presented in over a thousand schools across the country and abroad, regularly delivers keynote addresses at national education and counseling conferences, and has 72 published children's books. The goal behind all of her books and efforts is to actively involve young people in her fun and creative stories and teach them to become life-long problem solvers. Inspirations for her books come from working with children and carefully listening to parents and teachers. Ms. Cook is the recipient of numerous book awards including the National Parenting Seal of Approval, the Mom's Choice Gold Award, and the Association of Educational Publisher's Distinguished Achievement Award.

Ashley Pugliese is a graduate student at Temple University working toward her master's degree of Education in Counseling Psychology with a focus in school counseling. After graduating with her bachelor's degree in psychology from the University of Delaware, she worked as the case manager/care coordinator at Drexel University's Student Counseling Center in Philadelphia for 3 years. Ms. Pugliese interns at an elementary school in Montgomery County, Pennsylvania.

Additional Resources

Cook, J., & Hyde, H. M. (2015). *I can't find my whatchamacallit!!* National Center for Youth Issues.

Appendix A
Pretest/Posttest

1. I believe that being organized can help me find personal items quickly, such as homework or toys:
   a. True
   b. False

2. I believe that organizing my personal items, such as my homework or toys, is too difficult:
   a. True
   b. False

3. I believe that I can organize my personal belongings on my own:
   a. True
   b. False

4. I can name two ways to organize my personal belongings:
   a. _____
   b. _____

DECISION-MAKING SESSION **PLAN 5**

LEVEL	SESSION TITLE	TOPIC
Elementary	Making Good Decisions with Police	Decision-Making

STAGE ☐ Orientation   ☒ Working   ☐ Closing

ASCA Mindsets Standards

Belief in development of whole self, including a healthy balance of mental, social/emotional, and physical well-being.

ASCA Behavior Standards

Learning Strategies

Gather evidence and consider multiple perspectives to make informed decisions.

Self-Management Skills

Demonstrate self-discipline and self-control.

Demonstrate effective coping skills when faced with a problem.

Demonstrate personal safety skills.

Social Skills

Create relationships with adults that support success.

Demonstrate ethical decision-making and social responsibility.

Demonstrate social maturity and behaviors appropriate to the situation and environment.

Learning Objectives

1. Students will discuss their own feelings about police and law enforcement.
2. Students will practice specific skills to use when interacting with the police.
3. Students will describe the importance of utilizing these skills to foster relationships with law enforcement.

Materials

1. Law enforcement officer or school police officer as a guest speaker
2. News report about police shootings
3. Poster board
4. Markers
5. Two index cards

Session Procedure

Activity One: Our Ideas

1. The school counselor will have students break up into groups and verbally respond to the following questions:

   - How would you feel if the police approached you?
   - Name one thing you should do if approached by the police.
   - Name one thing you should *not* do if approached by the police.

- What can you do if you feel that you were mistreated by the police?
- What is one question you have for a police officer?

2. The school counselor will ask for volunteers to read each answer and have the students compare their responses.
   Discussion Questions: Why should you or should you not do that action? What may be the outcome? What do you think the police officer may be thinking?
3. The school counselor will monitor discussions and check to see if students' questions for the police officer are focused. The school counselor should take note of some of the best questions to ask later in the session.

Activity Two: Discussion With an Officer

1. The school counselor will have students gather into the large group and introduce the police officer.
   Note: The police officer will ideally have prepared their discussion with the school counselor prior to the session and discuss ways that students and police can work together to increase the likelihood of positive outcomes. The police officer should also reiterate to students that the vast majority of police officers do not want to harm anyone in the community. Additionally, the officer will emphasize that they are a resource to help students and their families.
2. The school counselor will allow students to share their perspectives about the dos and don'ts with each other and the police officer, discussing their rationale for these lists. The police officer should be engaged in this conversation.

Activity Three: Role-Play

1. The school counselor will ask a student to volunteer to role-play a scenario in which a police officer can help an individual who needs assistance.
2. The school counselor will ask students to provide positive feedback and offer suggestions to improve or create alternative ideas.
3. The school counselor will ask the police officer to lead a discussion with the students, while the school counselor takes notes on the poster for the students
   Discussion Questions: What would you like to see a police officer do if they stop you or a member of your family?

Closing Discussion Questions/Activities

1. Students will have the opportunities to ask their questions from the index cards. The police officer will answer the questions and offer insight about what to do if they feel the police mistreat them.
2. On the second index card, students will write a one-word response about their current feelings about the police after the session, which will be compared to previous feelings.
3. Have your feelings changed or stayed the same? How and why do you think this happened?
4. Can you name one skill you have learned and why it is beneficial if approached by the police?

About the Group Worker

Sarah Daly is a doctoral candidate in the Department of Criminal Justice at Rutgers University. She spent 11 years as a public school teacher and school counselor working with at-risk youth. She currently works as a professor of criminal justice at Saint Vincent College.

Additional Resources

U.S. Department of Justice. (n.d.). *Community oriented policing services*. https://cops.usdoj.gov/

U.S. Department of Justice. (2014). *Community policing defined*. https://cops.usdoj.gov/RIC/Publications/cops-p157-pub.pdf

Williams, B. N., Brower, R. S., & Earle Klay, W. (2016) Community-centered police professionalism: A template for reflective professionals and learning organizations with implications for the co-production of public safety and public order. *Police Journal: Theory, Practice and Principles, 89*(2), 151–173.

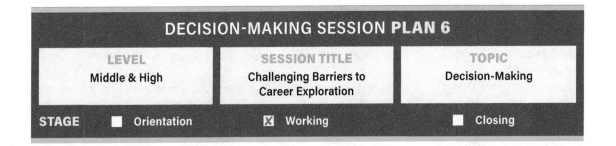

ASCA Mindsets Standards

Belief in development of whole self, including a healthy balance of mental, social/emotional, and physical well-being.

Self-confidence in ability to succeed.

Understanding that postsecondary education and life-long learning are necessary for long-term career success.

ASCA Behavior Standards

Learning Strategies

Demonstrate critical-thinking skills to make informed decisions.

Identify long- and short-term academic, career, and social/emotional goals.

Gather evidence and consider multiple perspectives to make informed decisions.

Self-Management Skills

Demonstrate ability to manage transitions and ability to adapt to changing situations and responsibilities.

Demonstrate ability to work independently.

Social Skills

Create positive and supportive relationships with other students.

Use effective collaboration and cooperation skills.

Demonstrate advocacy skills and ability to assert self, when necessary.

Learning Objectives

1. Students will communicate postsecondary interests and plans.
2. Students will develop awareness of barriers when making decisions toward their college and career planning.
3. Students will draw upon the insight of others to identify ways around barriers in pursuit of postsecondary plans.

Materials

1. Student Barrier Diagram (see Appendix A)
2. Pencils/pens
3. Paper
4. Whiteboard and dry erase markers

Session Procedure

Activity One: College and Career Exploration

1. The school counselor will ask students to take out a piece of paper and request that each student describe five different areas of interest toward a potential field of study in college or plans for employment.

2. The school counselor will assist students in communicating their interests by describing popular fields of study in college and professional fields in the workforce (e.g., nursing, accounting, entrepreneurship, architecture, construction, teaching). The school counselor should have a list of occupations and their connected courses of study regarding the following topics: 10 male-dominated occupations, 10 female-dominated occupations, 10 high-prestige professions, and 10 low-prestige professions. Suggested information for each of these topics can be accessed through the Additional Resources section.
   Note: The titles of these topics will function to guide the conversation with students. The topics should not be shared with students to encourage critical thought.

3. The school counselor will introduce the idea that sociological barriers and personal biases exist that can influence college and career decision-making using Linda Gottfredson's theory of circumscription (eliminating unacceptable alternatives because they do not fit personal expectations) and compromise (choosing accessible options over challenging options because they are more congruent with personal self-efficacy) to the students.

4. The school counselor should explain to the students that sociological barriers may pertain to gender stereotypes (e.g., females lack the initiative and confidence to function in high-responsibility management positions; males lack the caring and sensitive nature required to function as a nurse or caregiver); socioeconomic status (e.g., low-income students lack high-quality education, adult guidance, and the knowledge and motivation to succeed in a college atmosphere); and minority discrimination (e.g., students of African American and Hispanic backgrounds cannot enter highly respected professions with lucrative salaries in a similar manner as their White counterparts).

5. The school counselor should explain that personal biases may pertain to cultural values (e.g., expectations that students will contribute to the financial stability of the family during or immediately after receiving a high school education, thereby limiting opportunities for postsecondary education) and parental attitudes (e.g., messages encouraging students to enter similar professions as a mother or father; expectations that students will continue the family business).

6. The school counselor will request that the students rank the same five areas of college or career interest according to three different variables: sex roles (most male-oriented to most female-oriented), prestige (most difficult to succeed to least difficult to succeed), and preference (most interested to least interested).

Activity Two: Challenging Barriers to College and Career Exploration

1. The school counselor will explain that a student barrier diagram will be constructed on the whiteboard that demonstrates the various fields of interest all students have described. The diagram will include a *y*-axis (prestige) and an *x*-axis (gender).

2. The school counselor will facilitate a discussion about student perspectives. One area of interest for each student will be placed on the diagram and potential barriers to student achievement of college and career goals will be discussed. Potential barriers may include gender stereotypes, minority stereotypes, cultural values, a lack of adult guidance, parental expectations, little awareness of the college application and/or job application process, poor understanding of personal strengths, and a poor self-esteem regarding postsecondary success.

Discussion Questions: Where should the college and career interest of a doctor be placed on the diagram?

3. Through group facilitation of student perspectives, the school counselor will place a marker to distinguish the area of interest according to the two axes.

   Discussion Questions: What sociological barriers, such as discrimination or gender stereotypes, may influence your group decision-making to place this area of interest toward the high-prestige portion of the axis? What personal biases may influence your group decision-making to place this area of interest toward the female portion of the axis (e.g., cultural)?

Closing Discussion Questions/Activities

1. How does this activity change your perception of future college and career decision-making?
2. How can you overcome such barriers for college or career planning and success?

About the Group Worker

Patrick Rowley is a doctoral student in the Counselor Education program at Virginia Polytechnic Institute and State University. His dissertation topic focuses on improving school counseling practices toward effective postsecondary planning for emotional support populations in urban environments.

Additional Resources

Gottfredson, L. S. (1981). Circumscription and compromise: A developmental theory of occupational aspirations. *Journal of Counseling Psychology, 28*(6), 545–579. https://doi.org/10.1037/0022-0167.28.6.545

Brown, D., & Brooks, L. (1996). *Career choice and development* (4th ed.). Jossey-Bass.

Brown, S. D., & Lent, R. W. (2005). *Career development and counseling: Putting theory and research to work* (2nd ed.). Wiley.

Appendix A
Student Barriers Diagram

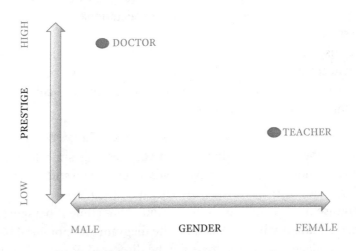

Appendix B
Pretest/Posttest
Please describe any barriers or biases that may influence your college and career planning:

1. _____

2. _____

3. _____

4. _____

5. _____

6. _____

7. _____

8. _____

9. _____

10. _____

ASCA Mindsets Standards

Belief in development of whole self, including a healthy balance of mental, social/emotional, and physical well-being.

Self-confidence in the ability to succeed.

Understanding that postsecondary education and life-long learning are necessary for long-term career success.

ASCA Behavior Standards

Learning Strategies

Demonstrate critical-thinking skills to make informed decisions.

Apply self-motivation and self-direction to learning.

Identify long- and short-term academic, career, and social/emotional goals.

Self-Management Skills

Demonstrate ability to assume responsibility.

Demonstrate perseverance to achieve long- and short-term goals.

Social Skills

Use effective oral and written communication skills and listening skills.

Learning Objectives

1. Students will be able to identify three new roles that they will embrace as a college student.
2. Students will be able to identify three individuals who can assist them with being successful in these new roles.

Materials

1. Two Blank Face templates per student (see Twinkl, 2010)
2. Scissors
3. Markers/colored pencils/crayons

Session Procedure

Pregroup Preparation

The school counselor will ask the students to prepare for the next group by writing a reflection about their thoughts and feelings about becoming a first-generation college student.

Activity One: Myself Today, My Role Today

1. The school counselor will remind students that they have been reflecting on their identities as they prepare to transition into becoming first-generation college students.
2. The school counselor should explain to students that they have made great accomplishments academically and personally in order to soon be starting this new phase of their lives, and

that sometimes students feel both excited and anxious about the idea of becoming the first college student in their families.

3. The school counselor should explain that art is often used to help individuals of every age express their thoughts and feelings.

4. The school counselor should show students the blank face templates and invite them to choose the set of two faces that best represents them.

5. The school counselor will explain that the students will create the first face template, which represents them as they think and feel about themselves today. Students should be asked to include some symbols, elements, or an expression that tells the group who they are presently.

6. The school counselor should stress that artistic ability is not the point of the activity—the art should instead be a vehicle for processing students' thoughts and feelings.

Activity Two: My Future College Self, My Future Role

1. After 10 minutes has passed, the school counselor will inform the group that they will be working on the second face template. Students should choose symbols, elements, or an expression that they think will show who they aim to be in college.
   Discussion Questions: What symbols, elements, or expressions from the first face template will be the same? What might be new when you create this second self-expression?

2. The school counselor should stress that this face template might reflect how students are feeling and what thoughts or anticipations they might have when they are a college student.

Activity Three: My College Role—What It Might Look Like?

The school counselor should invite the students to share their two representations of themselves to the group and explain what each face represents.

Closing Discussion Questions/Activities

1. What academic achievements have you accomplished that make you look forward to going to college?

2. What concerns or emotions have you felt as a result of this activity?

3. What can you do beginning today that will assist you in preparing for your upcoming role and responsibilities as a college student?

4. What barriers do you anticipate as you move into your new role?

5. What support do you have now, and what type of support will you need in your new role?

6. What did you learn from others in the group as they presented their face templates and discussed their future roles in college?

About the Group Workers

Lee Edmonson Grimes, PhD, NCC, LPC, is a counselor educator at Valdosta State University. As a school counselor for 10 years, Dr. Grimes has led small groups on a variety of topics at all levels of education.

Natoya Haskins, PhD, LPC, is a counselor educator at the University of William and Mary. Dr. Haskins has led groups specifically for marginalized groups of students at the middle and high school levels, addressing topics such as anger, academic success, behavior modification, empowerment, grief, and self-esteem.

References

Twinkl. (2010). *Blank faces templates*. Retrieved from http://www.twinkl.co.uk/resource/t-t-2151-blank-faces-templates

Additional Resources

Borrero, N. (2011). Shared success: Voices of first-generation college-bound Latino/as. *Multicultural Education, 18*(4), 24–30.

Chang, J., & Nylund, D. (2013). Narrative and solution-focused therapies: A twenty-year retrospective. *Journal of Systemic Therapies, 32*(2), 72–88. https://doi.org/10.1521/jsyt.2013.32.2.72

National Center for Educational Statistics. (2010). *Status and trends in the education of racial and ethnic groups.* http://nces.ed.gov/pubsearch/pubsinfo.asp?pubid=2010015

Smith, W. L., & Zhang, P. (2010). The impact of key factors on the transition from high school to college among first- and second-generation students. *Journal of the First-Year Experience and Students in Transition, 22*(2), 49–70.

White, M., & Epston, D. (1990). *Narrative means to therapeutic ends.* Norton.

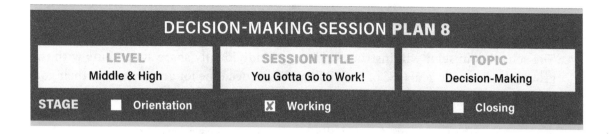

ASCA Mindsets Standards

Belief in development of whole self, including a healthy balance of mental, social/emotional, and physical well-being.

Positive attitude toward work and learning.

ASCA Behavior Standards

Learning Strategies

Apply self-motivation and self-direction to learning.

Self-Management Skills

Demonstrate perseverance to achieve long- and short-term goals.

Demonstrate ability to overcome barriers to learning.

Social Skills

None

Learning Objectives

1. Students will understand how their actions have positive and negative consequences, which directly impact their stress levels.
2. Students will be able to identify current barriers to their academic motivation and success.
3. Students will develop short- and long-term goals that can contribute to academic success, while lowering stress levels.

Materials

1. Actions & Consequences worksheet (see Appendix A)
2. SMART Goals worksheet (see Appendix B)
3. Paper
4. Pencils/pens

Session Procedure

1. The school counselor will engage the students in a discussion about the importance of attendance and going to school. Some students may need additional prompting to understand the connection between school and work, as well as understanding that consequences can be both positive and negative.
2. The school counselor will distribute the Actions & Consequences worksheet to the students and have students complete three to five statements using the following sentence frame:

    a. If I do/do not _____, then _____ will/will not happen and this will/will not cause stress.

3. The school counselor will instruct students to review or reflect on their written statements and identify at least one short-term goal and one long-term goal, using the SMART Goal prompts.

4. The school counselor will instruct students to individually share statements with the group, their specific goal ("S" of SMART) and their deadline for accomplishing their goal ("T" of SMART).

5. Depending upon the developmental levels of the students, it is possible to have Steps 3 and 4 occur within another session. Additionally, as a follow-up, the school counselor can use these goals as the check-in activity for subsequent group counseling sessions or after termination of the group.

Closing Discussion Questions/Activities

1. What is the relationship between school attendance, college, and/or the world of work?
2. Our behaviors and actions have consequences, both positive and negative. What are some positive and negative consequences?
3. What is a positive consequence of going to school? What is a positive consequence of going to college or work?
4. What is a negative consequence of not going to school? What is a negative consequence of not going to college or work?
5. How is your stress impacted by your decisions?

About the Group Worker

Sandra Logan, PhD, CSC, NCC, NCSC, DCC, ACS, is a clinical assistant professor at the University of Alabama. She has been employed as a professional school counselor and loves working with groups, especially those focused on academic improvement and attendance. Additionally, Dr. Logan enjoys incorporating expressive arts into her clinical and supervisory practices.

Additional Resources

Doran, G. T. (1981). There's a S.M.A.R.T. way to write management's goals and objectives. *Management Review, 70*(11), 35–36.

Appendix A
Actions & Consequences

Complete the following statements that outline your actions and their consequences:

If I do/do not _____ , then _____ will/will not happen and this will/will not cause stress.

If I do/do not _____ , then _____ will/will not happen and this will/will not cause stress.

If I do/do not _____ , then _____ will/will not happen and this will/will not cause stress.

If I do/do not _____ , then _____ will/will not happen and this will/will not cause stress.

If I do/do not _____ , then _____ will/will not happen and this will/will not cause stress.

Appendix B
SMART Goals

SMART Goals Specific — Measurable — Achievable — Relevant — Time Specific	
Stress Goal #1 (Short-Term)	**Stress Goal #1 (Long-Term)**
Specific (Describe your goal: What exactly will you accomplish?)	**Specific** (Describe your goal: What exactly will you accomplish?)
Measurable (How can you track your progress? How will you know when you have reached this goal?)	**Measurable** (How can you track your progress? How will you know when you have reached this goal?)
Achievable (Can you achieve this goal with effort and commitment? Do you have the resources to achieve this goal? If not, how will you get them?)	**Achievable** (Can you achieve this goal with effort and commitment? Do you have the resources to achieve this goal? If not, how will you get them?)
Relevant (Why is this goal significant in your life?)	**Relevant** (Why is this goal significant in your life?)
Time Specific (When will you reach your goal?)	**Time Specific** (When will you reach your goal?)

Appendix C
Pretest/Posttest

1. I believe that I can be successful in school:
   a. All of the time
   b. Sometimes
   c. Once in a while
   d. Never

2. I believe that if I attend school every day, I can learn:
   a. True
   b. False

3. The reason why I don't come to school every day is:
   a. I don't know
   b. I don't feel safe
   c. I am too stressed out/overwhelmed
   d. I have to take care of my family or obligations

4. I believe that I can meet my short-term goals:
   a. True
   b. False

5. I believe that I can meet my long-term goals:
   a. True
   b. False

DECISION-MAKING SESSION PLAN 9

LEVEL	SESSION TITLE	TOPIC
Middle & High	Sugar and Spice and Everything Nice	Decision-Making

STAGE   ☐ Orientation   ☒ Working   ☐ Closing

ASCA Mindsets Standards

Belief in development of whole self, including a healthy balance of mental, social/emotional, and physical well-being.

Positive attitude toward work and learning.

ASCA Behavior Standards

Learning Strategies

Gather evidence and consider multiple perspectives to make informed decisions.

Self-Management Skills

Demonstrate ability to assume responsibility.

Social Skills

Demonstrate advocacy skills and ability to assert self, when necessary.

Learning Objectives

1. Students will gather information to support nontraditional career decision-making.
2. Students will demonstrate personal responsibility for career choice.
3. Students will reflect upon their self-efficacy to pursue a nontraditional career.

Materials

1. Blank, full-face costume masks (e.g., purchased from a craft store or constructed out of plaster, clay, plastic, styrene, cardboard, construction paper)
2. Craft items (e.g., glue gun, craft glue, tape, paint, feathers, beads, flowers, ribbon, glitter)
3. Paper
4. Pencils/pens
5. Scissors
6. Printouts of nontraditional careers
7. Computer lab

   Note: This is a group for girls to learn more about nontraditional careers.

Session Procedure

1. The school counselor will provide a list of nontraditional, male-dominated (75% or more of the employees) careers provided by the U.S. Department of Labor.
2. The school counselor will ask the students to select one of the careers that is interesting to them.
3. The school counselor will ask the students to read about the career they've chosen and print at least one picture or symbol that represents that nontraditional career.

4. The school counselor will ask the students to take out a piece of paper and a pen/pencil.
5. On one side of the paper, the school counselor will ask students to create a list of the reasons the nontraditional career is interesting to them and the personal attributes that would make them a good fit for that career; on the other side of the paper, students will be asked to list the reasons they are hesitant to pursue the nontraditional career.
6. After each student's list has been created, the school counselor will ask the students to decorate the front of their masks with pictures and symbols that represent the nontraditional career and their personal attributes that would make them a good fit for the that career.
7. When finished, the school counselor will ask students to decorate the inside of the mask with symbols that represent their concerns about the career or their own characteristics that make them hesitant to pursue that career.

Closing Discussion Questions/Activities

1. Describe why this nontraditional career is interesting to you.
2. How would you be able to express yourself and your ideas through this nontraditional career?
3. What is your perception of your competency in this nontraditional career?
4. What are the reasons that you would be successful in this nontraditional career?
5. Who would encourage and/or discourage you to pursue this nontraditional career?
6. What barriers would you encounter working in this nontraditional career?
7. What resources do you have that would support your work in this nontraditional career?
8. How would you advocate for yourself and overcome barriers in this nontraditional career?
9. What nongender-dominant perspectives do you believe you could bring to this nontraditional career?
10. What are the benefits of being "unique" in a male-dominated career?
11. How would having a more balanced gender representation be beneficial to this career?

About the Group Worker

Jake J. Protivnak, PhD, LPC, is an associate professor and chairperson of the Department of Counseling, Special Education and School Psychology at Youngstown State University. He is a professional school counselor with primary teaching responsibilities in school counseling.

Additional Resources

Betz, N. E., Klein, K. L., & Taylor, K. M. (1996). Evaluation of a short form of the career decision-making self-efficacy scale. *Journal of Career Assessment, 4*(1), 47–57. https://doi.org/10.1177/106907279600400103

Tang, M., Pan, W., & Newmeyer, M. D. (2008). Factors influencing high school students' career aspirations. *Professional School Counseling, 11*(5), 285–295. https://doi.org/10.1177%2F2156759X0801100502

Appendix A
Pretest/Posttest
How many nontraditional male-dominated careers can you list?

1. _____

2. _____

3. _____

4. _____

5. _____

6. _____

7. _____

8. _____

9. _____

10. _____

Which nontraditional career is the most interesting to you?

_____

ASCA Mindsets Standards

Belief in development of whole self, including a healthy balance of mental, social/emotional, and physical well-being.

Belief in using abilities to their fullest to achieve high-quality results and outcomes.

ASCA Behavior Standards

Learning Strategies

Demonstrate critical-thinking skills to make informed decisions.

Self-Management Skills

Demonstrate ability to assume responsibility.

Social Skills

Create relationships with adults that support success.

Learning Objectives

1. Students will be able to describe the three types of decisions.
2. Students will be able to name positive and negative consequences of decisions that relate to future choices.
3. Students will identify at least two adults to support them in the decision-making process.

Materials

1. "Would You Rather …" questions (see Appendix A)
2. Five Steps of Responsible Decision-Making handout (see Appendix B)
3. Container or basket
4. Paper
5. Pencils/pens
6. Whiteboard/chalkboard

Session Procedure

1. Before the start of the group session, the school counselor should select 10 questions from the "Would You Rather …" questions, which should be cut into separate pieces and placed in a container or basket.
2. The school counselor will invite the students to play "Would You Rather …" to start the group's transition to the topic of making decisions. Students should be invited one at a time to select a slip of paper, share their question with the group, and then select a choice.
   Discussion Questions: How did you make the decision when you were asked to choose between two options? Were some options more challenging than others? If yes, how so?
3. The school counselor should briefly explain that each student quickly made choices and decisions. The school counselor should reflect what themes were heard from the students regarding how they made their decisions during the game.

4. The school counselor will provide a piece of paper for each student.

5. The school counselor should invite students to write down 10 to 15 decisions they have made in the last month. The counselor can adjust the time frame as needed and can give the group a few examples if students get stuck starting this activity. For example, a few common decisions that will help students with this activity can include What did you eat for breakfast? What time did you go to bed? Did you make your bed? Did you do your homework last night?

6. When the school counselor notices that students are finishing writing their decisions, he or she should ask students to put their papers down so they can share three basic types of decisions. The counselor should encourage students to record these types of decisions on their own papers.
   Decision Types:
   a. No Decision: Letting others decide what you will do.
   b. Snap Decision: A quick choice individuals make with no consideration of the result and little thought.
   c. Responsible Decision: Taking time to consider others and your future when individuals make a decision.
   Discussion Questions: Which type of decision category do you think you make most often? What do you think is the best category?

7. The school counselor should write these three categories on the chalkboard.

8. The school counselor will go around the group and invite students to share a decision on their lists, and then identify what category they believe it fits under. If time permits, the counselor should allow students to share multiple decisions from their lists.

9. As the school counselor helps students draw connections, he or she should refer back to the opening game as there was little time to think before having to make a quick decision, which is an example of a snap decision. It is important that the counselor provides students with examples of each type of decision.
   Discussion Questions: What are some instances when you have made responsible decisions? Who helped you with that decision? What do you think is easy or challenging about making decisions? Are there times when it is okay to make a snap decision? How do you make a challenging decision? What else do you consider when you are making a challenging decision?

10. The school counselor will distribute the Five Steps of Responsible Decision-Making handout to each student.

11. The school counselor should briefly discuss the five steps of responsible decision-making with students.
    Discussion Questions: Can you identify two or three adults from whom you can seek guidance and support when making decisions? Who can help you think about the choices relating to a decision and any possible consequences or outcomes?

12. The school counselor will review the three types of decisions and the steps of decision-making on the handout.
    Discussion Questions: How can you use these decision-making steps?

Closing Discussion Questions/Activities

1. What skills can you improve in order to become better at decision-making?

2. To close this session, we are going to go around the circle and share one word or phrase to summarize what you learned today that has a big role in the decisions you make.

About the Group Worker

Brandie Oliver, PhD, is an assistant professor in the School Counseling Department at Butler University. Previously, she worked as a middle school counselor. She has taught the group counseling course and has experience facilitating numerous groups. Dr. Oliver strongly believes in the power of group counseling and its benefit to students learning in this format of counseling. She is dedicated to the training, development, and supervision of school counselors who strive to be change agents in PreK–12 education.

Additional Resources

Bridges Transitions. (2012). *Teacher guide to Choices® explorer: Decision making guide.* https://access.bridges.com/usa/en_US/choices/pro/content/lessons/decisionmakingguide/dmg_usa_teachers.pdf

Appendix A
"Would You Rather ..."

Would you rather:

Visit the doctor or the dentist?

Eat broccoli or carrots?

Watch TV or listen to music?

Own a lizard or a snake?

Have a beach holiday or a mountain holiday?

Eat an apple or a banana?

Be invisible or be able to read minds?

Be hairy all over or completely bald?

Be the most popular or the smartest person you know?

Make headlines for saving somebody's life or win the Nobel Peace Prize?

Go without TV or fast food for the rest of your life?

Always be cold or always be hot?

Not hear or not see?

Eliminate hunger and disease or be able to bring lasting world peace?

Be stranded on a deserted island all alone or with someone you don't like?

See the future or change the past?

Be 3 inches taller or 3 inches shorter?

Wrestle a lion or fight a shark?

Walk 5 miles or bike 10 miles?

Go skydiving or swim with dolphins?

Meet the president of the United States or your favorite musician?

Appendix B
Five Steps of Responsible Decision-Making

1. Identify Your Choices
   a. Brainstorm options. Make a list.
   b. There are always more solutions than the obvious ones.
   c. Start by building yourself a good list of choices.

2. What's Best for You Now?
   a. If you only thought of yourself right now, which of the choices is your favorite?
   b. What is your "gut response" or that snap decision?

3. Consider Others
   a. What point of view will other people have about your various decisions?

4. Consider Your Future
   a. What is the best choice for your future or which one has the best possible future benefits?
   b. What are the potential consequences?

5. Make a Choice and Go for It!
   a. What are some of the choices you have identified?
   b. Did you consider the future and the social implications of each choice?
   c. Remember, we can learn along the way and make adjustments to our choices/decisions.

(Adapted from https://access.bridges.com/usa/en_US/choices/pro/content/lessons/decision-makingguide/dmg_usa_teachers.pdf)

Appendix C
Pretest/Posttest

1. I know the five steps to responsible decision-making:
   a. Yes
   b. No

2. I know the three types of decisions:
   a. Yes
   b. No

3. I can identify at least two adults who I can ask to help me make a decision:
   a. Yes
   b. No

4. I make several decisions every day on my own:
   a. Yes
   b. No

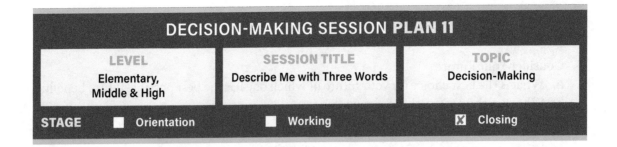

DECISION-MAKING SESSION **PLAN 11**

LEVEL	**SESSION TITLE**	**TOPIC**
Elementary, Middle & High	Describe Me with Three Words	Decision-Making

STAGE   ☐ Orientation   ☐ Working   ☒ Closing

ASCA Mindsets Standards

Belief in development of whole self, including a healthy balance of mental, social/emotional, and physical well-being.

ASCA Behavior Standards

Learning Strategies

Demonstrate critical-thinking skills to make informed decisions.

Identify long- and short-term academic, career, and social/emotional goals.

Gather evidence and consider multiple perspectives to make informed decisions.

Self-Management Skills

Demonstrate ability to manage transitions and ability to adapt to changing situations and responsibilities.

Social Skills

Demonstrate ethical decision-making and social responsibility.

Learning Objectives

1. Students will understand informed decision-making processes that contribute to life-long learning and career success.
2. Students will understand that data from a single source will not be enough to make a decision about a person's career or life plan.
3. Students will demonstrate critical thinking skills to make informed decisions by collecting and using data from multiple sources.
4. Students will understand the different results, analyze them, and demonstrate informed decision-making.

Materials

1. Jung Typology Test, completed a week before this session
2. Describe Me handouts

Session Procedure

Activity One: Jung Typology Test

1. The school counselor will explain each category of the Jung Typology Test (Extroverted vs. Introverted; Sensing vs. Intuition; Thinking vs. Feeling; and Judging vs. Perceiving).
2. The school counselor will ask students to write one or two paragraphs about their reaction/reflection regarding the results of the Jung Typology Test.

Discussion Questions: Do you agree or disagree with the results? Why or why not? How can you use these results to further your career planning process, whether it is choosing a major in college or choosing a career path?

Activity Two: Describe Me

1. The school counselor will distribute the Describe Me handouts to the students. For example, there will be seven handouts for each student in a group of eight.
2. The school counselor will call each student's name and ask the other students to describe the student whose name is called with three adjectives. The school counselor will also ask students to write the person's name on the handout.
3. The school counselor will collect the handouts after each student has been described.
4. The school counselor will give completed handouts to the student it corresponds to and ask them not to look at the papers before all students' descriptions are completed.
5. After each student's descriptions are completed, the school counselor will ask students to look at their descriptions.

   Discussion Questions: Do you agree or disagree with these descriptions/adjectives? Why or why not?

Closing Discussion Questions/Activities

1. The school counselor will explain that the Jung Typology Test results are based on our answers to instrument questions. The Describe Me activity results/descriptions are based on responses to our verbal and nonverbal communications with group members, our body language, and our actions in the group.
2. The school counselor will make the connection between the Jung Typology Test and Describe Me activity. Since one adjective cannot be enough to describe a person, one instrument also cannot be enough to give us 100% accurate information about our personality, career, and life planning.
3. The school counselor will facilitate a final discussion in regard to what applicable information students have learned and how they would be able to use them.

About the Group Worker

Bilal Kalkan is a doctoral candidate at Ohio University working toward his dissertation in Counselor Education and Supervision. He is interested in career counseling, group counseling, addiction counseling, online counseling and supervision, and ethical issues in counseling and supervision.

References

HumanMetrics. (n.d.). *Jung typology test.* http://www.humanmetrics.com/personality

Grief Groups

Introduction

Many students experience some type of loss during their educational careers. This cannot be overstated given the consequences of COVID-19. The need to support students post-COVID-19 in dealing with grief and loss will likely increase exponentially. A natural reaction to loss is a period of grief that can be categorized by feelings of deep sadness, anger, relief, loneliness, and/or confusion. While some may consider the loss or the death of a loved one as the primary impetus for grief, it is important to recognize that the loss of a beloved pet, parental divorce, parental incarceration, loss of security, or loss of a particular identity may also precipitate a period of grieving for children and adolescents. One of the most challenging aspects of supporting a grieving student is that this process is neither linear nor predictable. Instead, grief is unique to each individual and does not necessarily go away after a particular amount of time.

Grief can permeate all settings and can result in unexpected behavioral issues and/or an inability to focus on academics. School counselors hold a privileged and vital role in assisting grieving students as they begin to adjust to their "new normal." On an individual level, school counselors may meet with students to allow space for them to process their emotions related to grief. At this time, school counselors assist students in finding their voices so that they learn to ask for support from adults or peers when feeling particularly challenged by these emotions. This can then set the stage for productive small-group membership with peers who are grieving.

Although individual counseling offers many positive benefits to grieving students, it does not as readily afford students the opportunity to experience cathartic release and the sense of universality that comes from disclosing emotions and information with peers. Empathic responses and support can likewise help students develop important coping skills that facilitate the grieving process. The small-group session plans in this chapter address various forms of grief and loss as experienced by children and adolescents.

Data Discussion

Being able to collect and analyze data effectively is key to developing your comprehensive school counseling program, and is also important for your small-group counseling program (see Chapter 3 for more). Examining data that are accurate and appropriate for the goals of your small group is imperative in garnering support for a more robust small-group counseling program. Here are steps we hope you undertake as you review the sample sessions on grief.

Discuss Data Collection With a Peer/Colleague

As a school counselor or school counselor-in-training you will find that collaborating with peers (other school counselors or school counseling students) helps you both build confidence about the interventions you are planning and also align your interventions with the ASCA National Model for School Counseling programs. Collaboration and consultation also represent school counseling best practices and help us remain data driven and intentional with intervention planning. Based on the sessions you choose when considering your particular school, consult with a peer or colleague about your rationale/selections and your data collection plan.

Take a Walk With Data Related to Grief

For each of the sessions included here on grief, we ask that you engage in the following four steps for thought and discussion either with your colleague(s) or your course instructor(s):

Step 1 — General Data Consideration

Read the Learning Objectives for each small group on grief and then:

Ask yourself, What kinds of data might be relevant to collect based on the learning objectives stated? Are you most interested in the number of students served (participation) or are you more concerned with how your small group meets the mindsets and behaviors that were the target of your group (surveys, pretest/posttest)? Are you most concerned with examining the number of students for whom grief is so large an issue that it is likely impacting student academics (outcome)?

Disaggregating your data to determine if certain subgroups of students are disproportionately impacted is essentially important to the small-group planning process. Do you have any suspicions that grief plays a role in how underserviced or marginalized students are treated in the school? Does grief impact any underserved or marginalized groups of students more than others (e.g., students who are economically disadvantaged who are also grieving separation from a parent due to incarceration)?

Step 2 — Thoughts on Participation Data

After reading the general outline for the session:

Develop a data collection plan related to participation data. What will the collection of participation data look like in your grief group? How will you track this data? Some school counselors prefer traditional paper/pencil options (i.e., notebook with attendance rosters), but there are plenty of high-tech options available, including Microsoft and Google applications (i.e., Word, Docs, Excel, and Sheets) and even web-based school counselor data organization tools such as SCUTA (a school counselor's advocate). Whichever option you select, be sure to commit to it with fidelity! There is nothing more frustrating for a school counselor than delivering an intervention and not having the data to support your efforts when it is requested by an administrator or other stakeholder.

Step 3 — Thoughts on Mindsets and Behaviors Data

After reading the Closing Discussion Questions/Activities section for each session, ask:

When considering mindsets and behaviors data, what pretest/posttest instrument might help you collect the data needed for you to know if the group was successful? What questions would you want to ask to determine if the mindsets and behaviors you targeted were achieved? When looking to answer these questions, for yourself, consider the enduring skills and knowledge you anticipate participants will possess once they have participated in the group.

For example, when thinking about a grief group, you might be most interested in Mindset Standard M1., "Belief in development of whole self, including a healthy balance of mental, social/emotional and physical well-being"; Behavior Standard B-SMS 6., "Demonstrate ability to overcome barriers to learning"; and/or B-SMS 7., "Demonstrate effective coping skills when faced with a problem." Remember, you can access the *ASCA Mindsets and Behaviors Database* (https:// scale-research.org/mandb/public_html/) for a quick reference and additional resources as you develop group interventions to support students who are facing grief.

Step 4 — Thoughts on Outcome Data

Upon reading the entire group plan, consider this:

Outcome data most often refers to metrics associated with attendance, behavior, and academics. Accordingly, what data point could you examine to determine if this group helps with a measurable data point? Are you most concerned with examining students' abilities to attend class (despite the grief they may be experiencing) (attendance)? Or perhaps it feels more appropriate to measure students' classroom behaviors (e.g., office referrals) (behavior) resulting from shutting down or acting out due to their grief. Is the grief that the group's members experience negatively impacting their ability to be successful academically? If so, what might you examine to determine if your group is having an impact (e.g., improved test scores, greater rates of turning in homework)? Consider what metric would be best to determine intervention effectiveness. One final note about outcome data: pick one! It is not always necessary to evaluate all three areas—attendance, behavior, and academics—for your small group. Target one area and let that guide your evaluation of the group's impact!

ASCA Mindsets Standards

Belief in development of whole self, including a healthy balance of mental, social/emotional, and physical well-being.

ASCA Behavior Standards

Learning Strategies

Identify long- and short-term academic, career, and social/emotional goals.

Self-Management Skills

Demonstrate ability to overcome barriers to learning.

Demonstrate effective coping skills when faced with a problem.

Demonstrate ability to manage transitions and ability to adapt to changing situations and responsibilities.

Social Skills

Demonstrate empathy.

Demonstrate social maturity and behaviors appropriate to the situation and environment.

Learning Objectives

1. Students will be able to define grief.
2. Students will be able to identify three personal levels of support.
3. Students will be able to accurately identify their emotions.

Materials

1. Magazines
2. Scissors
3. Glue
4. Paper
5. Pencils/markers/colored pencils/crayons
6. Notebook and paper dividers

Session Procedure

1. The school counselor will ask students to make a picture collage out of magazine scraps. Students will cut out pictures, words, or phrases within the magazine that express how they currently feel.
   Discussion Questions: The pictures and phrases you used seem to express a variety of emotions; can you tell me about your choices and what they mean to you?
2. The school counselor will help students label and identify their emotions.

3. The school counselor will lead a discussion about the normalcy of grief reactions after the death of a loved one.

4. The school counselor will ask the students to draw a picture of someone who helps them when they are experiencing strong emotions.
   Discussion Questions: How does this person help you process your emotions?

5. The school counselor will discuss the importance of identifying support systems when the student is having an emotional reaction.
   Discussion Questions: Why is it important for you to have a support system in place after the death of a loved one?

6. The school counselor will ask students to list three places where they feel comfortable and safe on a sheet of paper.

7. The school counselor will ask the students to list three people who they feel that they can talk to when experiencing an emotional reaction.

8. The school counselor will ask the students to list three positive coping skills the students can use to express or release emotions.
   Discussion Questions: What types of positive coping skills have you used in the past? What were the results of using these skills?

9. The school counselor will provide students with a handout of resources that can be useful for students who are recovering from trauma or sudden loss. This list should include information about local counselors, support websites, churches, grief centers, or local helping agencies, in addition to facts about how the individuals may be affected by the encountered death of a loved one.

10. The school counselor will combine all of the materials into a notebook called the "Pillars of My Life."

11. The school counselor will give this book to students at the end of their group session to take with them as a reminder of the support systems they have in place to help them when they are experiencing difficult times.

Closing Discussion Questions/Activities

1. How can you use this book when you are having an emotional reaction?
2. What other resources would you like to include in your book?

About the Group Workers

Sarah Kitchens, PhD, is an assistant professor and instructional mentor at Liberty University. She was previously a K–12 school counselor in both a public and a private school.

Lacey Ricks, PhD, is an assistant professor in the Department of Clinical and Professional Studies at the University of West Georgia. She has eight years of experience working as a school counselor in the public school setting.

Additional Resources

Balk, D. E., Zaengle, D., & Corr, C. A. (2011). Strengthening grief support for adolescents coping with a peer's death. *School Psychology International, 32*(2), 144–162. https://doi.org/10.1177/0143034311400826

Tillman, K., & Rust, J. (2011). Kids supporting kids. *School Counselor, 49*(1), 18–23.

ASCA Mindsets Standards

Belief in development of whole self, including a healthy balance of mental, social/emotional, and physical well-being.

Sense of belonging in the school environment.

ASCA Behavior Standards

Learning Strategies

Demonstrate critical-thinking skills to make informed decisions.

Self-Management Skills

Demonstrate effective coping skills when faced with a problem.

Demonstrate ability to manage transitions and ability to adapt to changing situations and responsibilities.

Social Skills

Create positive and supportive relationships with other students.

Create relationships with adults that support success.

Learning Objectives

1. Students will increase their awareness of their emotional and physiological responses to grief.
2. Students will utilize individual coping skills.
3. Students will increase their awareness of supportive adults who may assist them with coping with feelings of grief.

Materials

1. *Liplap's Wish* by Jonathan London & Sylvia Lane
2. Paper
3. Pencils/markers/colored pencils/crayons

Session Procedure

1. The school counselor will introduce *Liplap's Wish* to students by discussing the cover picture, in which a child rabbit and his mother are wishing upon a star.
   Discussion Questions: What have you wished for when you've wished upon a star?
2. The school counselor will transition to reading the book by saying, "Let's find out what Liplap is wishing for."
3. As the story progresses and Liplap thinks about his grandmother who has died, the school counselor will ask students who they miss.

4. The school counselor will highlight the physical and emotional symptoms of grief that Liplap experiences in the story: (a) yearning to see his grandmother again, (b) suddenly wanting to cry, (c) loss of appetite, and (d) feelings of sadness.
   Discussion Questions: Have you ever felt these feelings when you think of the loved one who you miss?

5. The school counselor will tell the students, "Let's find out who helps Liplap feel better when he misses his grandmother."

6. The school counselor will read the portion of the story where Liplap's mother tells him a story to remember his grandmother, as they both wished upon a star in her memory.
   Discussion Questions: Who helps you feel better when you miss your loved one?

7. When the students have identified who helps them to feel better at home, the school counselor should expand the discussion to identify who might help them feel better at school.

8. The school counselor will provide drawing materials to the students and prompt them to draw by instructing them to "Draw how you help yourself feel better when you miss your loved one."

Closing Discussion Questions/Activities

Discuss and share drawings.

About the Group Worker

Laura Tejada, PhD, LMFT, LPC, Registered Play Therapist-Supervisor, is a former elementary classroom teacher and school counselor who earned the Registered Play Therapist credential during her years as a school counselor. Dr. Tejada is an assistant professor in the Department of Counselor Education at Northeastern Illinois University.

Additional Resources

Children's Grief Education Association. (2011). *About childhood grief.* https://childrengrieve.org/resources/about-childhood-grief

Freeman, S. J. (2008). *Grief and loss: Understanding the journey.* Brooks/Cole Learning.

Jackson, K. (2015). How children grieve: Persistent myths may stand in the way of appropriate care and support for children. *Social Work Today, 15*(2), 20. http://www.socialworktoday.com/archive/030415p20.shtml

Mundy, M. (1998). *Sad isn't bad: A good-grief guidebook for kids dealing with loss.* Abbey Press.

National Alliance for Grieving Children. (n.d.). *Education.* https://childrengrieve.org/

Perry, B. D. (n.d.). *Death and loss: Helping children manage their grief.* http://teacher.scholastic.com/professional/bruceperry/death_and_loss.htm

Rando, T. A. (1984). *Grief, dying, and death: Clinical interventions for caregivers.* Research Press.

Tillman, K. S., & Rust, J. P. (2011). Kids supporting kids. *School Counselor, 49*(1), 18–23.

Vitas Healthcare. (n.d.). *Guidelines for helping grieving children.* http://www.vitas.com/resources/grief-and-bereavement/helping-grieving-children

Appendix A
Pretest/Posttest

Note: This is for the adult to read to students and is not intended as an assessment that students complete independently.

Student: _____ Date: _____

1. Sometimes I miss someone who has died so much that I cannot do my schoolwork.

     I am sad but I can do it!   I'm not sure.   Lots of times.

2. Sometimes I miss someone who has died so much that I don't want to play with my friends.

     I am sad but I can do it!   I'm not sure.   Lots of times.

3. When I am at school and feel sad because I miss someone who has died, I can help myself feel better.

     Yes! I know what to do!   I'm not sure.   I need help with this.

4. When I am at school and feel sad because I miss someone who has died, I know of an adult I can talk to who will help me handle my feelings.

     Yes! I know what to do!   I'm not sure.   I need help with this.

GRIEF SESSION **PLAN 3**

LEVEL	SESSION TITLE	TOPIC
Elementary	Family Constellations & Star Strategies	Grief

STAGE ☐ Orientation ☒ Working ☐ Closing

ASCA Mindsets Standards

Belief in development of whole self, including a healthy balance of mental, social/emotional, and physical well-being.

ASCA Behavior Standards

Learning Strategies

Demonstrate critical-thinking skills to make informed decisions.

Self-Management Skills

Demonstrate effective coping skills when faced with a problem.

Demonstrate ability to manage transitions and ability to adapt to changing situations and responsibilities.

Social Skills

Create relationships with adults that support success.

Demonstrate social maturity and behaviors appropriate to the situation and environment.

Learning Objectives

1. Students will evaluate the level of connection they feel with family members.
2. Students will think critically about the relationships that they have with their family and identify the reasons they may or may not feel close with certain family members.
3. Students will identify and use one coping strategy to handle emotions.

Materials

1. Star Strategies handout (see Appendix A)
2. Twelve smaller stars and one large star per student (see Appendix A)
3. Black construction paper
4. Pencils/markers/colored pencils/crayons
5. Glue/glue sticks

Session Procedure

1. The school counselor will ask students what they know about constellations.
2. The school counselor will compare families to stars in a constellation by telling students that some stars and families are closer with each other and some are further apart.
3. The school counselor will tell each student that they will be creating a family constellation and ask them to write their name on the large star and the names of their family members on the small stars, writing one name per star.

4. The school counselor should explain that each student can determine who is considered part of the family. For example, some students can determine that extended family members such as grandparents or cousins are a key part of their family constellation.

5. As students are creating their family constellations, the school counselor will begin a discussion on closeness.
   Discussion Questions: What does it mean to feel close to someone? How do you know if you are close with or connected to family members? How does it feel to be disconnected from specific family members?

6. The school counselor will invite students to share about one family member with whom they feel close and one from whom they feel disconnected.

7. The school counselor will reiterate that some of the feelings that come up while talking about disconnected family members are likely to be painful feelings (e.g., sadness, anger, frustration, worry, jealousy, mistrust).

8. The school counselor will explain that while individuals cannot choose how their family members behave or interact with them, each student has the power to take care of and control how they react to these painful feelings.

9. The school counselor will distribute the Star Strategy handout to each student.

10. Using the handout, the school counselor will highlight different actions that students can take in order to deal with the painful feelings that sometimes accompany feeling disconnected.

Closing Discussion Questions/Activities

1. Which strategy would you like to try this week? Color or check the star in front of the strategy for the week and try this strategy at home.

About the Group Worker

Jeanne Winters Morriss earned her master's degree in School Counseling from Syracuse University. She has been a school counselor for 8 years, working in a small school district in rural southern Missouri and in a culturally and economically diverse urban school district in Salt Lake City, Utah.

Star Strategies For Coping

 #### Say What You Feel

> Talk to the family member you DON'T feel
> close to about your painful feelings. Use your
> magic feeling word: I feel ... when ...

 #### Take a Note

> Write a letter or note to the person you DON'T
> feel close to about your painful feelings. You
> can give it to them or keep it to yourself.

 #### Ask a Trusted Adult for Help

> If you can't talk or write to the adult involved
> with your painful feelings, talk to another
> adult you trust at home or at school.

 #### Reset to Calm

> When painful feelings come up, do something
> that helps you feel happy, safe or calm.

Directions: Color the star next to the strategy you will try
this week. Come prepared to write and talk about your
experience next week!

Directions for the Counselor:
- Cut one large star for each group member
- Cut up to 12 small stars per group member (they will need
  one for each family member)
- Provide dark colored paper for a background. Markers or
  pencils for writing names and glue for securing stars to
  the background

ASCA Mindsets Standards

Belief in development of whole self, including a healthy balance of mental, social/emotional, and physical well-being.

ASCA Behavior Standards

Learning Strategies

Demonstrate critical-thinking skills to make informed decisions.
Demonstrate creativity.

Self-Management Skills

Demonstrate effective coping skills when faced with a problem.
Demonstrate ability to manage transitions and ability to adapt to changing situations and responsibilities.

Social Skills

Demonstrate empathy.
Demonstrate social maturity and behaviors appropriate to the situation and environment.

Learning Objectives

1. Students will gain emotional self-awareness regarding feelings of grief and loss.
2. Students will be able to express one or more emotions associated with grief and loss.
3. Students will be able to identify one strategy for managing emotions of grief and loss.

Materials

1. Washable paint
2. Multiple-sized paintbrushes
3. Rocks of different shapes and sizes
4. Paper towels
5. Cups
6. Water
7. Paper plates
8. Photos, pictures or books of different types of rock art (e.g., cave paintings, Egyptian hieroglyphics, modern rock art)

Session Procedure

1. The school counselor will ask students what they know about the history of rock art and provide different examples to pass around the group.
   Discussion Questions: Why do you think people throughout history, such as cave people, ancient Egyptians, or Native Americans, have painted on rocks?

2. The school counselor will summarize students' individual thoughts by stating that throughout human history, rocks have been used to memorialize or create memories of important people, places, and events in time.
   Discussion Questions: Was there an important person or pet in your life that you would like to memorialize or remember using rock art? Can you tell us a little about this person or pet?

3. The school counselor will discuss emotions associated with grief and loss with students and ask them to think about the loved one or animal that they mentioned.

4. The school counselor will ask students to clean their rocks and set them down on the space prepared for them to paint.

5. The school counselor will encourage students to think about how they are feeling in the moment—or in the here-and-now—while painting their rocks. Sample language may include, "Think about the rock you are going to paint. Would you like it to tell a story about your lost loved one or pet? While you are painting, try to connect with your emotions in the moment. For instance, ask yourself, 'Am I feeling sad, mad, or happy while remembering my loved one?' It's okay if you don't know how you are feeling or if you are having more than one emotion right now."

6. The school counselor will invite students to paint their rocks using any colors, designs, letters, or numbers of their choice.

7. The school counselor will ask students to share their rock art with the group if they feel comfortable and to talk about it with the rest of the students.

8. The school counselor will ask students to identify where they would like to place their individual rocks (e.g., home doorway, bedroom, outside, at the gravesite) and why they would choose these locations.
   Discussion Questions: How will you use your rock art as a strategy to help manage or express emotions of grief and loss?

9. The school counselor will suggest to the students that they can use their respective rocks to share their memories and emotions with others and/or as a way to remember and reassure themselves that their loved one is always with them and will never be forgotten.

Closing Discussion Questions/Activities

1. How did you feel while creating your memory rock?
2. How do you feel now that you are telling us about it?

About the Group Worker

Deborah L. Duenyas, LPC, is an assistant professor in the Department of Counselor Education at Kutztown University and has experience working as a full-time school-based counselor.

Additional Resources

Kanyer, L. A. (2004). *25 things to do when Grandpa passes away, Mom and Dad get divorced, or the dog dies: Activities to help children suffering loss or change.* Parenting Press.

Appendix A
Pretest/Posttest

1. I can identify one or more emotions regarding my feelings of grief and loss:
   a. All of the time
   b. Sometimes
   c. Once in a while
   d. Never

2. I can identify one or more strategies for managing emotions of grief and loss:
   a. All of the time
   b. Sometimes
   c. Once in a while
   d. Never

3. I can use one or more strategies for coping with emotions of grief and loss:
   a. All of the time
   b. Sometimes
   c. Once in a while
   d. Never

ASCA Mindsets Standards

Belief in development of whole self, including a healthy balance of mental, social/emotional, and physical well-being.

ASCA Behavior Standards

Learning Strategies

Demonstrate creativity.

Self-Management Skills

Demonstrate ability to manage transitions and ability to adapt to changing situations and responsibilities.

Social Skills

Demonstrate empathy.

Create positive and supportive relationships with other students.

Learning Objectives

1. Students will understand that change is a part of growth.
2. Students will be able to identify and express feelings in a productive manner.
3. Students will identify and recognize changing family roles.

Materials

1. My Two Tanks worksheet (see Appendix A)
2. Bubbles: Likes & Dislikes worksheet (see Appendix B)
3. Pencils/markers/colored pencils/crayons

Session Procedure

1. The school counselor will distribute pencils, crayons, or markers with the My Two Tanks worksheet to students.
2. The school counselor will instruct students to creatively draw each of their homes in the two tanks.
3. The school counselor will ask students to discuss their tanks.
   Discussion Questions: Why do you live in two homes? How long has your family lived like this?
4. After each student has had an opportunity to talk about their two homes, the school counselor will distribute the Bubbles: Likes & Dislikes worksheet to the students.
5. The school counselor will instruct students to fill out the bubbles with a few reasons why they like and dislike living in two different homes.
6. Once students have completed this worksheet, the school counselor will encourage them to share at least one like and one dislike about living in two homes.

Discussion Questions: What is difficult about splitting your time between two homes? What do you enjoy about splitting your time between two homes?

7. The school counselor will ask students what it was like to hear each other's experiences with living with divorced parents.

   Discussion Questions: What does it feel like to hear others' likes and dislikes? What similarities and differences do you notice between your and others' experiences? What does it feel like to hear that you have some things in common with group members? What does it feel like to hear that we can all experience a similar situation differently?

8. The school counselor should discuss the value of looking at situations from multiple perspectives by telling the students that talking about our experiences can help us to know that we are not alone, and it also allows people to learn about other ways to see various situations.

Closing Discussion Questions/Activities

How has your view of living in two homes changed after listening to your classmates?

About the Group Worker

Karen Szilli is working toward her master's degree in School Counseling at Kutztown University and is currently completing the requirements for her internship in elementary school counseling in southeastern Pennsylvania. Ms. Szilli earned her bachelor's degree in Clinical and Counseling Psychology at Kutztown University.

Appendix A
My Two Tanks

Name: _____   Date: _____

My Two Tanks

Let's think about our homes as fish tanks! In a fish tank, there would be a place to swim, eat, and sleep, right? Draw a picture of both of your homes in the tanks. Make sure to include all of the people you live with, just like you'd include the fish swimming around!

Tank 1: _____'s House

Tank 2: _____'s House

Name: _____   Date: _____

Bubbles: Likes & Dislikes

Think about what it is like having two homes. What are some things you like about having two homes? What are some things you dislike about having two homes? Write your thoughts in the bubbles.

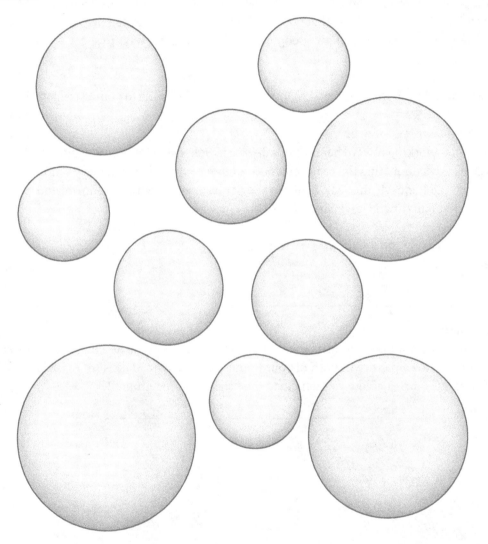

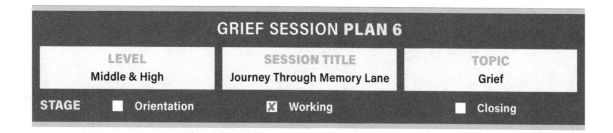

ASCA Mindsets Standards

Belief in development of whole self, including a healthy balance of mental, social/emotional, and physical well-being.

ASCA Behavior Standards

Learning Strategies

None

Self-Management Skills

Demonstrate effective coping skills when faced with a problem.

Social Skills

Create positive and supportive relationships with other students.
Use effective oral and written communication skills and listening skills.

Learning Objectives

1. Students will reflect on their feelings related to the death of a loved one.
2. Students will artistically express their memories using Play-Doh®.

Materials

1. Different colored Play-Doh® or clay
2. Poster board

Session Procedure

1. The school counselor will have students sit on the floor or at a table with the poster board to act as a buffer for the Play-Doh® or clay.
2. The school counselor will place the different colored Play-Doh® in the middle of the floor or table.
3. The school counselor will explain that students will be using the Play-Doh® to create a memory of the person who died or something that represents that person.
4. The school counselor will facilitate student discussions after all students have finished creating their symbol(s).

Closing Discussion Questions/Activities

1. What is special about this memory?
2. What kinds of things did you like to do together?
3. What types of feelings does this memory bring to the surface for you?
4. What do these feelings make you want to say or do?
5. What is unpleasant about this memory?

6. How do you cope with these unpleasant memories?
7. What would your loved one say or think about this symbol?

About the Group Worker

Eliese M. Keith, M.Ed, EdS, is an affiliate member of ASCA, FSCA and FCCA. She is currently working as an elementary school counselor in Jacksonville, Florida. Ms. Keith has 13 years of elementary school counseling experience in low socioeconomic-status public schools within Duval County, facilitating multiple and varied small counseling groups, based on student and teacher needs surveys.

Additional Resources

Boulden, J., & Boulden, J. (1992). *Bereavement activity book: Saying goodbye.* Boulden.

Brown, L. K., & Brown, M. (1996). *When dinosaurs die: A guide to understanding death.* Little, Brown.

Gray, R. E. (1988). The role of school counselors with bereaved teenagers: With and without peer support groups. *School Counselor, 35*(3), 185–193.

Ingpen, R., & Mellonie, B. (1983). *Lifetimes: A beautiful way to explain death to children.* Bantam Books.

LaTour, K. (1983). *For those who live: Helping children cope with the death of a brother or a sister.* Centering Corporation.

Maple, M. (1992). *On the wings of a butterfly: A story about life and death.* Parenting Press.

Papenbrock, P. L., & Voss, R. F. (1990). *Loss: How children and teenagers can cope with death and other kinds of loss.* Medic.

Rogers, F. (1988). *When a pet dies.* G. P. Putnam's Sons.

ASCA Mindsets Standards

Belief in development of whole self, including a healthy balance of mental, social/emotional, and physical well-being.

ASCA Behavior Standards

Learning Strategies

Demonstrate creativity.

Identify long- and short-term academic, career and social/emotional goals.

Self-Management Skills

Demonstrate effective coping skills when faced with a problem.

Demonstrate ability to manage transitions and ability to adapt to changing situations and responsibilities.

Social Skills

Use effective oral and written communication skills and listening skills.

Create positive and supportive relationships with other students.

Demonstrate empathy.

Use effective collaboration and cooperation skills.

Learning Objectives

1. Students will identify specific emotions related to their grief and loss.
2. Students will gain knowledge about the process of grief, which promotes adaptation to the difficult situation.

Materials

1. Paper
2. Markers/colored pencils/crayons
3. Picture of a large pot of soup
4. *Tear Soup: A Recipe for Healing After Loss* by Chuck DeKlyen & Pat Schwiebert
5. Tangled ball of yarn with no visible beginning or end

Session Procedure

Activity One: Tangled Ball of Emotions

1. The school counselor will distribute a piece of paper to each group member.
2. The school counselor will ask students to select colors that represent the top three emotions related to their grief and loss.

3. The school counselor will discuss the process of grieving with students by using a tangled ball of yarn to represent mixed emotions.
   Discussion Questions: When you look at this tangled ball of grief, what feelings come to mind? Are there other emotions you would like to add? What are they?

4. The school counselor will introduce the idea that grief is not a linear, structured process but involves numerous feelings and stages (e.g., denial, anger, bargaining, depression, acceptance) (Kubler-Ross & Kessler, 2005) and by identifying and verbalizing these emotions, students may more effectively cope with the loss, communicate with others, enlist support, and demonstrate empathy toward one another.

5. The school counselor will ask students to share which emotions they colored. Students may pass if they are not comfortable doing so.

6. The school counselor will utilize the tangled ball of yarn analogy to increase understanding of the complexity of grief and loss.
   Discussion Questions: When your emotions are all mixed up, sometimes it's hard to know what you are feeling and how you are dealing with things—how many of you can relate with that?

7. The school counselor will explain that the students may experience different feelings on different days or even later in the same day. Recognizing what the emotions are can provide an opportunity to attend to self-care, increase self-awareness, and help to promote ability to verbalize to friends and family.

8. The school counselor will explain that certain harder feelings, like anger and guilt, are common experiences after loss or death and that talking about those feelings is helpful.
   Discussion Questions: How do you receive comfort? What may benefit others when they are upset? How would you like others to support you through this time? What are some new things that you can think of to support each other?

Activity Two: Making Tear Soup

1. The school counselor will pass out paper and coloring supplies and instruct students to draw a soup bowl on their paper.

2. The school counselor will direct students to write or draw ingredients in their tear soup as the school counselor reads *Tear Soup: A Recipe for Healing After Loss.*

3. Depending on the total number of students, the school counselor will ask students to separate into pairs or groups of three to share what is in their pots with one another.

4. The school counselor will lead students in a discussion about what they experienced when creating their "soup" and during their dyads or groups of three.

Closing Discussion Questions/Activities

1. What would you like to share with the entire group about what's in your pot?
2. What did you learn from seeing what was in your classmates' pots?
3. What are some other ingredients you may add to your tear soup in the coming week?
4. Share one goal you have to attend to your grief and loss this week.

About the Group Worker

Jennifer Park, PhD, earned her doctorate in Counselor Education and Supervision from Regent University and her master's degree from the BTS-Graduate School of Counseling at the University of Pennsylvania. She taught guidance and math classes to middle school students for a decade and is an adjunct professor at Grace College and Regent University. Dr. Park is currently practicing at the Engle Center for Counseling and Health Services at Messiah College and is a private contractor within a church setting.

References

Kubler-Ross, E., & Kessler, D. (2005). *On grief and grieving: Finding the meaning of grief through the five stages of loss*. Scribner.

Additional Resources

Schwiebert, P., & DeKlyen, C. (2005). *Tear soup: A recipe for healing after loss*. Grief Watch.

Victim Relief Ministries. (n.d.). *Grief: A tangled 'ball' of emotions*. http://myaccesscounseling.com/wp-content/uploads/2016/12/GRIEF-handout.pdf

Appendix A
Pretest/Posttest

1. I feel that I understand myself and how I respond to grief and loss:
    a. Strongly agree
    b. Agree
    c. Neither agree nor disagree
    d. Disagree
    e. Strongly disagree

2. I am familiar with the stages of grief and loss:
    a. Strongly agree
    b. Agree
    c. Neither agree nor disagree
    d. Disagree
    e. Strongly disagree

3. I feel comfortable crying:
    a. Strongly agree
    b. Agree
    c. Neither agree nor disagree
    d. Disagree
    e. Strongly disagree

4. I can handle my sadness:
    a. Strongly agree
    b. Agree
    c. Neither agree nor disagree
    d. Disagree
    e. Strongly disagree

5. I can express my grief to others appropriately:
    a. Strongly agree
    b. Agree
    c. Neither agree nor disagree
    d. Disagree
    e. Strongly disagree

6. I felt supported in this group:
   a. Strongly agree
   b. Agree
   c. Neither agree nor disagree
   d. Disagree
   e. Strongly disagree

ASCA Mindsets Standards

Belief in development of whole self, including a healthy balance of mental, social/emotional, and physical well-being.

ASCA Behavior Standards

Learning Strategies

None

Self-Management Skills

Demonstrate ability to manage transitions and ability to adapt to changing situations and responsibilities.

Social Skills

Demonstrate advocacy skills and ability to assert self, when necessary.
Use effective oral and written communication skills and listening skills.

Learning Objectives

1. Students will reflect on memories of a person in their lives who has died.
2. Students will be able to process their emotions with others specific to the death of a loved one.

Materials

1. Pencils/pens
2. Paper
3. Books, pamphlets, and handouts from local hospice and bereavement organizations
   Note: This session will be cathartic for students, especially if the death was unexpected and the student didn't have the chance to say goodbye prior to their loved one's death. This letter will serve as one way in which the student can find closure with their loved one.

Session Procedure

1. The school counselor will state that each student takes their own time to heal and that feelings of grief are real for each individual, especially when members are sharing the death of a pet compared to students who are sharing the death of a friend or relative.
2. The school counselor will have students sit at a table with a piece of lined paper and compose a letter to a loved one who has passed.
3. When students have finished, the school counselor will provide students with the choice of either editing their letters or exploring supplemental bereavement-focused materials.
4. The school counselor will tell students that they should not feel pressured to finish their letters and that they will have the option of taking them home in order to complete them at a later time; however, students may read their letters aloud to the group if they wish.

5. The school counselor will stress the importance of the other students remaining supportive and understanding while each member is sharing with the group.

6. The school counselor will facilitate student discussions as students share their letters.

Closing Discussion Questions/Activities

1. How did you feel before writing this letter?
2. How did you feel after composing this letter?
3. What, if anything, did you leave out of the letter?
4. What would your loved one say or think about this letter?

About the Group Worker

Eliese M. Keith, M.Ed, EdS, is an affiliate member of ASCA, FSCA and FCCA. She is currently working as an elementary school counselor in Jacksonville, Florida. Ms. Keith has 13 years of elementary school counseling experience in low socioeconomic-status public schools within Duval County, facilitating multiple and varied small counseling groups, based on student and teacher needs surveys.

Additional Resources

Aliki. (1984). *Feelings.* Mulberry Books.

Balk, D. (1983). How teenagers cope with sibling death: Some implications for school counselors. *School Counselor, 31*(2), 150–158.

Balter, L. (1991). *A funeral for Whiskers: Understanding death.* Barron's Educational Series.

Boulden, J., & Boulden, J. (1992). *Bereavement activity book: Saying goodbye.* Boulden.

Boulden, J., & Boulden, J. (1992). *Self-esteem activity book: Feeling good!* Boulden.

Brown, L. K., & Brown, M. (1996). *When dinosaurs die: A guide to understanding death.* Little, Brown.

Gray, R. E. (1988). The role of school counselors with bereaved teenagers: With and without peer support groups. *School Counselor, 35*(3), 185–193.

Ingpen, R., & Mellonie, B. (1983). *Lifetimes: A beautiful way to explain death to children.* Bantam Books.

LaTour, K. (1983). *For those who live: Helping children cope with the death of a brother or a sister.* Centering Corporation.

Maple, M. (1992). *On the wings of a butterfly: A story about life and death.* Parenting Press.

Miller, J. H., & Rotatori, A. F. (1986). *Death education and the educator.* Thomas Books.

Morgan, J. D. (1991). *Young people and death.* Charles Press.

Myrick, R. D. (1987). *Developmental guidance and counseling: A practical approach.* Educational Media Corporation.

Papenbrock, P. L., & Voss, R. F. (1990). *Loss: How children and teenagers can cope with death and other kinds of loss.* Medic.

Rogers, F. (1988). *When a pet dies.* G. P. Putnam's Sons.

Simon, N. (1986). *The saddest time.* Albert Whitman.

Smilansky, S. (1987). *On death: Helping children understand and cope.* Peter Lang.

Valente, S. M., Saunders, J., & Street, R. (1988). Adolescent bereavement following suicide: An examination of relevant literature. *Journal of Counseling and Development, 67*(3), 174–177.

Vigna, J. (1991). *Saying goodbye to Daddy.* Albert Whitman.

Wittmer, J., & Myrick, R. D. (1989). *The teacher as facilitator.* Educational Media Corporation.

Worden, J. W. (1982). *Grief counseling and grief therapy.* Springer.

Appendix A

Pretest/Posttest

Read each of the statements below. Circle the number underneath that best describes how you feel (1 = Strongly Agree, 2 = Agree, 3 = Undecided, 4 = Disagree, 5 = Strongly Disagree).

1. The idea of death or dying is frightening.

    1   2   3   4   5

2. Everyone understands how I am dealing with this death.

    1   2   3   4   5

3. I have felt very different from my peers since the death occurred.

    1   2   3   4   5

4. I am angry with my loved one who passed away.

    1   2   3   4   5

5. I could not have prevented this death from happening.

    1   2   3   4   5

6. I believe that things in life take place in random order or no fixed order.

    1   2   3   4   5

7. Death is unfair to those people who are left behind.

    1   2   3   4   5

8. I do not blame myself for this death.

    1   2   3   4   5

9. I am afraid that whenever people leave, they will never come back.

    1   2   3   4   5

10. I feel comfortable sharing my feelings of grief with others.

    1   2   3   4   5

ASCA Mindsets Standards

Belief in development of whole self, including a healthy balance of mental, social/emotional, and physical well-being.

ASCA Behavior Standards

Learning Strategies

Demonstrate creativity.

Self-Management Skills

Demonstrate effective coping skills when faced with a problem.

Social Skills

Demonstrate empathy.

Demonstrate social maturity and behaviors appropriate to the situation.

Learning Objectives

1. Students will share feelings about death.
2. Students will share what they think happens after death and how these beliefs impact how they live their lives on a day-to-day basis.

Materials

1. Pencils/markers/colored pencils/crayons
2. Notecards

Session Procedure

1. The school counselor will ask students to share an experience that they have had with death in their lives.
   Discussion Questions: When you hear the word *loss*, what thoughts or feelings come to mind? Can you share an experience you have had with death or loss in your life? This could be a family member, relative, friend, pet, or even someone you were close to on social media.
2. The school counselor will reflect on each answer and draw similarities together that the students share.
3. The school counselor will hand out note cards and ask the students to write an emotion that comes to mind when they consider this death.
4. The school counselor will mix the cards in a hat and ask students to draw one card out and read it out loud.
   Discussion Questions: Who can relate to that feeling? What does it feel like in your body? Has anyone else felt the same way?

5. The school counselor will allow each student to draw a different card.
6. If the card has the same emotion, the school counselor can see if any of the students have something else to add to it.
7. After all of the cards have been drawn, the school counselor will move onto the next processing questions, which involve students sharing what they believe happens after death. The school counselor should explain that this part of group is not a place for debate but a place for each student to have their beliefs respected, particularly as they relate to different cultures or religious affiliations.

   Discussion Questions: How does what you believe about death impact how you live your life? Knowing what you believe about what happens after death, is there anything you want to change about your life now?

Closing Discussion Questions/Activities

1. What are you taking away from our discussion today?
2. What is one thing someone else said in group that really hit home for you today?

About the Group Workers

Penny Dahlen, EdD, LPC, has been a practicing counselor for more than 25 years and currently works for her local hospice as a bereavement counselor. She has served as a faculty member training counselors at a variety of universities for 20 years. Dr. Dahlen also specializes in both traditional counseling approaches and alternative healing practices with extensive experience healing trauma and grief, as well as using spiritual practices to help life flow smoother. She also provides executive and career consulting.

Nancy L. A. Forth, PhD, LPC, NCC, is a professor and chair in the Department of Counselor Education at the University of Central Missouri. Dr. Forth has over 15 years of experience in teaching content and clinical courses as well as providing supervision to master's level counselors-in-training. Her research interests include using creativity in counseling and supervision and counselor development. Additionally, Dr. Forth has had varied clinical experience.

GRIEF SESSION PLAN 10

LEVEL	SESSION TITLE	TOPIC
Middle & High	The Soundtrack of Hope	Grief

STAGE   ☐ Orientation   ☒ Working   ☐ Closing

ASCA Mindsets Standards

Belief in development of whole self, including a healthy balance of mental, social/emotional, and physical well-being.

ASCA Behavior Standards

Learning Strategies

Demonstrate creativity.

Apply self-motivation and self-direction to learning.

Self-Management Skills

Demonstrate the ability to work independently.

Demonstrate the ability to overcome barriers to learning.

Social Skills

Create positive and supportive relationships with other students.

Demonstrate empathy.

Learning Objectives

1. Students will be able to effectively communicate feelings about the person they have lost.
2. Students will be able to demonstrate empathy toward each other and create supportive relationships with each other.

Materials

1. Media device
2. Markers/colored pencils/crayons
3. Paper

Session Procedure

Two Weeks Prior to This Session

The school counselor will explain that each student will need to think about a song that reminds them of the person in their lives who has passed away. This can be a special song they sang or listened to together or one that reminds the student of that person.

One Week Prior to This Session

1. The school counselor will meet with students individually to ask what songs they have chosen.
2. The counselor can either instruct the students to bring their songs on whatever media device is preferred/available to them or the school counselor can download them for the students.

Activity: The Soundtrack of Hope

1. The school counselor will have each student individually play their song for the group.
2. After each song is over, the school counselor will ask each student to discuss their song with the group.

   Discussion Questions: How does this song remind you of the person you have lost? How does it make you feel to play this song for the group? What is one thing you would want the group to know about the person you have lost? Are there questions or comments that the group has for the student who has shared this song?

Closing Discussion Questions/Activities

1. What was it like to hear everyone talk about their songs?
2. How did that make you feel?
3. What did you learn from today's experience?

About the Group Worker

Dana Unger is a doctoral candidate at Kent State University. Prior to her doctoral work, she worked as both an elementary and secondary school counselor in Nevada.

ASCA Mindsets Standards

Belief in development of whole self, including a healthy balance of mental, social/emotional, and physical well-being.

ASCA Behavior Standards

Learning Strategies

Demonstrate critical-thinking skills to make informed decisions.

Self-Management Skills

Demonstrate effective coping skills when faced with a problem.

Social Skills

Create positive and supportive relationships with other students.
Create relationships with adults that support success.

Learning Objectives

1. Students will move through the group closure stage and recognize the many gifts that they learned throughout the group.
2. Students will be able to positively manage their experiences with individual grief and loss.

Materials

1. Gift package printouts (see Appendix A)
2. Pencils/markers/colored pencils/crayons

Session Procedure

1. The school counselor will remind students that the group is in the closure stage and that this will be the last group session.
2. The school counselor will distribute printouts of the gift package (see Appendix A).
3. The school counselor will instruct students to write their names on the handout and encourage students to decorate their gift package.
4. The school counselor will facilitate a discussion with students about the possible "gifts" that they have received for participating in the group.
   Discussion Questions: What are some of the things that you have learned throughout the group process that will be helpful to you as you continue to manage your own grief and loss? How did you feel supported throughout the group process? What did you learn about yourself from participating in the group? What did you learn from other students?
5. The school counselor will tell students that they are going to have an opportunity to share their gift packages as a "gift" to share with each group member.
6. The school counselor will instruct students to write a brief positive statement on other students' packages by having them pass their gift package handout to the right until each student has their own package back.

7. Once all students have their respective gift package handouts back, the school counselor will allow a few minutes for each student to read and individually process the statements written on them. Students may be encouraged to think about how their body feels as they are reading these "gifts."

8. The school counselor will give students the opportunity to share their responses to the activity before moving into the closing discussion questions.

9. The school counselor will suggest that students take their gift packages with them as they leave the group and encourage them to post them somewhere that will serve as a visual reminder of their group experience.

Closing Discussion Questions/Activities

1. How did it feel to share your "gifts" with other group members?
2. How would you describe your reaction to the other students' statements on your own gift package?
3. What specific "gifts" from the group do you see yourself using in the future?

About the Group Worker

Christy Land, PhD, LPC, has her doctorate in Counselor Education and Supervision. Dr. Land worked as a school counselor for 14 years and believes in a comprehensive and collaborative approach to ensure young people's academic and personal success. Additionally, she is experienced in the availability of student supportive services delivered by the school system. Dr. Land is a full-time faculty member at Grand Canyon University. She has numerous professional publications, holds leadership positions in numerous counseling organizations, and has been recognized at the local, state and national levels for her contributions to the field of counseling.

Appendix A
Gift Package Printout

CREDITS

Grief Session Plan 2 Design Image: Copyright © 2014 Depositphotos/kanate.

Grief Session Plan 3 Design Image: Copyright © 2016 Depositphotos/kchungtw.

IMG 14.8: Copyright © 2012 Depositphotos/interactimages.

Index

About the Editors

Dr. Sarah I. Springer is an associate professor in the Department of Professional Counseling at Monmouth University. She received her Bachelor of Music Education degree in voice at Mason Gross School of the Arts at Rutgers University and Master of Arts and Master of Education degrees in psychological counseling from Teachers College, Columbia University. In addition to her New Jersey School Counselor Certification, she is also certified as a Daring Way™ Facilitator (CDWF) and Licensed Professional Counselor. Before moving into higher education, Dr. Springer provided counseling in the high school and elementary settings for a decade, most recently developing an elementary school counseling program from the ground up in Mendham Township, New Jersey. Through her private practice, Dr. Springer has worked as a mental health counselor in a school running groups for children with special needs and provided individual counseling to children, adolescents, and parents, as well as LPC supervision to pre-licensed counselors. She has had the privilege of providing professional development faculty presentations for K-12 educators and presentations about counselor leadership to several area universities. Most recently, Dr. Springer created a graduate counseling course, Courageous Connections, which incorporates the Daring Way™ Curriculum, a highly experiential methodology based on the research of Dr. Brené Brown into pre-service school and mental health training. She regularly researches and publishes on topics specific to school counselor education, counselor supervision, ethics, and group work.

Dr. Lauren J. Moss is an associate professor at Kutztown University in the Department of Counselor Education and Student Affairs, where she teaches coursework related to school counseling, group work, and career development. She serves as the clinical co-coordinator of the School Counseling Program at Kutztown, allowing her to directly support school counselors-in-training as they navigate their school counseling practicum and internship experiences. Dr. Moss has extensive experience in the public school setting at the middle school level as a professional school counselor and special educator. As a licensed professional counselor, she maintains a small private practice working with children, young adults, and parents. Dr. Moss provides educational advocacy services for school-aged children and clinical supervision for pre-licensed counselors. She is actively involved in her county and state school counseling associations and is currently serving as President of the Berks Area School Counselors Association to support the important work of school counselors in her area. Her professional experiences working with diverse populations have led her to research interests, which include group work, bullying prevention, social justice, and advocacy, topics on which she has presented at international, national, regional, and state conferences and produced over 25 practitioner-oriented publications and peer-reviewed journal articles. Dr. Moss prides herself in working as a change agent for the field of counseling, particularly in the school setting, to best support and advocate for and with all clients.

Dr. Christine J. Schimmel is an associate professor and associate department chair in the Department of Counseling and Learning Sciences at West Virginia University. She coordinates the school counseling program and serves as a field placement coordinator. She specifically focuses her energies working with and training pre-service school counselors. In that role, Dr. Schimmel provides supervision to students in field experiences. A former school counselor herself, Dr. Schimmel has spent the last 20 years providing staff development and conference workshops on topics relevant to school counselors, clinical mental health counselors, and teachers. She has presented on topics such as Impact Therapy, creative counseling techniques, counseling theory, dealing with students who exhibit problematic behaviors, growth mindset, protective factors, and group counseling. Dr. Schimmel has published more than 10 articles, books, book chapters, and monographs on these subjects as well. Along with her colleague, Dr. Ed Jacobs, they have published one of the most widely used group counseling textbooks on the market, *Group Counseling: Strategies and Skills,* which is now in its 8th edition. In December 2018, her newest textbook with co-editor Dr. Ann Vernon, *Counseling Children and Adolescents,* was released. It is currently Cognella's top-selling textbook.

About the Contributors

Chapter Contributors

Zyer Beaty, PhD, NCC, High School Counselor, Bard High School, Washington D.C.

Annie Carro, Graduate Student and Research Assistant, George Mason University

Raven K. Cokley, PhD, NCC, Counseling Lecturer, Johns Hopkins University

Carol Dahir, EdD, Professor & former chair of School Counseling, New York Institute of Technology

Jason T. Duffy, PhD, Assistant Professor, SUNY Oswego

Sean Finnerty, PhD, Assistant Professor & Coordinator of School Counseling Program, SUNY Oswego

Shelby Gonzales, Department of Education Studies, University of South Carolina

Wilson Harvey, MA, Provisionally Licensed Counselor, School Counselor, Buckhannon-Upshur High School, Buckhannon, West Virginia

Trish Hatch, PhD, Professor Emeritus, San Diego State University, Chief Executive Officer & President of Hatching Results, LLC

Ed Jacobs, PhD, LPC, Associate Professor, West Virginia University

Jennifer Melfie, Graduate Student & School Counseling Intern, George Mason University

Clare Merlin-Knoblich, PhD, Assistant Professor, University of North Carolina at Charlotte

Ashley Kruger, Adjunct Faculty, San Diego State University, Hatching Results, LLC

Jonathan H. Orht, PhD, Associate Professor, Department of Education Studies, University of South Carolina

Nicole Pablo, Adjunct Faculty, San Diego State University, Hatching Results, LLC

Christine J. Schimmel, EdD, NCC, LPC, Associate Professor, West Virginia University

Megyn Shea, PhD, Core Faculty – School Counseling, Capella University

Anneliese A. Singh, PhD, LPC, Provost for Diversity and Faculty Development, Tulane University

Carla Smith, M.Ed, LPC-S, School Counselor, PhD Student, University of the Cumberlands

Sam Steen, PhD, Associate Professor & Academic Program Coordinator, George Mason University

Carolyn B. Stone, EdD, Professor & Counselor Educator, University of North Florida

Matthew B. Tolliver, MA, LPC, NCC, ALPS, School Counselor, Adjunct Instructor, West Virginia University, PhD Student, University of the Cumberlands

Group Session Contributors

Anxiety

Susannah Coaston, EdD, LPCC-S, CWC, Associate Professor of Counselor Education, Northern Kentucky University

Christine Ebrahim, PhD, LPC-S, NCC, Associate Professor, Loyola University New Orleans

Carey Gilchrist, MS, NCC, PLPC, CCC, Senior Class Counselor, Cabrini High School

Christina N. Jurekovic, MA, LPC, School Counselor, Doctoral Student, Adjunct Instructor, Adams State University

Keith LaBadie, MA, School Counselor

Nader Manavizadeh, MS, School Counselor, Kutztown University of Pennsylvania

William A. McAleenan, MA, NCC, Lead 11/12 School Counselor, Gilbert A. Dater High School – Cincinnati Public Schools

Rebecca L. H. Meidinger, PhD, Assistant Professor & Graduate Counseling Program Chair, Adams State University

Megan Numbers, MA, LPC, LCMHC, RPT, Doctoral Student, Adams State University

Brandie Oliver, PhD, Associate Professor, Butler University

Johnsa B. Phares, MA, School Counselor, Doctoral Student, Assistant Professor, Adams State University

Stephanie Probert, MA, School Counselor

Phillip Waalkes, PhD, Assistant Professor, University of Missouri St. Louis

Cindy Weiner, LPC, NCC, ACS, School Counselor

Social Skills

Allison Crowe, PhD, NCC, LPC, Associate Professor and Acting Chair of the Department of Interdisciplinary Professions, East Carolina University

Teddi Cunningham, PhD, Associate Professor, Valdosta State University

Kylie P. Dotson-Blake, PhD, NCC, LPC, NBCC President and Chief Executive Officer

J. Scott Glass, PhD, NCC, LPC, Professor of Counselor Education and Acting Associate Dean for Graduate Education & Faculty Affairs, East Carolina University

Glenda S. Johnson, PhD, LPC, NCPSC, Associate Professor, Appalachian State University

Heather Kelley, PhD, Associate Professor and Department Head of Human Services, Valdosta State University

Jered Kolbert, PhD, LPC, NCC, Professor, Counselor Education Program Co-Director, Duquesne University

Ashley Lopez, BS, School Counseling Student, Loyola University New Orleans

Hennessey Lustica, PhD, LMHC, ACS, Assistant Professor, Medaille College

Jill Schwarz, PhD, NCC, Associate Professor and School Counseling Program Coordinator, The College of New Jersey

Julia V. Taylor, PhD, Assistant Professor, University of Virginia

Laura Tejada, PhD, LMFT, LCPC, RPT-S, AAMFT Approved Supervisor, Associate Professor, Northeastern Illinois University

Malti Tuttle, PhD, LPC, NCC, Assistant Professor and School Counseling Program Coordinator, Auburn University

Cheryl Pence Wolf, PhD, LPCA (KY), NCC, GCDF, PHR, CHt, Associate Professor, Western Kentucky University.

Decision-Making

Cassandra Allen, MA, NCC, School Counselor

Christian D. Chan, PhD, NCC, President of the Association for Adult Development and Aging, Assistant Professor, University of North Carolina Greensboro

Julia Cook, MS, School Counseling, Children's Author

Sarah Daly, PhD, Assistant Professor, Saint Vincent College

Lee Edmonson Grimes, PhD, LPC, CPSC, Associate Professor, Valdosta State University

Amanda R. Friday, LPC, NCC, Doctoral Candidate, George Washington University, Adjunct Professor, Georgetown University

Natoya Haskins, PhD, LPC, Associate Professor, University of William and Mary

Bilal Kalkan, PhD, Assistant Professor, Adıyaman University, Turkey

Sandra Logan-McKibben, PhD, NCC, NCSC, ACS, BC-TMH, Clinical Assistant Professor and Program Director, Florida International University

Brandie Oliver, PhD, Associate Professor, Butler University

Patrick Perry, EdD, Director of Luckyday Scholarship Program and Instructional Assistant Professor of Higher Education, University of Mississippi

Jake J. Protivnak, PhD, LPCC-S, LPSC, Associate Professor and Department of Psychological Sciences and Counseling Program Director, Youngstown State University

Ashley Bleakley, M.Ed, Middle School Counselor

Rebekah Reysen, PhD, NCC, LPC, DCC, Assistant Director of Academic Support Programs at the Center for Student Success and First-Year Experience, University of Mississippi

Patrick Rowley, EdD, Assistant Professor, Rosemont College

Diana L. Wildermuth, PhD, NCC, LPC, Associate Professor and Counseling Psychology Program Coordinator, Temple University

Grief

Penny Dahlen, EdD, LPC, Senior Core Faculty, Walden University

Deborah L. Duenyas, PhD, LPC, Assistant Professor, Kutztown University of Pennsylvania

Nancy L. A. Forth, PhD, LPC, NCC, Professor and Program Coordinator, University of Central Missouri

Eliese M. Keith, EdS, School Counselor

Sarah Kitchens, PhD, LAPC, NCC, Associate Professor, Liberty University

Lacey Ricks, PhD, NCC, Assistant Professor, Liberty University

Christy Land, PhD, LPC, Assistant Professor, Grand Canyon University

Jennifer Park, PhD, NCC, LPC, ACS, Assistant Professor of Counseling, Colorado Christian University

Karen Szilli-Potharaju, MS, School Counselor

Laura Tejada, PhD, LMFT, LCPC, RPT-S, AAMFT Approved Supervisor, Associate Professor, Northeastern Illinois University

Dana Unger, PhD, LSC, LCMHCA, NCC, Assistant Professor of Professional School Counseling & Wilmington Initiative Coordinator, University of North Carolina at Pembroke

Jeanne Winters Morriss, MS, School Counselor